CONT

C000149596

HI, I'M LONDON

REGENT'S
CANAL
P.58

10 BRIDGES
LOOP
P.274

THE GRAND
TOUR
P.52

WHEN YOU KNOW WHERE TO GO LONDON IS A RUNNER'S PARADISE. Canals, riverside paths, woodlands, abundant countryside, huge Royal Parks, narrow green corridors, all-weather tracks, even cemeteries—this city has it all and is arguably the world's best major city in which to live and

EAST
LONDON
MARITIME
P.242

SOUTHWARK
PARK
P.48

THAMES
PATH
P.278

run. But knowing where to run is the great challenge and that's where this book steps in. Keep it close in a backpack or glove box or atop a coffee table ready to inspire you off the couch. Read it whenever you, your trainers, and this incredible city need to share some quality time.

FROM THE AUTHOR

I've run in cities all over the world but, with its combination of environment and culture, there is something truly special about running in London.

On the environment front, London has a mind-boggling acreage of parks and green spaces. I remember running through Richmond Park for the first time. I had never been so close to freely roaming deer before and the soft and perfectly undulating surface beneath my feet was a joy to run on. I had to keep reminding myself that I was still in the heart of suburban London.

Richmond Park and its neighbour, Bushy Park, are the shining jewels in a crown that boasts a lavish array of parks and woodlands all over the city. A glance at Google Earth's satellite imagery

HAYDEN'S TOP 3 LONDON RUNNING SPOTS ▸

Here are a few favourites of mine that may not make your typical top-three lists:

3. Epping Forest | If you don't like running loops of the same park for long runs, but don't mind getting lost occasionally, this is the spot.

2. Cray Riverway | Windswept and a little rough and ready, but its isolation and humble beauty is part of its attraction.

1. Home Park (Hampton Court Park) | I feel like this has become the neglected, less-appreciated sibling of Bushy and Richmond Parks. But I love its wide sweeping views, the swaying of its tall grasses, and its accessibility to the Thames Path just over the fence.

reveals that almost every home in London is within a mile or so of a greenspace in which to go running. The options are more limited out east but projects like Queen Elizabeth Olympic Park, the Greenway, and the Green Chain, are making a huge difference.

As if the parks weren't enough, waterways provide the setting for a huge percentage of the thousands of miles that London runners log each day. From the docklands to the Thames Path and from small meandering streams to Industrial Age canals, London provides many options for replacing busy roads with laid-back waterways. When running alongside a London canal it's incredible how fast you can disengage from the hustle and bustle to find a tranquil passageway beneath the city.

However, what would all this natural beauty and green infrastructure be without the people and culture to make it all accessible?

Over the centuries many grand estates and royal hunting grounds have been thankfully turned into public spaces. And the mayor's office seems committed to creating more and more accessible parklands and areas of conservation.

On the socialising front, Londoners have been getting together and going running since the first harriers clubs popped up in the late-1800s. Nowadays you can involve yourself at any point on the running spectrum: from elite athletics on the one hand (visit Teddington in the summertime to see the world's best in training) to the super casual beginner's jogging groups on the other.

When runners arrive in London from other cities, they are taken aback by the number of races available. If you want, you can run one every other day. In fact, when I first arrived, I embraced the smorgasbord of racing options a little too eagerly, by racing track meets and road races, that I quickly wound up injured. So, a word of warning, pace yourself. When you have more parkrun events than any other city on the planet, a thriving athletics scene, and arguably the world's most iconic marathon major, a runner can feel like a kid in a candy shop when inside the M25.

Rock up to any of these races and chances are you'll meet a friend for life—there's something eternally bonding about battling through a hard race together. And it's this friendliness that ultimately makes London such a special place in which to be a runner.

Finally, when running in London, you become part of the furniture. You're meant to be there. The jogger pounding the pavers next to the Thames has become about as iconic an image as a red double-decker bus. Runner's are an integral part of the fabric of this city—and there are few places on Earth for which that statement is true.

Happy running.

Hayden Shearman
runnersguide.org

Hayden dodging the crowds on The Serpentine's two-mile loop.

7

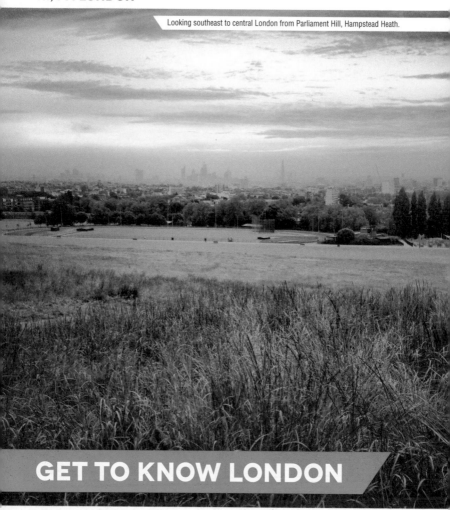

Looking southeast to central London from Parliament Hill, Hampstead Heath.

GET TO KNOW LONDON

"It is not a pleasant place; it is not agreeable or cheerful or easy or exempt from reproach. It is only magnificent." - Henry James, 1869.

London the magnificent. It sounds more like a magician than a modern city, but, given its changing guises and incredible feats, the magical analogy is perhaps not too far from the truth.

CHANGING FACES ▶ Two millennia ago London was just an outpost of the Roman Empire. It had a 3mi stone wall around it (of which you can still see the remnants) and a single bridge spanning the Thames (in a similar location to the current London Bridge).

At the collapse of the Roman Empire in the fifth century, London went from outpost to backwater, until the Anglo-Saxons arrived from modern day Germany and spied its value as a centre for trade.

The wide tidal river of the Thames provided the perfect harbour for shipping, and from then on London became intimately tied to the sea and to the trade it could bring. Once national identity had been established—following several Viking invasions, a nation-defining Norman invasion (from northwest France), and the odd civil war—London gradually found itself at the centre of the world.

By the 1800s, with an industrial revolution on its doorstep, a navy that ruled the waves, and an empire that circumnavigated the globe, London had come of age. During this time the city had two faces: one an imperial upper class of palaces and sprawling estate grounds and the other of over-crowded slums and Dickensian poverty.

Over the next 100 years, as the city grew, London's extremes began to be ironed out and, with that ironing process, came some innovations and social developments that have had surprisingly positive spin offs for today's runner.

First of all, many estates and royal hunting grounds became spaces set aside for public enjoyment. Victoria Park is a perfect example when: In 1839, east Londoner's life expectancy was shockingly low and Queen Victoria was petitioned to provide residents with a park for health and wellbeing reasons. Four years later, Londoners were making use of the world's first public park.

The second nineteenth century innovation was the installation of a complex sewer system to relieve some of the stench that came from the Thames. Combine this with the world's first underground rail network (opened in 1863) and you have the makings of a far more liveable and,

as a result, runnable city.

The other major benefit London's industrial revolution had on the runner is the construction of waterways. All over London are canals and docks that were initially built as transport hubs, but have become redundant with the evolution of technology, leaving behind peaceful waterside alcoves and passageways throughout the city.

London took a battering during the first half of the twentieth century with two world wars and a depression, but in the booming 50s and the liberating 60s and 70s, a new, grittier, and creative society emerged. The London we see now oozes art, music and innovation. It dramatically renovates dilapidated docklands, it transforms power stations into modern art galleries, it embraces cycle transport as though it were another Amsterdam, and it builds creatively-stunning (and sometimes strange) glass skyscrapers.

Today, London carries visible souvenirs of all its chapters, which at times can be frustrating as you get lost in twisting medieval streets. Yet, on the whole, once you appreciate the history of the place, you can extend a little more grace to things like the 150-year-old underground being late and learn to look for those little quirks and surprises that make London so magnificent.

GEOGRAPHY › London's obvious geographic feature is the meandering Thames River that cuts the city in two, west to

HI, I'M LONDON

east. It is tidal to Teddington Lock—a whopping 17mi west of London Bridge.

The land surrounding the Thames is usually flat—but don't let that fool you, there are some substantial hills to be found in the suburbs: Westerham Heights in the southeast stands 245m above sea level, Shooters Hill in Greenwich 132m, and Hampstead Heath 134m. Although these won't cause too many cardiac episodes, there are enough undulations to keep you from becoming a purely flat-land mammal.

One feature of London's geography that affects runners almost year round is the boggy soil, particularly in wooded areas. It means that after rain most of the forest trails (e.g. in Epping Forest or Wimbledon Common) are tough going and should be avoided unless you love slipping and sliding, muddying your new kicks.

WEATHER ▶ From an overseas perspective, London often conjures images of being damp and grey. But this isn't entirely accurate. In fact, although it can remain cloudy or drizzly for many days (or weeks) on end, London actually has far less rainfall than most of Europe and only half the annual precipitation of New York.

In general, summers are warm, but temperatures often soar into the 30s Celsius when weather patterns move up from the Mediterranean. These spells of fine weather can catch people off guard as the Tube sweats and the lack of air-conditioning stifles the city—sending everyone to their nearest park or rare outdoor swimming spot. With limited drinking fountains throughout the city, it pays to take fluids or a credit card with you in order to stay hydrated.

London winters are cold, but, compared to much of continental Europe, snowfall and frosts are relatively few and far between, with snow settling on the ground about five days per year and falling on 16 days per year.

Winds are typically light in London (which probably hasn't helped the problem below) and only reach gale force (a mean speed of 34 knots or more) on one or two days per year. The stillest months are during summer, generally making it a good time to go for that track or road PB.

Londoners coined the word "smog" back in the early 1900s, but, thanks to the 1956 Clean Air Act and a decline in factories, its air quality has improved hugely. The worst air pollution is probably to be found in the dusty old Tube network—look out for that black snot after a long journey.

Mean Daily Maximum:
Mid-summer = 23c (73F)
Mid-winter = 8c (46F)

Note: The inner city has the effect of retaining heat, and so can be much warmer than the outer suburbs.

Mean Monthly Sunshine:
July = 190.3 hours
January = 45.9 hours
Annual Average = 1460 hours

In winter you can expect to see the sun on average for about 1.5 hours per day (ouch!) and for

The remnants of many thirsty London runners.

A boggy trail in Wimbledon Common.

six or more hours each day in summer.

Mean Monthly Rainfall
July = 38mm (1.51in)
January = 52mm (2.04in)
Annual Mean Rainfall = 601mm (23.7in)

Autumn is typically the wettest time of year.

Keep a website like metoffice.gov.uk on your favourites list for regular, quick reference.

INNER SUBURBS▶ In Trafalgar
Square is a plaque that marks the official centre of London. Distances to the running routes and hotspots in this book are measured to this point.

Immediately surrounding Trafalgar Square are the inner city areas of Westminster City (home to the royal palaces and to parliament) and the City of London (the original city containing the old financial district and the Tower of London).

The running around here is best done either in the Royal Parks (Hyde, Kensington, Green and St James's) or alongside the Thames. The hectic nature of the roads and pavements making any other alternative practically a death wish (although early Sunday mornings can be a great time to explore the centre city).

Just to the north of the city centre you'll find excellent running in Regent's Park, Primrose Hill and Regent's Canal.

East from here, amongst an area that was known for over-crowding and poverty, are rejuvenating suburbs and, in Canary Wharf, an old docklands that is now one of the world's key financial hubs. Running spots around here include Victoria Park, Queen Elizabeth Olympic Park, several great canals, and the waterside paths of Canary Wharf (and the rest of the Isle of Dogs).

St Paul's Cathedral.

retain something of their own identity as part of a larger city. Newcomers are often surprised at the diversity and dramatic change from one suburb to the next in wealth, culture and feel.

All this makes it difficult to generalise, but when generalisations are made the west and north suburbs are typically seen as more desirable. Interestingly, running regions roughly follow this same pattern with many wonderful green spaces to run out west (most notably Richmond and Bushy Parks) and north (Hampstead Heath). The main hotspot for running in the northeast is the lengthy Epping Forest and otherwise you're looking at smaller and/or less developed parks, the River Lea and some country parks on the outskirts. In the southeast there is Greenwich Park, the wonderful initiative of the Green Chain (50mi of trails stretching from three points on the Thames to Dulwich Park, Nunhead Cemetery and Chislehurst West) and several woodlands.

In the southwest, as well as the big parks (of Richmond, Bushy, Home and Wimbledon Common) there are many extremely popular medium sized parks (like Clapham Common) and several waterways with paths alongside. The northwest of London has a good collection of medium sized parks and waterways with some top-notch country parks in the outer boroughs.

South of the centre city is Southbank—a revitalised creative district that was once a place predominantly of heavy industry. Running around here is typically done on the banks of the Thames and at Battersea, Burgess and Southwark Parks.

West of the city centre the Paddington Branch of the Grand Union Canal couples with the Thames Path to make excellent traffic-free running routes further west, while Wormwood Scrubs Park, several cemeteries and several smaller parks provide further running options.

OUTER SUBURBS ▶ As it has
expanded, London has swallowed up dozens of small villages, and these communities still

TRANSPORT ▶ Many London runners
use the public transport network to get to and from a particular run. However, during peak times this can make you the stinky one squashed in a full train carriage. But, hey, if people complain just explain that it's the smell of your incredible self-discipline oozing from your pores. Also wear woollen garments (like Icebreaker) that avoid gathering odour rather than synthetics that seem to breed bad smells.

Alternatively, you can always take a change of

clothes with you and utilise one of the multitude of leisure centres around the city (just plug "leisure centre" into Google Maps). These centres, as well as having pools, gyms and other sporting facilities, also provide showers and lockers for a small charge (up to £2).

The new contactless payment system makes public transport super easy by just tucking your credit card into a pocket and swiping on and off. It also manages daily and weekly fare caps.

Rail: London has a well-developed network of regular underground trains (called the Tube). However, additionally, and rather confusingly, London also has several other rail services: the London Overground, multiple National Rail services, the Docklands Light Rail, and trams. Fortunately, these fall under the same ticket system and the variety of services means that most areas of London are accessible by rail.

The train lines generally spread out from the city centre like spokes on a wheel, providing effective access from the outskirts of London into the centre (and vice versa). However, it can be a challenge to move from suburb to suburb in a circular motion around the city. In such cases, the London Overground can help or buses may prove faster and much cheaper.

In general, the cheapest way to buy tickets for trains is to get an Oyster Card and top it up at rail stations or online. Alternatively, if you're doing a lot of travel over a week go for the seven-day Travelcard (which can be loaded to your Oyster Card). Travel prices are calculated depending on how many zones (1-9) you are travelling between. Scan your Oyster Card in and out at stations, thus recording how many zones you've travelled and the cost of your trip.

Bus: The red double-decker bus is a London icon. And, not only are there lots of them circling all over Greater London, they are regular, cheap (at £1.50 per ride, no matter how long that ride might be) and, from the top deck, a good way to sightsee. The only trouble is that they're

Trafalgar Square, the centre of London.

The former bustling port, now financial district, Canary Wharf.

slow—it's not outside the realms of possibility to beat your local bus by running. Also, buses no longer accept cash—you'll need an Oyster card, contactless credit card, Travelcard or a Bus & Tram Pass.

Taxi: The London black cabs use the same express lanes as buses (but obviously avoid stopping every few hundred metres) so, apart from cycling and running, are probably the fastest mode of inner city travel (being more direct than the Tube). A 10-minute ride will cost about £10.

Car: With the congestion, lack of free parking, often-erratic street layouts, and central city congestion charge (£11.50 per day), car transport is not recommended near the city centre. However, for exploring running areas further afield, particularly the country parks, a car can be a great option. As such, this book only provides information on parking for the running spots outside of the city centre. For visiting runners, remember vehicles travel on the left in the UK and urban speed limits are usually 30mph.

Bike: Londoners are gradually turning their city into another Amsterdam with bike lanes everywhere and hordes of commuting cyclists using them (to the point where cycle congestion is actually becoming a problem at peak times). Overall, if you don't mind braving the traffic and the weather, cycling is a brilliant, and surprisingly fast, way to get around. Central London is perfectly flat, but you will encounter some quad-burning hills in the 'burbs.

Throughout the centre city there are thousands of Barclay's Bikes (called "Boris Bikes") available for hire. The maps that populate the inner city can point you to your nearest Boris Bike stand. They're certainly not made for speed, but can be a good alternative for sightseeing or getting across town. And they're cheap too at only £2 for a day or £10 for a week's hire (assuming you just use the bikes for stints of less than 30 minutes).

There are a few things you will need if you own a bike. Helmet: though not compulsory, when you get a taste for the traffic you will definitely want one. Two locks: bike theft in central London is a huge problem and the thieves are so crafty that you will need both a U-lock and a chain lock securing both wheels and frame to a fixed point. Lights and hi-vis gear: in the gloomy winter months these are an absolute must. Puncture repair kit/spare tube: potholes and broken glass abound on city roads and especially on designated cycleways unfortunately. Finally, Transport For London has produced a great series of free maps with every on- and off-road cycle route in the city. Pick these up from your local bike store.

While on the bike remember to keep left, use the cycle lanes when provided, signal when turning, and stay alert at all times (no ear buds).

River: There are various river bus services on the Thames and they're good for seeing the sights and avoiding traffic at the same time. They're generally slightly more expensive than the equivalent journey on the Tube. On most services you can get a discount of up to 33% if you have a Travelcard and/or Oyster Card.

See tfl.gov.uk for further transport information.

NAVIGATION ▶ Being such an old city that has sprawled over equally old country lanes, London's roads are notorious for playing havoc with visitor's (and even locals') internal compasses. Seemingly parallel streets often diverge to end up heading in opposite directions. For this reason it's always recommended to carry a good map or smart phone and check it regularly when venturing somewhere new.

In central London, on almost every street corner, are handy information stations with local maps and approximate distances and walking times. Most parks, especially the Royal Parks, have detailed maps at park entrances.

This book splits London into five geographic sections: the centre and then the four quarters of southeast (south of the river), southwest (either side of the river but generally south of Trafalgar Square), northwest, and northeast. To help you pinpoint the location of each run we provide the suburb, the borough (of which London has 32), and the postcode. Combined with the distance and direction from Trafalgar Square (central London) this should give you a clear idea of where each run is located.

An iconic London sight that needs no introduction.

London Marathon twists through Canary Wharf.

A CITY OF RUNNERS

Ever since the mid-1800s, Londoners have been leading the world of running. Here's a snap shot of the city's proud running heritage and an insight into what is to come.

THE EARLY YEARS ▶ London holds claim to the oldest cross country running club in the world. In the 1860s the Thames Hare and Hounds got the ball rolling with social running and throughout that century running clubs sprung up all over London and the world. So, in being the first amongst many, it was inevitable that a Londoner would soon become the best.

Early London-based Olympic champions include Charles Bennett (originally from Dorset, he won gold at the 1900 Paris Games in the 1500m and the 5000m teams race), Harold Abrahams

of *Chariots of Fire* fame (1924 100m Olympic gold), Albert Hill (won gold at the 1920 Antwerp Olympics in both the 800m and 1500m), Douglas Lowe (won gold in the 800m in 1924 and 1928), and Tommy Hampson (gold in 1932 in the 800m—completing a four-straight run in the event by Londoners).

London has an early running claim to fame that doesn't involve any particular athlete, in fact it has more to do with the Royal Family. In 1908 the Olympic Marathon in London was planned to start at Windsor Castle and finish at the Olympic Stadium about 40km later. However, due to complaints from the athletes about the course and complaints from the Royals about their viewing options, the distance was stretched out to 42.195km (26 miles 385 yards). In 1921 the IAAF officials decided they liked this strange distance because of the epic drama that unfolded in the race, with the Italian winner, Dorando Pietri, being disqualified for receiving help while staggering through the final 385 yards to the finish. And so the distance stuck.

THE GOLDEN AGE ▶ Skipping

forward a few decades, Chris Brasher won gold at the 1956 Olympics in the 3000m steeplechase and helped to pace Sir Roger Bannister to the world's first ever sub-4-minute mile. He also co-founded the London Marathon in 1981 (of which he ran in just under three hours when aged 52).

Later to become the London Marathon Race Director (from 2002 to 2012), Dave Bedford is a colourful character in the London running scene. In the 70s, while wearing bright red socks and a handlebar moustache, he set a new world record in the 10,000m (27:30.80).

In 1971, the Barnet-raised Joyce Smith broke the world record for the 3000m, won the first two London Marathons, and was the first British woman to run under 2:30 for the distance.

The great British mile era of the late 70s and 80s was headed by Sebastian Coe who held numerous world records and won gold in the 1500m at both the 1980 Moscow Games and the 1984 Los Angeles Games (as well as the silver in the 800m in both). He was born in Chiswick, London, and raised in Sheffield, but also represented Haringey Harriers, in north London, once he had left Loughborough University.

Daley Thompson (born in Notting Hill, London) ran his way to a gold medal in the decathlon at both the 1980 and 1984 Olympic Games. All done while sporting another great moustache.

Linford Christie (born in Jamaica, but raised in Acton, northwest London) won the 100m bronze in 1988 Seoul Olympics behind Carl Lewis, but

was later upgraded to silver after the winner, Ben Johnson, tested positive for a drug violation. Christie then came back to win gold four years later in Barcelona. At those same Games in 1992, Sally Gunnell, from northeast London, won gold in the gruelling 400m hurdles.

THE NEW MILLENNIUM ▶ In

2004, Kelly Holmes replicated Albert Hill's 1920 double by winning the Olympic 800m and 1500m gold medals. She grew up just southeast of London at Tonbridge and later competed for London club Ealing, Southall and Middlesex.

Christine Ohuruogu grew up less than one mile from what is now Queen Elizabeth Olympic Park where she won a silver medal in the 2012 Olympics, backing up her previous gold from Beijing 2008. She also has two 400m world championship titles to her name.

Mo Farah, who learnt his craft at Newham and Essex Beagles, is the man of the moment in British athletics having claimed double gold (5000m and 10,000m) at the London Olympics and three world championship titles.

London has a host of current competitive distance runners, including miler Andy Baddeley, top 5 and 10k performer Julia Bleasdale, marathoner Scott Overall, 800m speedster Andrew Osagie, 5 and 10k contender Andy Vernon, and 5k-turned-marathon-runner Chris Thompson.

Not to be out done by the endurance junkies, London's top current sprinters include 2014 European Champions James Dasaolu (100m) and Adam Gemili (200m), 2014 World Junior 100m Champion Dina Asher-Smith, 2007 World Junior 100m Champion Asha Philip, and Bianca Williams (2014 Commonwealth Bronze 200m).

Safe to say there must be something speedy in London's water.

TRAINING TIPS

This book details thousands of miles of running terrain just waiting to feel the soft tread of your trainers. But before you jump off the couch and suddenly start running 100mi each week, here are some training and safety ideas.

GRADUAL CONSISTENCY ▶ Our bodies are designed for running, but they are also creatures of habit and don't respond well to sudden changes. So if you're new to running or looking to increase your mileage, remember that, although your mind might be willing, your body will take time to adjust to new training demands.

Most runners need to take breaks from running each year because of overuse injuries which are typically caused by a sudden jump in either overall mileage or speed work (or both). A simple rule to help keep these injuries at bay is to only increase your weekly mileage by a maximum of 10 per cent each week (or 3mi—whatever is longer).

Structure your training so you increase your workload for three weeks and then take an easy week every fourth to allow your body and mind to recover.

The key to developing your running, beyond any magic training formulas or gadgets, is simply stringing weeks, months and years together of consistent training. So aim to take gradual steps forward in your training and racing goals in order to develop your fitness but not break this consistency with injuries.

LONG RUNS ▶ A big component of that development will be gradually increasing the length of a weekly long run. Increasing this by 1mi or 10 per cent (which ever is more) each week is typically a safe approach. Here are some ideas for long run courses around London:

- **Ruislip Woods Perimeter** (NW, p.166) 9.0mi
- **Chiswick & Twickenham Loop** (Thames, p.18) 9.1mi
- **Regent's Canal** (Central, p.58) 9.3mi
- **10 Bridges** (Thames, p.18) 9.4mi
- **Woolwich, Oxleas & Plumstead** (SE, p.100) 10mi
- **Cray Riverway** (SE, p.92) 11.3mi
- **Tower Bridge & Greenwich Loop** (Thames, p.18) 11.4mi
- **Dollis Valley** (NW, p.200) 13.2mi
- **Greenwich to Erith** (Thames, p.18) 13.3mi
- **Paddington Branch**, Grand Union Canal (NW, p.204) 14mi
- **Epping Forest** (NE, p.212) 15mi
- **Julia's Loop** (SW, p.151) 19.2mi

WORKOUTS ▶ Imagine if you owned a Ferrari and never took it out of first gear—how tragic would that be? It's the same with our running: if we do it all at an easy jogging pace, we become single speed runners and don't maximise both the fitness benefits and enjoyment of running. So here are some workout ideas for changing gears (start with one speed session per week and work up to a maximum of three per week to prepare for a key race):

- **Barefoot Strides:** Finish off an easy run with some short controlled fast runs on the

Wilson Kipsang (who trains a lot with fartlek and tempo runs) on his way to winning the London Marathon.
Photo: Pete Sheffield, flickr.com/twosheffs (CC BY ND 2.0)

grass to develop good running form e.g. 4x20 seconds. Do it at Parsloes Park (NE, p.232); Hampstead Heath Extension (NW, p.181); Hanworth Park (SW, p.138); and Dulwich Park (SE, p.82).

- **Fartlek:** This is a Swedish word that means "speed play". A fartlek workout usually starts and ends with 10-20mins easy jogging and in the middle has periods of faster running intermingled with recovery jogs e.g. 5x3mins with 2min jogs. Do these workouts on rolling terrain with interesting surfaces under foot. The following spots are perfect: Hainault Forest (NE, p.222), Horsendon Hill (NW, p.164), Wimbledon Common (SW, p.123), and Petts Wood (SE, p.72).

- **Tempo Runs:** This is an extended period of faster running usually performed at your lactate threshold (the pace at which you could race for an hour flat out). Do this on flat and, ideally, measured courses: Hyde Park's Serpentine (Central, p.38); Danson Park (SE, p.68); Bushy Park (SW, p.132); Grand Union Canal (NW, p.204); and Hornchurch Country Park (NE, 228).

- **Intervals & Reps:** These are shorter speed efforts (typically 200m to 1mi) repeated multiple times with recovery jogs or walks after each effort. Run these on measured circuits (you can also use a GPS watch) like an athletics track (for a list of London tracks see **runnersguidetolondon.co.uk**). Other good locations for interval sessions include Southall Park (NW, p.171), Fairlop Waters (NE, p.221), Battersea Park (Central, p.36), and Surrey Canal Path (Central, p.47).

Hills, like this one in Greenwich Park, reward the runner with both views and speed.

HILLS ▶ Running uphill isn't just about hunting out a good spot to take a selfie; leading running coaches call this lactate-inducing running terrain "speed work in disguise".

Just like speed work, you don't want to rush into a diet of hill training all in one go. Ease yourself in once a week doing an easy run over hilly terrain. Then step up to a couple of times per week and eventually do repetition workouts on hills.

Some top London locations for hill training include Hampstead Heath (NW, p.181), Greenwich Park (SE, p.64), Crystal Palace (SE, p.80), Richmond Park (SW, p.130), Farthing Downs (SW, p.118); Primrose Hill (Central, p.44), Ally Pally (NE, p.246) and many more (look for the hilly icon in this book).

SHOES ▶ The routes in this book will take you across a massive variety of surfaces, some of which can be slippery and uneven. So be sure to find a shoe that fits well and has suitable tread (remember that cobbled urban environments can be particularly perilous in wet and icy weather).

CLOTHING ▶ High visibility clothing is a must after dark and in winter, even consider wearing a head lamp. Plus, it's always safest to assume that vehicles can't see you and to giveway to all types of traffic.

It pays to have a water-resistant and breathable running coat ready to go in the wardrobe as well as warm layers that can be easily removed and tied around your waist once you are warmed up. A pair of gloves and hat go along way to preventing chills in winter (even when racing in just singlet and shorts) and a cap is ideal for keeping the rain off your face when it's wet. Avoid chaffing on the long runs by applying baby oil beforehand and use liquid soap (from public toilets) if you get a mid-run irritation.

SAFETY ▶ It's always a good idea to carry a phone whether you're going off-road or just roaming the streets. Plus, GPS-capable phones are great for bringing up a map if needed and for recording workouts.

A simple little note or a text is enough to let close friends or family know where you're going and when you'll be back. This is particularly important when running after dark and when in the larger green spaces like Epping Forest. Better yet, take someone with you so you can look out for each other—a running buddy is also an excellent motivator.

Unfortunately it's the reality that women need to take extra care when running. Find a running club or regular running buddies (see p.26), wear loose fitting clothing, run in the day time in well-populated areas, and interpret whistles as compliments (all the running is obviously paying off!).

CONSERVATION ▶ We all know the saying "take only photos and leave only footprints" but even your footprints can be nasty to London's wonderful undergrowth. So stick to marked trails and take those energy gel wrappers with you.

TOILETS ▶ This book details the location and opening times of many public toilets, however, if you find yourself in a rush to unload the goods (as often happens with runners—this is commonly called "the runner's trots") you'll find that local businesses are receptive to allowing desperate runners use their facilities. Otherwise, find a bush or two (preferably with large leaves for wiping) and be sure to bury the evidence.

FOOD & HYDRATION ▶ With a general lack of drinking fountains, your best bet for staying hydrated in most London running environments is to either carry a credit card or some coins (as you're never far from a store or cafe) or carry a fuel belt/hydration pack. On long runs (an hour or more) consider carrying or buying energy gels (or sweets) as well as isotonic fluid for more effective hydration.

DISCLAIMER

Although this book has been thoroughly proofed and checked, it may contain errors and inaccuracies in relation to distances, directions, and other descriptions. We take no responsibility for any injuries or mishaps that occur as a result of any of these errors or inaccuracies. The maps are produced from openstreetmap.org and are to be used only as guides; they may not be perfectly to scale. We also remind readers that they undertake the routes described in this book at their own risk and encourage everyone to enjoy their running but not push themselves too far in one single run when you do not have the people and medical support nearby to offer assistance.

RUN EVERY BOROUGH

As runners we often have dreams of bounding along a Rift Valley trail in Kenya or traversing a snowy Swiss mountain pass or battling the heat on America's Death Valley, but what about fully exploring your own hometown?

London is perfectly set up for the local runner to be a tourist in their own town. It has brilliant public transport, is easily accessible for day trips, and, as you'll find out scrolling through the pages of this book, has oodles of great running terrain in all of its 32 boroughs (well, 33 boroughs if you count the City of London, which technically isn't a borough).

To encourage this local exploration we've put together the *Run Every Borough Challenge*. The rules are simple and quite self-explanatory, to be honest: Find somewhere beautiful to run in every borough of London, run it, then tell the world how amazing it is on social media using the hashtag #runeveryborough (use photos and GPS records).

To provide added motivation, why not set a time frame to the challenge? Six months is achievable for most if you aim to set out on an exploration run 2-3 times per month. Three months (or one season, like summer or winter) requires weekly adventures. A month demands some serious planning and, most likely, some annual leave. And a week is reserved for the crazy.

Tip: A great way to tick off a bunch of boroughs in one run is to find a point-to-point course on a canal or way-marked walkway. For example, Regent's Canal will take you through five boroughs in just over 9mi of running.

Using bridges and tunnels to cross the Thames is a great way of ticking two or more boroughs in one run. The Greenwich Tunnel connects the Boroughs of Tower Hamlets and Greenwich.

Add a ✔ when you have run in a borough.

INNER BOROUGHS ▶

1 Westminster: Spoilt for inner city options here with the Royal Parks of Hyde, Kensington, St James's, Green and Regent's.

2 Kensington & Chelsea: Check out the sanctuary that is Holland Park (especially good for romantic date runs) and a couple of cemeteries (slightly less romantic).

3 Hammersmith & Fulham: From the smaller parks of Bishops and Ravenscourt to the large expanse of the Scrubs. Plus, plenty of Thames Path.

4 Camden: This is all about Hampstead Heath with notable mentions going to Waterlow Park and Primrose Hill.

5 Islington: The largest park here is Highbury Fields (12ha), also only slithers of Regent's Canal and the Parkland Walk.

6 Hackney: Hackney Marsh, the lower reaches of the River Lea and the parks that surround are great starting points. Plus, London Fields and Hackney Downs.

7 Tower Hamlets: From the Isle of Dogs and Canary Wharf to the canals of Limehouse and Regent's and on to Mile End Park and Victoria Park, the East End has plenty of running.

8 Greenwich: Greenwich Park is the obvious attraction. Combine it with the Green Chain and Thames Path to create exceptional long runs.

9 Lewisham: Beckenham Place Park in the south and Hilly Fields and Blackheath in the north—all connected by the Waterlink Way.

23

HI, I'M LONDON

Can you run in all of London's boroughs during spring?

Or would you prefer to tackle the challenge in winter?

10 Southwark: Has an impressive section of Thames Path (from Blackfriars Bridge to Greenland Dock) as well as parks (Dulwich, Peckham Rye, Southwark & Burgess), short canals, and cemeteries.

11 Lambeth: Thames Path in the north and parks further south (Streatham Common, half of Clapham Common, Norwood, Brockwell & Ruskin).

12 Wandsworth: Putney Heath in the west, the upper River Wandle, Wandsworth Common, the remainder of Clapham Common and Battersea Park (and the neighbouring Thames Path).

13 City of London: Aside from sprinting for the bus, running through here is best kept to the river's north bank.

OUTER BOROUGHS ▶

14 Hillingdon: In the south you have Harmondsworth Moor, Cranford Park and Stockley Country Park. Then use the Celandine Route and the Grand Union Canal to head north toward Park Wood and Ruislip

Woods.

15 Ealing: With many smaller parks, the Grand Union Canal's Paddington Arm and the River Brent serve to connect the majority of them.

16 Harrow: Many small parks and reserves. Use the LOOP in the north and the Capital Ring in the south to join the dots.

17 Brent: It's central highlight is Fryent Country Park, plus a selection of compact parks and the upper reaches of the River Brent.

18 Barnet: Together the Dollis Brook Walk and Pymmes Brook manage to connect most of this borough's commons and greenspaces.

19 Haringey: The must-do run here is Finsbury Park to Ally Pally via Parkland Walk.

20 Enfield: A collection of medium-sized parks in the south, the River Lea in the east, and some large country parks in the north (notably Forty Hall, Whitewebbs and Trent).

21 Waltham Forest: Run the length of the borough in Epping Forest and explore Walthamstow Marshes in the southwest.

22 Newham: From the Thames north check out the Royal Docks, Beckton District Park, the Greenway, West Ham Park, and, of course, Queen Elizabeth Olympic Park.

23 Redbridge: On top of several smaller suburban parks and woodlands, Redbridge has Wanstead Flats & Park, Valentines Park, Fairlop Waters, and Hainault Forest.

24 Barking & Dagenham: Suburban parks are your main port of call here with Barking, Mayesbrook, Parsloes, Central and Eastbrookend.

25 Havering: Run one of the many country parks that create a green belt on the outer fringes of the borough. Also visit Hornchurch and Harrow Lodge Park.

26 Bexley: Use the Green Chain and Thames Path to connect Erith and Thamesmead, run the Cray Riverway, and do a workout at Danson Park.

27 Bromley: Find a wood and explore it. Better yet, connect several woods together like in our Three Commons route (see p.90).

28 Croydon: From South Norwood Country Park in the north, follow the string of woods and greenspaces south to Selsdon Wood and all the way west to Farthing Downs and Happy Valley.

29 Sutton: The Wandle Way will get you started in the northern end of the borough with a couple of smaller parks and reserves to entice you further south.

30 Merton: Wimbledon Common is the great attraction here, with the mid-Wandle Way an option, and other parks worth a visit (Wimbledon, Morden, Mitcham Common and Canon Hill Common).

31 Kingston: Run along the river near Kingston-upon-Thames, otherwise it's just small unconnected parks and woodlands.

32 Richmond: If there were a competition for best borough for running on the planet, here's your winner. Thames Path connects Richmond, Bushy, Home, and Old Deer Parks—and we're just getting started.

33 Hounslow: With Osterley Park in the north and Hounslow Heath, Hanworth Park, and Bedfont Lakes in the south, there's plenty to take your mind off the constant hum of planes overhead.

LONDON RUNNING CLUBS

Clubs are perfect for meeting other runners, for regular competition and training, and for getting kids into athletics. If you have any doubts about whether your current running ability will be catered for, just ask the club, they're typically always friendly.

CENTRAL CLUBS ▶

London City Runners (Bermondsey)
londoncityrunners.com

London Frontrunners (Central London)
londonfrontrunners.org

Mornington Chasers (Kentish Town)
chaser.me.uk

Serpentine RC (Central London)
serpentine.org.uk

Victoria Park & Tower Hamlets AC
(Hackney) vphthac.org.uk

SOUTHEAST CLUBS ▶

Bexley AC (Erith) bexleyac.org.uk

Blackheath and Bromley Harriers Athletic Club (Hayes) bandbhac.org.uk

Bromley Veterans AC (Beckenham)
bromleyvetsac.org.uk

Croydon Harriers (South Norwood)
croydonharriers.com

Cambridge Harriers (Eltham)
cambridgeharriers.org.uk

Crystal Palace Fun Runners (Crystal Palace)
crystalpalacefunrunners.co.uk

Dulwich Park Runners (Dulwich)
dulwichparkrunners.co.uk

Dulwich Runners AC (Dulwich)
dulwichrunners.org.uk

Gmax TrackStars AC (Eltham)
gmaxtrackstars.com

Greenwich Tritons Triathlon Club
(Greenwich) greenwichtritons.org.uk

Kent AC (Lewisham)
ilfordathleticclub.co.uk

New Eltham Joggers (New Eltham)
newelthamjoggers.co.uk

Orpington Road Runners (Orpington)
orprunners.com

Petts Wood Runners (Petts Wood)
pettswoodrunners.org

Plumstead Runners (Welling)
plumsteadrunners.co.uk

SOUTHWEST CLUBS ▶

26.2 Road Runners Club (Surbiton)
26point2.co.uk

Barnes Runners (Barnes)
barnesrunners.org

Belgrave Harriers (Wimbledon)
belgraveharriers.com

Clapham Chasers (Clapham)
claphamchasers.co.uk

Clapham Pioneers (Clapham)
claphampioneers.co.uk

Clapham Runners (Clapham)
claphamrunners.com

Collingwood AC (Wallington)
collingwoodac.org.uk

Hercules Wimbledon AC (Wimbledon)
herculeswimbledonac.org.uk

Herne Hill Harriers (Tooting Bec)
hernehillharriers.org

Kingston AC And Poly Harriers (Kingston-upon-Thames) kingstonandpoly.org

Ranelagh Harriers (Richmond)
ranelagh-harriers.com

South London Harriers (Coulsdon)
southlondonharriers.org

St Mary's Richmond AC (Teddington)

smrac.org.uk

Striders Of Croydon (Croydon)
stridersofcroydon.org.uk

Sutton & District AC (Carshalton)
suttondistrictac.co.uk

Sutton Runners (Carshalton)
suttonrunners.org

The Stragglers Running Club (Ham)
stragglers.org

Thames Hare & Hounds (Wimbledon)
thameshareandhounds.org.uk

Wimbledon Windmilers (Wimbledon)
windmilers.org.uk

Veterans AC (South London) vetsac.org.uk

NORTHWEST CLUBS▶

Barnet & District AC (Southgate)
barnetadac.com

Ealing Eagles Running Club (Ealing)
ealingeagles.com

Ealing Southall & Middlesex AC (Greenford)
esm.org.uk

Fulham Running Club (Fulham)
fulhamrunningclub.org.uk

Harrow AC (Harrow Weald) harrowac.co.uk

Hayes & Harlington Road Runners (Hayes)
hhroadrunners.com

Highgate Harriers (Hampstead Heath)
highgateharriers.org.uk

Hillingdon AC (Ruislip) hillingdonac.co.uk

Metros RC (Pinner) metros.org.uk

Queen's Park Harriers (Willesden)
queensparkharriers.org.uk

Shaftesbury Barnet Harriers (Hendon)
shaftesburybarnet.co.uk

Sudbury Court Running Club
(Wembley) sudburycourt.org.uk

Trent Park Running Club (Oakwood)
trentparkrc.org

Thames Valley Harriers (White City)
thamesvalleyharriers.com

Tri London (Gospel Oak) trilondon.com

West 4 Harriers (Chiswick) west4harriers.com

NORTHEAST CLUBS▶

Barking Road Runners (Barking)
barkingroadrunners.org.uk

Dagenham 88 Runners (Dagenham)
dagenham88runners.com

East End Road Runners (Newham) eerr.org.uk

East London Runners (Wanstead)
eastlondonrunners.org.uk

Edmonton RC (Winchmore Hill)
edmontonrc.co.uk

Enfield and Haringey AC (Edmonton)
ehac.co.uk

Eton Manor AC (Leyton) eton-manor.com

Hackney Hurricanes AC (Hackney)
hackneyhurricanes.co.uk

Havering '90 Joggers (Hornchurch)
h90j.org.uk

Havering AC (Upminster)
havering-mayesbrook.org

Ilford AC (Ilford) ilfordathleticclub.co.uk

London Heathside Runners AC
(North London) londonheathside.org.uk

Newham & Essex Beagles AC (Plaistow)
newhamandessexbeagles.co.uk

Orion Harriers (Chingford)
orionharriers.org.uk

Synergy Running Club (Crouch End)
crouchendrunning.co.uk

Woodford Green AC with Essex Ladies
(Woodford Bridge) wgel.org.uk

*Visit **runnersguidetolondon.co.uk** or **clubfinder.englandathletics.org** to search for a club near you.*

Aside from the registered running clubs also check out London Athletic's RUN! programme (run-london.org), many social running groups organised by stores (such as Nike, Sweat Shop and Sweaty Betty), and innovative run groups like Run Dem Crew, GoodGym, and HomeRun.

RACE LONDON

Chances are, right now, as you are reading this, there is a running race going on somewhere in London. To complete the quintessential London racing experience, we recommend trying each of the following race types at least once in your running lifetime.

We should also point out that parkrun is technically not a race. It's a timed run. So it doesn't matter what place you come or what time you get; it's a chance to make friends, run in beautiful places, and challenge yourself to keep the running habit strong.

See if you can reach the 50 parkrun club. Or, even better, take on the challenge to get Lon-Done status by participating in every parkrun in the city.

Sign up for free at **parkrun.org.uk** (and don't forget your barcode). Plus read our parkrun reviews to find a parkrun that suits you at **runnersguidetolondon.co.uk**.

Charity fun runs are hugely popular and a great way to get started.

PARKRUN ▶

With 46 events inside the M25 (and growing monthly), London is the spiritual home of parkrun. So it makes sense that the first dip of your toe in the sea of London running races should be at one of these super friendly runs.

Yet another happy parkrun finisher.

The leading woman makes her kick for home in the British 10K.

10K ▸

This is the next step up from a 5k and London has plenty of regular 10k (or 6.2mi) races. Look out for The British 10k (July), London 10000 (May), Run to the Beat (Sep—formerly a half marathon), Croydon 10k (Oct), and the Regent's Park Summer 10k Series. These events can be perfect for targeting PBs or for tuning up for a longer race. Several charities, like Cancer Research, put on regular 10k events that have wonderfully relaxed and supportive atmospheres. Most half marathons will also have 10k options.

HALF MARATHON ▸

Possibly the most popular race distance on the planet, everyone who can put one foot in front of the other should have running a half marathon on their bucket list.

Finding a race in London at which to tick that box will be easy, there's the Royal Parks Half (Oct), East London Half (Apr), Richmond Running Festival (Sept), Hampton Court Half (Feb), Richmond Half (Mar), North London Half (Mar), Ealing Half (Sep), Dartford Half (Mar) and more.

There are also many smaller local half marathons, some great trail half marathons just on the outskirts of London, and several iconic races within an hour or two of London (like Bath, Reading and Hastings).

CROSS COUNTRY ▸

Before we move up to the big 26.2mi distance, there are several types of races that are great for developing strength and for getting those competitive juices flowing. Cross country perfectly fits this bill.

You'll need to sign up to a club to take

HI, I'M LONDON

The masses of the London Marathon.

Cross country clubs also offer various road racing events throughout the year as well. Notably, the 6 and 12 Stage Relays are great events that epitomise running as a team.

ATHLETICS ▸

Most London athletics clubs have programmes for children. These are great for developing foundational skills that kids can use for life. But the athletics track is also a destination for the adult runner as well.

Many London clubs hold open nights/days where races cost about £5 (or free for registered runners) and you can have a crack at anything from 100m to 10k. These events often have a wide range of abilities and ages.

If you want to take things more competitively, all athletics clubs compete in regional and/or national leagues, which, like cross country, accumulate team points. The British Milers Club also host some of the UK's top athletics meets—perfect if you want to nail a really fast time.

The athletics season runs from May to September with indoor racing at select locations during the winter months and a couple of mass participation road mile races in early summer (City of London and Westminster).

part (see p.26 for a club near you) and will probably need a pair of spikes (otherwise you'll be slipping everywhere!).

Adult cross country races are 2-10mi long and have a good spread of abilities. At most races, you'll receive an individual place and a team place for your club—great for adding a team camaraderie dynamic to the race.

The cross country season runs from October to March and very few things can improve your mental toughness like a series of hard cross country races. Be prepared to get muddy.

Local speedsters in the London Marathon.

OFF ROAD & ADVENTURE ▸

Within a few hours of London you can find yourself running on all sorts of terrain, over all sorts of distances. Fell running (or mountain running) finds the biggest hills in the neighbourhood and makes you run up and down them as fast as you can. Trail running tends to be a little less vertical and there are plenty of trail races near London, particularly on the North and South Downs. Obstacle races and mud runs have become hugely popular and are ideal for making use of your running fitness while having a fun day out with friends.

MARATHON ▸

As one of the world's most iconic races, London Marathon (Apr) is the premier running event on the London calendar. But it can be a tricky one to get into.

Charity spots are usually your best bet, however, if you have some wheels you can improve your chances by applying under the good-for-age category (with proof of a recent marathon time) or, if you are registered to a UK club, through the championship category (sub-2:45 for men and sub-3:15 for women).

For a more low-key local marathon, check out Richmond Park (May) and Thames Meander (Nov) Marathons. There are also plenty of nearby rural and off road marathons and Brighton (Apr), Bournemouth (Oct), Leicester (Oct), and Milton Keynes (May) Marathons all have good sized fields.

ULTRA MARATHON ▸

Once your running addiction has got seriously out of control, a mere 26.2mi simply won't do. So for you there's the Royal Parks Ultra (50k in Oct), Thames Path 100 (100mi in May), and North Downs Way 100 (100mi in Aug). Plus the charity events of the Thames Path Challenge (25, 50 & 100k in Sep) and the London 2 Brighton Challenge (100k in May).

See **runnersguidetolondon.co.uk/races** for dates and further details on all races.

ICON DESCRIPTIONS

MAP KEY

**ROADS/
TRAILS:**
— Main Road — Road — Minor Roads

— Main Run — Trails

········ Railway Tracks (underground tracks are not shown)

WATER:
■ River or Lake ～ Stream/Canal

LAND:
■ Grass/Farm ■ Woodlands — Park Fence

■ City & Suburban Zones ■■ Buildings

ICONS:
⬭ Athletics Track 🚻 Toilet

🅿 Parking 📷 Scenic Lookout

🍴 Cafe/Restaurant ⛲ Drinking Fountain

⊙ Underground Rail (Tube) Station

⇌ National Rail Station

🚆 Tram Station DLR DLR Station

⊙ London Overground Rail Station

▸ Park Entrance

RUN KEY

SURFACE: Road/Pavement   Grass

   Dirt/Mud   Gravel

   Limestone/Cinder   Cobbles/Pavers

TERRAIN: Hills   Mild Undulations

   Serious Hills   Mostly Flat (some undulations)

   Mostly Flat w/ some steeper hills   Flat

TRAFFIC & PARKS: High Foot Traffic   High Vehicle Traffic

   Congested Park   Closed at Various Times

WEATHER WARNINGS: No go in Wind   Caution in Wind

   No go in Rain/Ice   Caution in Rain/Ice

DISTANCES: **1.8mi / 2.8k**   Distance (loop/point-to-point or perimeter)

◀ ▶   Various Distances

Note: Distances are typically given in both miles (mi) and kilometres (km). When a distance is less than a kilometre it is given in metres (not yards). Areas are given in hectares (ha), which are 100m by 100m or roughly equal to 2.5 acres (ac). All distances are approximate only and maps may not be perfectly to scale.

CENTRAL HOTSPOTS

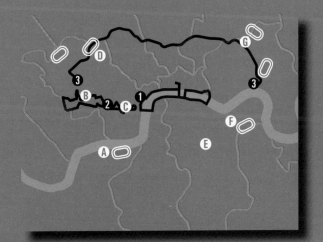

CENTRAL ROUTES

ALSO SEE THE THAMES PATH SECTION (P258) FOR MORE CENTRAL RUNS ▶

BATTERSEA PARK

1.8mi / 2.8k [i] [🔥] [⠿] [🏃]

Nestled on the south bank of the Thames, this inner city park still maintains an air of suburban life: casual sports, kids feeding ducks, families flying kites, plus plenty of runners.

LOCATION ▸ Battersea, Wandsworth, SW11 (2.6mi SW of central London)

INFO ▸ Battersea Park opened in 1854 and was part of a citywide plan to improve the living conditions of an industrialised, increasingly crowded London. At 83ha there's plenty to keep a runner busy, especially with the athletics track and direct access to the Thames Path.

Carriage Drive is the main sealed path and creates a loop around the entire park. Within the loop are several playing fields, a lake, gardens, two cafes, an impressive fountain display (goes on the hour for 15 minutes), and even a children's zoo. There are many trails through the interior. Most are short but the best are the crushed-limestone paths on the northwest side of the lake. Great for a quick explore.

Carriage Drive itself is a 1.75mi loop and has a crushed-limestone bridal path on either side—handy for mixing up surfaces. The park perimeter is 2.2mi (3.5km).

The athletics track (in the northeast of the park) is open 7am to 10pm weekdays and 7:30am to 7:30pm weekends. Next to the track is a selection of free-to-use outdoor gym equipment.

Battersea Park hugs the riverbank all the way

from Albert Bridge to Chelsea Bridge. This creates a straight, wide path that is just over kilometre long (0.7mi). So it makes for a great spot for 1km reps if you don't mind dodging the tourists and romantics who frequent the scenic stretch of river.

GETTING THERE ▸

Rail: Battersea Park National Rail Station (Southern; 0.2mi SE); Queenstown Road National Rail Station (South West, 0.3mi SE).

Bus: 44, 49, 137, 156, 319, 344, 345, 452, N19, N31, N44, & N137.

👍 ▸ A relatively quiet central-city park with a variety of running surfaces on offer.

👎 ▸ Unless you're on the track, it's off-limits before 8am.

MUST KNOW ▸

Circumference: 1.8mi (2.8km) main carriageway.

Surface: Sealed, grass, & crushed-limestone.

Terrain: Flat.

Weather Warnings: None.

Traffic Warnings: None.

Times: 8am till dusk (but you can still get in some gates to access the track and other sporting facilities).

Toilets: On Carriage Drive in both the southwest and northeast corners of the park, also by the water fountains.

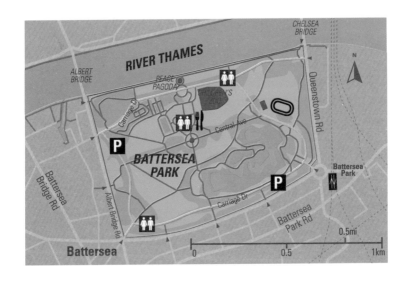

Runners finishing an evening 5k race at Battersea Park.

KENSINGTON GARDENS & HYDE PARK

4.3mi / 7.0k

A guide to running in London would be incomplete without a thorough going over of Hyde Park and its almost seamlessly conjoined neighbour Kensington Gardens.

LOCATION ▶ City of Westminster, W2 (1.2mi W of central London)

INFO ▶ With Kensington Gardens in the west and Hyde Park in the east, they are separated only by West Carriage Drive, which runs north-south across this otherwise roughly rectangular parkland. Most runners will incorporate portions of both parks into their run and a full loop around the edge of both parks is 4.3mi (7.0km).

Hyde Park | A perimeter of Hyde Park, following the trails closest to the fence line, is 3mi (4.8km). The park is packed full of trails, most of which are sealed. Construct your own favourite loops through formal gardens (in the southeast), grass fields, semi-woodlands, and of course around the Serpentine.

The Serpentine provides the perfect spot for 2mi loops or tempos. It's 100m longer than 2mi, but if you start from the cafe at the far eastern end of the lake (at the southern most point of the cafe's seating area) then run clockwise around the lake (keeping close to the shore except when you go around the Italian Gardens), and then finish

Looking north over The Serpentine. Kensington Gardens (left) and Hyde Park (right).

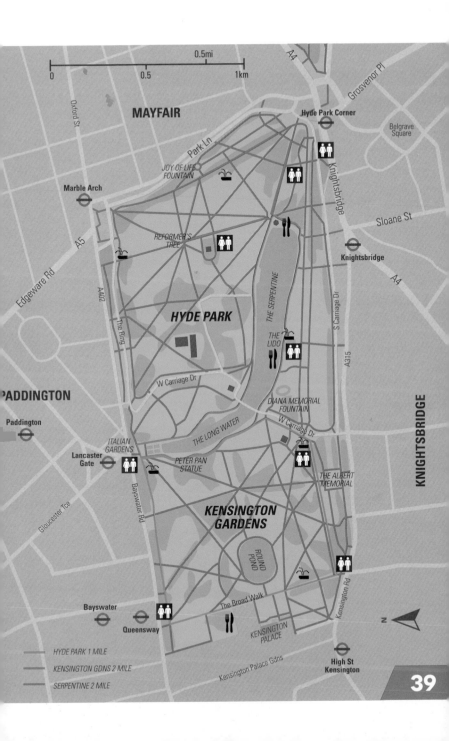

as soon as you meet the cafe again, that's 2mi exactly.

If the Serpentine is too busy, try a 1mi loop that starts just on the other side of Serpentine Road from the cafe. Run in an anti-clockwise direction past the bandstand, then turn left just before you meet The Broad Walk, using the final shortcut through to The Broadwalk. Follow this main path north until you pass the Joy of Life Fountain (on your right), make a gentle left here to cross the grass field to the Reformers Tree junction of paths. Turn left to run back to the start. This loop involves a 10m rise and fall and a full loop is about 20m longer than a mile.

Kensington Gardens | This is the more developed of the two parks, with plenty of landscaped symmetry, formal gardens and statues. Like Hyde Park, most of the paths (of which there are many again) are sealed, but there are also some nice grass trails in the interior. A full perimeter loop of the gardens is 2.7mi (4.3km).

A great 2mi loop starts from the Palace Gate (on Kensington Rd, south side of the park) and heads north along the Broad Walk past Kensington Palace. Just before you exit the park at Bayswater Road, turn right on to North Walk to reach the Italian Gardens. Turn right here to follow the water's edge south (on the west bank), but instead of going under the bridge into Hyde Park, turn right to follow the trail running parallel to West Carriage Drive. At the Mount Gate, turn right again onto the straight path heading to the Board Walk. The 2mi point is actually 100m before you reach the start point.

Options | Holland Park is a great nearby add-on. It's about 1km west by either following Bayswater Road (north Kensington Gardens) or Kensington High Street (south Kensington Gardens). By using Holland Walk in the east and then looping back through the western side of the park itself, the park's perimeter is 1.7mi (2.7km).

Finally, be sure to run the way-marked Diana Memorial Walk that charts a wonderful course

Hyde Park in all its spring glory.

through both parks as well as neighbouring St James's and Green Parks. Also, from the Italian Gardens, it's less than a mile north, past Paddington Station, to Little Venice from where you can run either east or west along the canal.

GETTING THERE ▶

Rail: Hyde Park Tube Station (Piccadilly line; SE corner of the parks); Marble Arch Tube Station (Central line; NE corner); Lancaster Gate Tube Station (Central line; near Italian Gardens); & Queensway Tube Station (Central line; NW corner).

Bus: 2, 9, 10, 14, 16, 19, 22, 36, 49, 52, 70, 73, 74, 82, 94, 137, 148, 274, 360, 390, 414, 436, & 452.

👍 ▶ It is hard to imagine two inner city parks that could match these beauties.

👎 ▶ Events and summer foot traffic can often render large sections of the parks non-runnable.

MUST KNOW ▶

Circumference: 4.3mi (7.0km)

Surface: Sealed (with grass options and even a bridle trail).

Terrain: Mild undulations.

Weather Warnings: None.

Traffic Warnings: This place gets very busy!

Times: Kensington Gardens is open from 6am to dusk and Hyde Park 5am to midnight. Check royalparks.org.uk/events/whats-on to see if there are any events on in the parks.

Toilets: Each of Kensington Gardens' four corners has a toilet, and in Hyde Park the Lido, Rose Gardens and south of the Reformer's Tree.

Winter on The Serpentine, Hyde Park. Photo: Indusfoto.

41

ST JAMES'S PARK & GREEN PARK

2.4mi / **3.9**k

The green lung of London's inner city, these two grand parks are regular stomping grounds for lunchtime joggers and early morning tempo runners.

LOCATION ▶ City of Westminster, W1J & SW1A (1mi W of central London)

INFO ▶ Running in these two parks, under Buckingham Palace's watchful eye, you feel like you're running on the front lawn of the Queen. Fortunately, the quality of the parks live up to this feeling.

Green Park | Sitting just north of Buckingham Palace, Green Park is furnished with long lines of beautifully mature trees and grassy meadows. There is a small rise from southeast to northwest and plenty of trails.

The perimeter is 1.2mi (2.0km) and you can follow it by starting at Canada Gate (near the Queen Victoria Memorial), while looking north, run along the fence line to your right. Then turn left to run north up Queen's Walk. Turn left again at Green Park Tube Station and follow the Piccadilly fence line until you reach the Memorial Gates at the western end of Constitution Hill. Follow Constitution Hill back to Canada Gate.

St James's Park | Dominated by the elongated lake, St James's is the more formal of the two

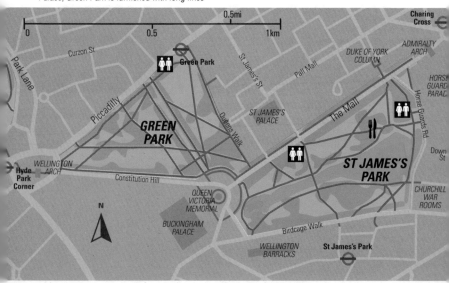

parks. This can make it rather congested but there is still plenty of running to be had within it.

Unless you run around the footpaths surrounding St James's Park, there isn't really a perimeter trail. Instead the most logical route is to run around the lake. One lap is 1.06mi (1.7km) so could potentially be run for mile intervals and tempos (accounting for the extra 100m).

The bridge that crosses the centre of the lake makes for some nice figure-of-eight loops and for half-lake loops. The eastern half is 70m longer (the length of the bridge) than 1km—so ideal for 1km reps (walking the bridge for recovery). The eastern loop (including the bridge) is 770m long.

Between the two parks is The Mall (which is emblazoned in many runners' minds as the long-awaited end of 26.2mi worth of suffering in the annual London Marathon). It has a nice wide, limestone footpath either side, so is perfect for connecting the two parks together.

Options | Definitely run the way-marked Diana Memorial Walk. Also the Thames Path is just a quarter mile east from the southeast corner of St James's Park. So with the combo of Kensington, Hyde, Green, and St James's, you can create a relatively traffic free, green corridor almost all the way to the river.

GETTING THERE▸

Rail: Green Park Tube Station (Victoria, Piccadilly, & Jubilee lines, NE corner of Green Park); & St James's Park Tube Station (District and Circle lines, 200m S of St James's Park).

Bus: 2, 3, 9, 11, 12, 14, 16, 19, 22, 24, 29, 36, 38, 52, 53, 73, 82, 88, 91, 148, 159, 211, 436, 453, & C2.

An inner city oasis of green and a photo-ready lake, all with palatial surrounds.

The leafy avenues of Green Park.

St James's Park Lake.

▶ Can get mighty crowded.

MUST KNOW ▶

Circumference: 2.4mi (3.9km)

Surface: Sealed & some crushed limestone.

Terrain: Slight slope.

Weather Warnings: None.

Traffic Warnings: Heavy pedestrian traffic and also take care when crossing The Mall (use the crossings).

Times: Green Park is always open and St James's 5am to midnight.

Toilets: Near the Green Park Tube Station, in the northeast of St James's Park and just north of the St James's Park bridge.

REGENT'S PARK & PRIMROSE HILL

4.0mi / 6.5k

Two parks with everything: lush gardens, large playing fields, wide sealed roads, narrow dirt trails, lakes, a running track, a hill with famous views of London, and even a zoo.

LOCATION ▶ Marylebone, City of Westminster, NW1 (2.1mi NW of central London)

INFO ▶ Unlike many London parks, which have wide sealed paths just inside their boundaries, Regent's Park has a road open to traffic just outside its fence line and several main paths that crisscross the centre of the park. This means that to do a full circumference you need to either run on the pavement of the surrounding Outer Circle road (2.7mi) or follow the paths and small dirt trails just inside the fence line (3.3mi, or 4.0mi when combined with a full circuit of Primrose Hill).

The southern end of Regent's is dominated by the dreamy Queen Mary's, English, Avenue and St John's Lodge Gardens. This area also boasts the Y-shaped boating lake and with so much to look at and so many fragrant flowers to enjoy, running around here is never boring.

The circular road surrounding the Queen Mary's Garden's makes for an interesting training loop. Running next to the inside curb is a perfect 1km loop. With traffic volumes it isn't always appropriate to use this loop, but choose your time wisely and it's a good spot to run your interval session. It also has a slight climb and descent.

The northern end of Regent's is predominantly sporting fields with plenty of opportunities for exploring and creating your own loops. And if you hear some monkey noises, it's not necessarily that the triathletes have arrived for a training

Boating Lake, The Regent's Park.
Credit: The Royal Parks.

session, but probably means you're running next to London Zoo, which sits right at the northern end of the park.

Also at this end is an old cinder running track. Being just outside the park it's open at all times and is free to use. It's only 386.8 metres but there are two lines marked on the road side of the track showing where a 400m loop begins and ends. Watch those tight turns though.

To the north of the park, just over Outer Circle Road, is Regent's Canal (which makes a great access point to and from the park) and then over one more road is Primrose Hill. With hills in short supply in central London, be sure to utilise the lung burning capabilities of Primrose and, of course, soak in its views.

Most trails on Primrose Hill lead up to the summit, but some, of which most are dirt, also skirt around the edges of the hill. The summit itself is about 30 metres higher than Regent's Park.

Helpful Hints | There are shower and locker facilities available for runners at The Hub—the sporting facility in the centre of the northern section of Regent's Park. There are several free toilet blocks (which close an hour before park closing) and several cafes and water fountains. Park maps are everywhere, so you shouldn't get lost.

GETTING THERE ▶

Rail: Baker Street Tube Station (Hammersmith & City, Circle, Metropolitan, Jubilee, & Bakerloo lines, 0.2mi SW); Regent's Park (Bakerloo line, 0.1mi S); & Great Portland Street (Hammersmith & City, Circle, & Metropolitan, 0.1mi SE).

Bus: 13, 18, 27, 30, 74, 82, 113, 205, 274, 453, & C2.

👍 ▶ Everything a runner could want with flat fields and hills, roads and dirt trails, and even a cinder track and nearby canal tow path.

👎 ▶ It's a shame the park doesn't connect directly to Primrose Hill and that London Zoo juts out into the park reducing its runnable area.

SEE MAP OVER PAGE ▶

The view from Primrose Hill. Credit: Giles Bernard.

MUST KNOW ▶

Circumference: 4.0mi (6.5km)

Surface: Sealed, grass, & dirt.

Terrain: Flat with a good hill.

Weather Warnings: None.

Traffic Warnings: It's a busy park and take care on internal roads, the Outer Circle, and when crossing Albert Road to Primrose Hill.

Times: Open from 5am to about dusk (4:30pm in winter & 9:30pm in summer).

Toilets: Wildlife Centre, Queen Mary's Gardens, Chester Road, The Hub, and the south side of Primrose Hill.

CENTRAL HOTSPOTS

REGENT'S PARK

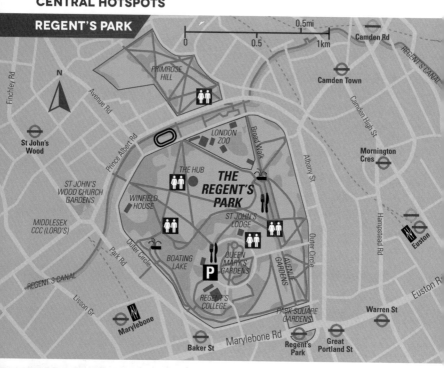

0.5mi
0 0.5
0 1km

Camden Rd

REGENT'S CANAL

Finchley Rd

N

PRIMROSE HILL

Avenue Rd

Camden Town

Camden High St

St John's Wood

Prince Albert Rd

LONDON ZOO

Broad Walk

Albany St

Mornington Cres

ST JOHN'S WOOD CHURCH GARDENS

THE HUB

THE REGENT'S PARK

WINFIELD HOUSE

St John's Lodge

Hampstead Rd

MIDDLESEX CCC (LORD'S)

Park Rd

Outer Circle

BOATING LAKE

P

QUEEN MARY'S GARDENS

AVENUE GARDENS

Outer Circle

Euston

Euston Rd

Lisson Gr

REGENT'S CANAL

Marylebone

REGENT'S COLLEGE

PARK SQUARE GARDENS

Warren St

Baker St

Marylebone Rd

Regent's Park

Great Portland St

BURGESS PARK

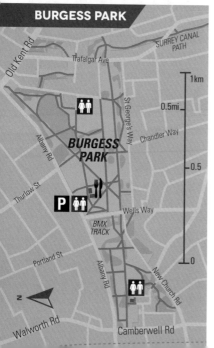

Old Kent Rd

SURREY CANAL PATH

Trafalgar Ave

1km

0.5mi

BURGESS PARK

St George's Way

Chandler Way

Albany Rd

0.5

Thurlow St

P

Wells Way

BMX TRACK

Portland St

Albany Rd

New Church Rd

0

Walworth Rd

Camberwell Rd

The fishing lake at Burgess Park.

BURGESS PARK

2.8mi / 4.5k 🚻 〰️ 🎴 🏃 🏌️

An long, narrow park that works more as a south-of-the-bridge thoroughfare (to places like Southwark Park and Surrey Canal Path) than a stand alone running destination.

LOCATION ▶ Camberwell, Southwark, SE5 (2.8mi SE of central London)

INFO ▶ A lot of money was poured into this park's refurbishment, however, it still provides little to entice the runner—except as a peaceful break away from the busy surrounding south London streets. Its main problem is that it's essentially just one long stretch of paved path, running east-west, surrounded by grass fields.

In the eastern end is a fishing lake that provides additional looping options and there are also some grass trails that can take you through the gardens and small hills that run parallel to the main path. A foot tunnel under Wells Way creates a seamless connection between the west and east sections of the park and a rough butterfly-shaped loop of the park will get you up close to 3mi.

There is a way-marked 5km jogging trail, but (at writing) the way-markers were tricky to follow.

From the east end of the park, cross over Trafalgar Avenue to find the 1km-long Surrey Canal Path. This was once a canal, but now provides an uninterrupted connection south to Peckham. It's ideal for 1km reps.

A great longer loop (about 10mi) can be made through Burgess Park, then onto Southwark Park and north to the Thames. Follow the Thames Path west all the way to Vauxhall Bridge where you can turn eastward past The Oval Cricket Ground to Kennington Park (ideal for a loop or two). Then follow Camberwell New and Wyndham Roads back to the start.

GETTING THERE ▶

Rail: Elephant & Castle Station (1.3mi NW; Bakerloo and Northern Tube lines, & Southeastern & Thameslink services).

Bus: 12, 21, 35, 40, 42, 45, 53, 63, 68, 78, 136, 148, 168, 171, 172, 176, 343, 363, 453, 468, & X68.

👍 ▶ Great for escaping nearby busy streets.

👎 ▶ Its irregular and elongated shape.

MUST KNOW ▶

Circumference: 2.8mi (4.5km)

Surface: Sealed (with grass options) & cobbles.

Terrain: Flat (with some man-made hills ideal for hill sprints on grass).

Weather Warnings: The cobbled area near Wells Way is uneven and can become slippery.

Traffic Warnings: It's a busy place on a hot summer's day so look out for other park users.

Times: Closes at dusk.

Toilets: Near the cafe (in the centre of the park) and also at the Tennis Centre (west end) and Sports Centre (east end).

SOUTHWARK PARK & DOCKS

1.4mi / 2.25k

A picturesque nineteenth century park handy to the Thames Path and waterside paths or green spaces.

LOCATION ▶ Bermondsey, Southwark, SE16 (3.8mi SE of central London)

INFO ▶ Southwark Park | A quiet road separates the northern end of Southwark Park from the south. In the south is a main trail that circumnavigates a large open sports field, a lake and formal gardens. There is also an athletics track, but is sadly in a state of disrepair. There

are plans to bring it back to life, but at the time of writing there is no ETA. However, the sealed loop around the sports field (including the small triangle at the northern end of the athletics track) is 1.03km around, so makes a good tempo or intervals location. A full loop of the park is 1.4mi (2.25km).

The central focus of the park's northern section is the replica of an 1833 bandstand, with most of the trails converging there. The tree-lined paths are truly beautiful, especially in autumn.

Directly north of Southwark Park (just over the road) is King's Stairs Gardens. This is a very small park but provides a green link to the Thames Path.

Greenland Dock | From Southwark Park's China Hall Gate (SE corner), jog southeast along Lower Road for a few hundred metres and then left onto Redriff, and you'll soon come to this large dock. There are maps on display that mark out a tranquil 1.4mi loop around the dock (including South Dock).

From Greenland Dock you can also explore the narrow, but beautifully green, corridor that is Russia Dock Woodland. This starts off with three parallel trails (a combo of sealed and dirt) that follow a small stream. It's about a mile north before you hit the Thames (after crossing a couple of roads and ducking through small public parks).

Canada Water | From China Hill Gate you can also run through the Canada Water shopping

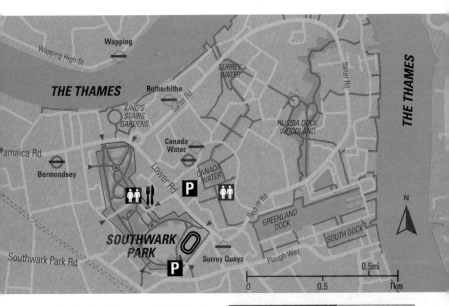

precinct and from there run north following the canal that connects Canada Water to the Thames.

Connect all these extras up by following the Thames Path back west to the King's Stairs Gardens and south to Southwark Park.

GETTING THERE▶

Rail: Surrey Quays Overground Station (0.1mi SE) & Canada Water Tube Station (Jubilee Line & Overground service, 0.4mi NE).

Bus: 1, 47, 188, 199, 225, 381, 395, C10, P12, & N381.

👍▶ A rare south bank inner-city green space. Being close to the Thames and other green areas provides plenty of extra options.

👎▶ The state of the athletics track.

VICTORIA PARK

2.7mi / **4.4**k

The model of the perfect inner-city park with large open fields, tree-lined avenues, ponds bordered by well manicured gardens—all making for an east London runners' haven.

LOCATION ▶ South Hackney, Tower Hamlets, E9 (4.1mi NE of central London)

INFO ▶ One of London's oldest public parks, Victoria Park was established in 1841 by Queen

Victoria after she received a signed petition from 30,000 Londoners requesting the park be set aside for public use. And by the number of locals who still frequent it, it's just as popular as it ever was.

Aside from its own virtues, Victoria Park makes a great connection point between various other parks (including Mile End which boasts a good athletics track), Lee Valley to the north, Olympic Park to the east, and the canals, two of which (Regent's and Hertford Union) run alongside the park. Use the many gates around Victoria Park to access these extra options.

The park itself is divided into two sections by Grove Road, which cuts through its middle, running north to south.

The western section has more developed gardens and, for the runner, has a main wide sealed road around its circumference (which also has a dirt trail and a crushed limestone bridal path alongside). There are several sealed paths through the interior that twist around the main lake and cross over a couple of bridges, making them well worth exploring.

The eastern portion of the park is more open and has the same wide path around its circumference (with accompanying dirt track) but in its interior, apart from a playground and a monument or two, are large playing fields. These are perfect for doing strides or finding your own favourite loop on the soft grass.

A full loop of the sealed perimeter road is 2.7mi

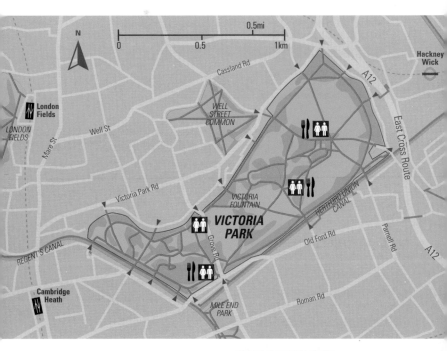

(4.4km). Victoria Park Harriers and Tower Hamlets Athletics Club has its home in the northeast corner of the park in St Augustine's Hall. The Pavilion Cafe offers organic food and coffee in the park's southern corner.

GETTING THERE ▶

Rail: Homerton Station (London Overground, 0.5mi N); Hackney Wick (London Overground, 0.4mi NE); Mile End Tube Station (Hammersmith & City, District, and Central lines, 0.7mi S), & Cambridge Heath National Rail Station (Greater Anglia service, 0.4mi SW).

Bus: 8, 276, 277, 339, 388, 425, 488, & N8.

👍 ▶ Access to many paths both inside and outside the park and lots of other runners to keep you company (or race!).

👎 ▶ The dusk closing times make this a lunchtime or before-work option in winter.

THE GRAND TOUR

7.0mi / 11.25k

For the visiting runner, why spend all day walking around London's main attractions, when you could run the whole thing in as little as an hour?

LOCATION ▶ Nelson's Column, Trafalgar Square, WC2N (central London)

MILE–BY–MILE ▶ Start: Trafalgar Square. From the base of Nelson's Column make your way south across the series of pedestrian crossings (or use the subways) to Whitehall Street.
Interest: Nelson's Column (commemorates Nelson's 1805 victory over Napoleon), National Gallery, and St Martin-in-the-Fields Church.

0.15mi: Whitehall. Keep to the right hand side of Whitehall Street and follow it all the way to Parliament Square (600m).

Interest: The Old Admiralty Offices (right), Horse Guards Parade (right), the Ministry of Defence (left), 10 Downing Street (right), and the WWI Cenotaph (centre of road).

0.5mi: Parliament Square. You may like to cross Parliament Square to get a closer look at Westminster Abbey, but otherwise turn left, crossing Whitehall via the subway (saves waiting for the lights and there are toilets here if needed). Then cross Westminster Bridge.
Interest: Westminster Abbey, Sir Winston Churchill Statue, Houses of Parliament, and the Queen Elizabeth Tower (Big Ben is the bell inside this tower).

0.8mi: Thames South Bank. Take the stairs to your left immediately after crossing the bridge and follow the Thames Path north (and then east) along the river's south bank.

Looking north along the Thames from Westminster Bridge.

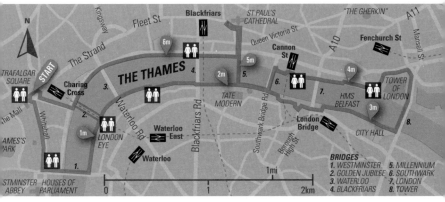

Interest: The River Thames, London Eye (marks 1mi), Jubilee Gardens, and the arts hub of the Southbank Centre.

1.8mi: Blackfriars Bridge. Carry on following the Thames Path past the hip apartment complexes, funky office blocks, art galleries, and bridge underpasses.

Interest: Tate Modern, Millennium Foot Bridge (we'll cross it shortly), and Shakespeare's Globe Theatre (modern reconstruction of the original).

2.25mi: Southwark Bridge. Carry on east following the Thames Path signs but be aware that you'll be heading away from the river for 600m. The Thames Path heads south just before the rail lines, and then goes under those lines via Clink Street. At the Golden Hinde (the sailing ship) turn right, briefly running on Cathedral Street, before turning left on to Montague Close, which will take you under London Bridge (the A3). 100m after exiting this tunnel, follow the Thames Path sign left along the walkway back to the river where you can now follow your nose east to Tower Bridge.

Interest: Clink Prison Museum, the ruins of Winchester Palace, the Golden Hinde, HMS Belfast, and City Hall.

3.2mi: Tower Bridge. Take the stairs from the Thames Path up on to Tower Bridge, and, keeping to the left (west) side of the road, cross the bridge. When you reach the north bank, continue following the road alongside the Tower of London. Complete an anti-clockwise 3/4 circuit around the Tower by hugging the pavement. Pass the main entrance to the Tower and join the Thames Path (heading west) via the Three Quays Walk.

Interest: Tower Bridge, Tower of London, plus excellent views of The Shard (310m high).

4.35mi: Steelyard Passage. 100m after exiting this unique tunnel take the stairs up to Southwark Bridge to cross the river back to the south bank again. Take the stairs on your left (east) down to the Thames Path and then head west under Southwark Bridge. Carry on for 200m, past Shakespeare's Globe, until you reach the Millennium Bridge outside the Tate Modern. Make a direct line for St Paul's Cathedral via this footbridge.

5.3mi: St Paul's Cathedral. The western face of St Paul's (on your left) is the best place for a quick photo opportunity. Then retrace your steps back to the river's north bank (take the stairs at the beginning of the Millennium Bridge). Head west along the Thames Path.

CENTRAL ROUTES

Interest: St Paul's (built following the Great Fire of 1666).

5.8mi: Blackfriars Bridge, North Bank.
Follow the riverside path under Blackfriars Bridge and Waterloo Bridge.
Interest: HMS President, HQS Wellington, and Cleopatra's Needle.

6.7mi: Northumberland Avenue. Immediately
after running under the Hungerford and Golden Jubilee Bridges (the adjoining foot and rail bridges) use the pedestrian crossing to reach Northumberland Avenue (heading northwest). Follow the street for 500m to reach Trafalgar Square once more.

Options | From Trafalgar Square it's easy to do a loop of a few miles through the West End. Start by heading northwest up to Piccadilly Circus (London's answer to Times Square) and then northwest again to the shopping hubs of Regent and Oxford Streets. Head east along Oxford and then south down Charing Cross Road through the dirty, but buzzing, theatre and social hub of Soho. Charing Cross Road will lead you back to Trafalgar Square. Have fun dodging shoppers.

Also consider joining this run with the Diana Memorial Run, which comes very close to Trafalgar Square halfway down The Mall.

GETTING THERE▶
Rail: Charing Cross Station is directly at Trafalgar Square (Northern & Bakerloo tube lines & Southeastern National Rail).

Bus: 3, 6, 9, 11, 12, 13, 15, 23, 24, 29, 53, 87, 88, 91, 139, 159, 176, & 453.

👍▶ Ideal for visitors wanting to tick off many of the key London icons in one run.

👎▶ Dodging pedestrians (be prepared to walk some sections).

Tower Bridge at sunset during the 2012 Olympic Games.

DIANA MEMORIAL RUN

7.2mi / 11.6k 🏃 🚴 🚚

Constructed to remember the late Princess Diana, this way-marked run of 7.2mi charts a course through London's top inner city parks, passing many iconic spots along the way.

LOCATION Hyde Park Corner, City of Westminster, W1J (2.5mi W of central London)

INFO ▸ This is a must-do run for both visiting runners and those who call London home. I say this not only because of the significant royal landmarks and for the wonderful collection of four inner city parks you will visit, but also for the memory of the incredible woman this route is constructed to remember.

The figure-of-eight course is marked with 90 brass plates (with a rose emblem) set in the ground. So navigation, once you know roughly where to go, is easy enough. Also, if you need to cut the distance down, you can always split the run into two separate loops (St James's and Green Park is 2.7mi, 4.4km; Hyde and Kensington is 4.5mi, 7.2km) or skip Kensington Gardens entirely.

MILE-BY-MILE ▸ Start: Hyde Park Corner. From the southeast corner of Hyde Park head east by crossing over the busy road (wait for the lights!), pass under Wellington Arch, cross the busy road again, and then head east down Constitution Hill (keep to the left side).
Interest: The Wellington Arch (commemorates Arthur Wellesley, the 1st Duke of Wellington, victory over Napoleon at Waterloo in 1815).

0.5mi: Buckingham Palace. When you reach Buckingham Palace, cross the road to run in front of the main gates (with the Queen Victoria Memorial to your left).
Interest: Buckingham Palace has been the royal residence since 1837.

0.6mi: Wellington Barracks. After passing the Palace, make two more crossings towards St James's Park. Enter the park from Birdcage Walk.

0.7mi: St James's Park. Head directly north to the lake and begin a clockwise 3/4-loop of it. At the 3/4 point, cross the bridge and head straight up to The Mall.
Interest: St James's Park is the oldest of the Royal Parks—acquired by Henry VIII in 1532 for

Children and families enjoying the Princess of Wales Memorial Fountain.

CENTRAL ROUTES

deer hunting.

1.7mi: The Mall. Cross to the north side of The Mall, turn left and run towards Buckingham Palace again. Turn right at the intersection and enter Green Park via the Canada Gate.
Interest: It is said that The Mall was coloured red to give the appearance of a royal red carpet. It's also almost exactly 1km long, so ideal for reps.

2mi: Green Park. Run up the straight line of trees, called the Broad Walk, to Piccadilly (the street). Turn left here and another quick left to follow this path west.

2.6mi: Wellington Arch. Back at the busy roundabout, cross over to Hyde Park Corner again and enter Hyde Park.

2.75mi: Rose Garden, Hyde Park. You'll see a long and wide bridle path stretching west, follow it briefly before turning into the Rose Garden on your right.
Interest: During the 1665 Great Plague, many Londoners escaped the city by camping in Hyde Park.

3.05mi: The Serpentine. When you reach the cafe, turn left and follow the south bank of The Serpentine all the way to the Princess of Wales Memorial Fountain (passing toilets and a drinking fountain on the way).
Interest: Surprising to many visitors, the murky waters of The Serpentine boast a popular paid swimming area (The Lido) used year round.

3.65mi: The Princess of Wales Memorial Fountain. At the fountain, turn left to reach West Carriage Drive, cross it and enter Kensington Gardens. Turn left and follow the trail parallel to the road. Then turn right as the trail veers towards the Albert Memorial.
Interest: The Diana Memorial Fountain was designed to be accessible for children and inclu-

sive of all, mirroring the life of Princess Diana.

4mi: Albert Memorial. With the Memorial and Royal Albert Hall to your left, carry on along South Flower Walk until you reach the large walkway (Broad Walk) heading north. Turn right.
Interest: The Albert Memorial was commissioned by a mourning Queen Victoria who lost her husband in 1861 to typhoid when he was just 42.

4.6mi: Kensington Palace. Carry on straight until you reach the Diana Memorial Playground. Turn right at the playground and, once you are directly in front of the palace again, turn left to connect back to the upper reaches of The Serpentine (called "The Long Water"). Turn left.
Interest: Princess Diana lived in Kensington Palace between 1981 and 1997.

5.4mi: Peter Pan Statue. Pass the statue and follow The Long Water north, around the Italian Gardens, then south, following the lake till you reach West Carriage Drive.
Interest: The Peter Pan Statue was erected overnight by the story's creator as a surprise. The Italian Gardens are believed to have been a gift from Prince Albert to Queen Victoria.

6mi: West Carriage Drive. Turn left to follow the road briefly before using the crossing to enter Hyde Park again. Turn left and then a quick right to run past the Police and Information Centre and reach the Reformers' Tree.

6.5mi: Reformers' Tree. Turn right, then left at the toilet block (on your right), and right again when you reach the wide Broad Walk. Follow it all the way back to Hyde Park Corner.
Interest: The Reformers' Tree is a monument to free speech and the right for all to vote.

GETTING THERE ▶

Rail: Hyde Park Corner Tube Station (Piccadilly Line).

Bus: 2, 9, 10, 14, 16, 19, 22, 36, 38, 52, 73, 74, 82, 137, 148, 414, 436, C2, N9, N16, N19, N22, N38, N52, N73, N74, N97, & N137.

👍 ▶ Brilliant parks, amazing palaces, and a generally easy to follow course.

👎 ▶ The scenery can distract your attention from spotting the brass way-markers, especially because the trail sometimes does not follow the straightest or most obvious route.

These inviting deck chairs will be waiting for you as you finish your run in Hyde Park.

MUST KNOW ▶

Distance: 7.2mi (11.6km)

Surface: Sealed.

Terrain: Mild undulations.

Traffic Warning: Road crossings and pedestrian traffic can be busy, particularly near Buckingham Palace.

Weather Warning: None.

Time Restrictions: Kensington Gardens open from 6am to dusk (Hyde and St James's Parks 5am to midnight).

Toilets: Hyde Park Corner; St James's Park (halfway down The Mall); northeast Green Park; Hyde Park (Rose Garden, Lido & near Reformers Tree); Kensington Gardens (Flower Walk & Italian Gardens).

REGENT'S CANAL

9.3mi / **15**k

A largely traffic-free nine-mile jog through London's heart and soul. From the transforming East End, past the grand mansions surrounding Regent's Park, to the tranquillity of Little Venice—this is a bucket list London run.

LOCATION ▶

Start: Limehouse Station, Tower Hamlets, E14 (3.9mi E of central London).
Finish: Paddington Station, City of Westminster, W2 (2.8mi NW of central London).

INFO ▶ Regent's Canal was opened in 1820

to connect the Paddington Arm of the Grand Union Canal to the Thames. It was once a key transport route for the factories and industries of east London and, now that those factories have been replaced by apartments, the canal provides a brilliant car-free route through the city.

This route also has several world class add-on options at Victoria Park, Regent's Park, Primrose Hill, the Thames Path, and Grand Union Canal. You can also complete a full loop by running south once you hit Paddington Station. Run through Hyde Park, past Buckingham Palace and then Westminster Abbey, before following the north bank of the Thames all the way to

One of the many tunnels on Regent's Canal.
Keep an eye and ear out for oncoming cyclists.

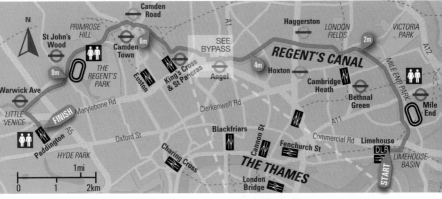

Limehouse Basin (makes a 17.7mi long run).

On the other hand if you're after a shorter run, you can cut this in half by finishing at Angel Tube Station in Islington. Finally, the paths running next to canals are called towpaths because horses were once used to tow the canal boats.

MILE–BY–MILE ▶ Start: Limehouse Station. From the Thames side of Limehouse Station make your way east to Limehouse Basin.

0.1mi: Limehouse Basin. Keep to the north banks of the basin, cross the footbridge over Regent's Canal and turn left to join the canal towpath heading north.

0.5mi: Mile End Park. On your right is the elongated Mile End Park. You can run through the meandering trail that runs parallel to the towpath through the park for a change of scenery. Also, the park has two half-mile circuits designed for walking, but can also be run as reps. Look for the yellow "Walk a Mile" signs.

1.7mi: Victoria Park. The towpath runs by Victoria Park which provides a great option for adding on.

2.4mi: Gas Holders. Keep on going along the towpath. Navigating this run couldn't be more

simple. On the other side of the canal there is a collection of the strange round steel structures that can be found all over London. These are gas holders that expand upwards inside the steel frame when filled with gas.

4.4mi: Islington Tunnel Bypass. With no footpath through the Islington Tunnel, it's time for runners to find their way through the city streets. This is a 1km detour (if you don't get lost) and the key is to stick as close as possible to the perfectly straight heading of the canal tunnel. There are small way-markers embedded in the pavement (look for either the brass "Towpath Link" plates or the newer blue plates with the wavy water symbol). Here are the directions:

- From the canal head straight along Duncan Street;
- Turn left onto Upper Street;
- Take the next right up Liverpool and

59

CENTRAL ROUTES

While taking in the beauty of the canal, keep an eye out for the traffic on the towpath.

the next left onto the busy Chapel Market;

- At Penton Street turn right and take the second left down Maygood;
- Follow the footpath through the residential area to Muriel Street where you'll find the canal directly opposite.

5.6mi: St Pancras Station. Through this rather industrial-feeling area the canal makes a hard right turn. St Pancras Station is just on the other side of the canal.

6.6mi: Camden Lock Markets. Pedestrian traffic can be a little heavy through here, so be prepared to walk some sections. And if you find that you're a little peckish or could seriously do with a caffeine boost for the rest of your run, this is the ideal spot for a pit stop. You can even get your latest PB time tattooed on your arm for all to see here, if you're that way inclined.

7.0mi: Regent's Park. When the canal next takes a 90-degree turn to your right you know you're at Regent's Park. If you want to explore this (to the south of the canal) or Primrose Hill (to the north) head up to road level at the next bridge.

8.0mi: Park Road. The canal passes under Park Road and then a rail bridge before reaching a large dock for narrowboats (a small but vibrant community).

8.4mi: Maida Vale Hill Diversion. Just after the narrowboat "village" there is another tunnel and diversion. This is only a short 400m detour via Aberdeen Place (runs in the same direction as the tunnel beneath it) and then Blomfield Road, which runs parallel to the canal with only a fence separating it from the towpath.

8.9mi: Little Venice. Begin an anti-clockwise

circuit of this junction of three waterways by running around the top of it (north side), crossing the Paddington Arm of the Grand Union Canal, and, when along the southern side, turning right into the Paddington Basin (running on its right hand or western side). Follow the signs to Paddington Station.

GETTING THERE (RAIL)▸

Start: Limehouse DLR/National Rail Station (c2c line).

Finish: Paddington Station (Bakerloo, District, Circle, Hammersmith & City; First Great Western; Heathrow Connect; & Heathrow Express).

👍▸ A long, largely uninterrupted, easy-to-follow run with some beautiful scenery and top notch options for adding on.

👎▸ Dodging cyclists in tunnels and navigating Islington.

The tranquillity of the canal belies the busyness of the surrounding city suburbs.

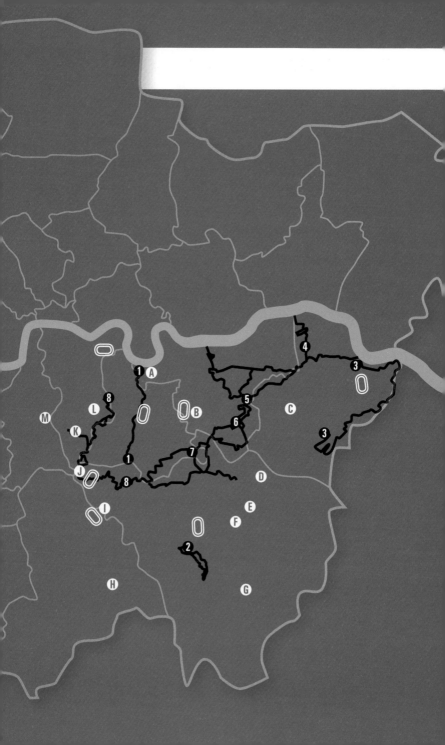

SOUTHEAST HOTSPOTS

SOUTHEAST ROUTES

GREENWICH PARK & BLACKHEATH

2mi / 3.2k

The oldest of the Royal Parks, Greenwich Park is also home to the Prime Meridian, making it the theoretical beginning and end of the world and also the home of time.

So in a roundabout way, runners owe a lot to Greenwich Park for helping provide time as a constant measure from which to gauge all our performances. And the popular park has another unforgiving measure in store for runners: hills!

LOCATION ▶ Greenwich, SE10 and SE3 (6.7mi SE of central London)

INFO ▶ Sitting just south of the Thames, behind Greenwich's historic buildings, Greenwich Park is famous for the Royal Observatory and the meridian line (longitudinal 0-point). But it's also a major hotspot for runners.

The northern section of Greenwich Park is flat with a pond and several open fields. Moving south it quickly rises up three hills that sit side-by-side, each with great views over the city. The centre hill is home to the Royal Observatory and meridian line, but each of the peaks is worth a climb and they're perfect for a post-run picnic on the grass.

South of these hills, the park plateaus and is dotted with trees and crisscrossed by many sealed (and some grass) trails. This flat plateau extends all the way to the wide, open expanse of Blackheath.

Just before you get to Blackheath, in the southeast corner of Greenwich Park, is the fenced Flower Garden and a woodland area (including deer sanctuary). Both provide some interesting twists and turns for a quick excursion away from the regular park.

It's easy to put together some nice loops through Greenwich Park, and a complete circuit around its circumference (including a diversion through the Flower Garden) is 2.0mi.

The Blackheath grassland is a large, open space not used for any particular sport. However, for

Bandstand, Greenwich Park.

the runner, it is crisscrossed by grass trails and it is possible to follow its perimeter for a 3.8mi (6.1km), zigzagging loop—great for combining with Greenwich Park.

GETTING THERE ▸

Rail: Cutty Sark DLR Station (0.3mi N) & Greenwich (Southeastern; 0.4mi W) & Maze Hill National Rail Stations (Southeastern; 0.1mi E).

Bus: 53, 54, 89, 108, 129, 177, 180, 188, 199, 202, 286, 380, 386, N1 & N89.

Riverboat: Hop off at Greenwich Pier (follow the signs 0.5mi to Greenwich Park).

👍 ▸ An historic site with great gardens, views, and hills. Plus longer open hours than many London parks.

👎 ▸ The squirrels are friendly, but sometimes a little too much so—seriously, make sure you don't accidentally step on one while flying down a hill.

SEE MAP OVER PAGE ▸

MUST KNOW ▸

Circumference: 2mi (3.2km) + Blackheath

Weather Warnings: Blackheath can be quite exposed to the wind.

Traffic Warnings: Take care on the busy Blackheath roads.

Times: Open year round at 6am and closes at various times between 6pm in winter and 9:30pm in mid summer. Blackheath is always open.

Toilets: Children's Boating Lake (the park's northeast corner), The Avenue (the centre of the park just beneath the observatory), and Blackheath Gate—keep 20p in your pocket when visiting Royal Parks (most toilets are charged).

The Avenue, Greenwich Park.

GREENWICH PARK

N

1km

0.5mi

0.5

0

OLD ROYAL
NAVAL COLLEGE

A206

Trafalgar Rd

Maze Hill

THE QUEEN'S
HOUSE

NATIONAL
MARITIME
MUSEUM

A206

King William Walk

Greenwich

ONE TREE HILL

Vanbrugh Hill

Westcombe Park Rd

The Avenue

King George St.

ROYAL
OBSERVATORY
GREENWICH

*GREENWICH
PARK*

Maze Hill

Croom's Hill

BANDSTAND

Hyde Vale

THE WILDERNESS
DEER PARK

P

THE ROSE
GARDEN

Charlton Way

Shooters Hill Rd

A2

A2

Blackheath Hill

A2

BLACKHEATH

Hare and Billet Rd

Goffers Rd

Watt Tyler Rd

Blackheath
Vale

Prince Charles Rd

Prince of Wales Rd

South Row

Mounts Pond Rd

Royal Parade

Granville Park

Eliot Heath Ln

St Joseph's Vale

Blackheath

Blackheath

Lee Rd

SUTCLIFFE PARK

0.85mi / 1.4k [!] 🏃

A small park with a great perimeter loop and several trails through a central wetland feature. All topped off with a good track.

LOCATION ▶ Eltham, Greenwich, SE9 (8.3mi SE of central London)

INFO ▶ Sutcliffe Park dates back to the 1930s but it wasn't until 2003 that it began to take its current shape as an important wetland area. The wetland was developed as a flood alleviation plan for the River Quaggy.

The result of these flood works is a wonderful network of ponds and streams with several well-positioned trails from which to explore them.

MUST KNOW ▶

Toilets: In athletics facility (when open).
Times: Closes at dusk..

In the northern half of the park the trails form a figure of eight and if you start from the centre and do a complete figure-of-eight it makes a perfect kilometre (0.62mi)—ideal for reps or for practising pacing.

The perimeter trail is a 0.85mi (1.4km) loop and lined with trees virtually the whole way—creating another quality alternative to the wetland. There are also three marked running routes on the paths that loop around the running track, with distances of 0.5mi (800m—so two laps will give a mile), 0.62mi (1km), and 0.78mi (1.25km—four laps give 5km).

In the southern end of the park (nearest to the A20) are grass fields that surround the track. The track is open on Tuesdays (4-9pm), Thursdays (4-9pm), Saturdays (9:30am-1:30pm), and Sundays (10am-1pm).

Options | Heading east along Eltham Road you will run into the Green Chain Walk near Eltham Palace (1.2mi from Sutcliffe Park). There are many options to follow the Green Chain signs either northeast or southwest.

GETTING THERE ▶

Rail: Kidbrooke National Rail Station (0.5mi N, Southeastern service).

Bus: 122, 160, 178, 321, B15, B16 & N21.

👍 ▶ Interesting wetlands, a tree-lined perimeter trail, and marked running routes.

👎 ▶ It's small size and extremely limited track open hours.

DANSON PARK

2.4mi / 3.9k

One of London's top suburban parks with grand old buildings, amazing play areas and sports facilities, a large boating lake, pockets of woodland, and, of course, great running terrain.

LOCATION ▶ Bexleyheath, Bexley (DA6, DA15, DA16) (11.7mi SE of central London)

INFO ▶ The hub of the park is the centrally located car park (paid during weekends and summer public holidays) that has two blocks of toilets, a refreshment kiosk and the Danson Stables Restaurant. Also just nearby are kids play areas (good for the baby-sitter), the grand Danson House (with tea rooms) and the Old English Garden.

From the car park is a 1500m loop (the Trim Trail) that heads northeast towards the tennis courts before turning left to follow the park fence line trail. This trail crosses over the stream that leads to the boating lake, and a few hundred metres later crosses it again to head back up to the car park. It's not way-marked but is easy to follow if you study the map at the car park.

The other trail marked on the map is the 2km

Danson House, Danson Park.

(1.25mi) Hard Surface Walk. You can start this on the sealed walkway just south of Danson House. Simply follow this path in either direction around the lake and the large grass field to the north of the lake. Except for the total of 30m vertical gain and descent, this is a great 2km training loop.

On top of these two trails are several grass or single trails. A complete circumference of the park, following the fence line, is 2.4mi (3.9km).

GETTING THERE ▸

Rail: Bexleyheath National Rail Station (0.6mi NE, Southeastern service).

Bus: 89, 96, 489, B13, B14, B16 & N89.

👍▸ Excellent facilities and two good running loops.

👎▸ It's a pity these loops aren't way-marked.

MUST KNOW ▸

Circumference: 2.4mi (3.9km)

Surface: Grass, sealed, dirt.

Terrain: A 20m rise from the lake up to Danson House, otherwise flat.

Weather Warnings: Woodland and some grass trails are boggy when wet.

Traffic Warnings: None.

Times: Open from 7:30am weekdays (9am weekends and holidays) and closes at dusk or 4:30pm (which ever is later).

Toilets: Two blocks near the central car park.

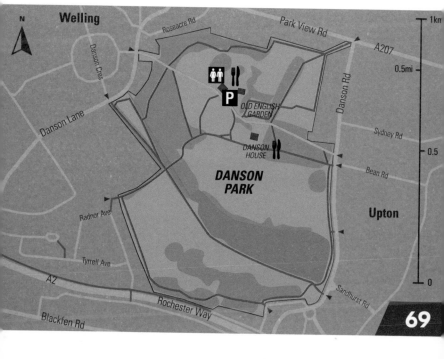

SCADBURY PARK

2.5mi / **4**k

A wonderful nature reserve with an easy-to-follow loop through woods and meadows. Plus plenty of nearby running spots for going longer.

LOCATION ▶ Chiselhurst, Bromley (BR7) (12.7mi SE of central London)

INFO ▶ The Acorn Trail is approx. 2.5mi and marked with wooden way-markers (running anti-clockwise). The markers are a little irregular and not always in the most obvious places, but the loop is still reasonably easy to follow.

The ideal start/finish point is the car park off Old Perry Street (with the Sydney Arms not far away for post-run refreshments). There is another car park in the south, off St Paul's Wood Hill.

The western side is mostly flat and wooded with dirt trails, some of which are incredibly soft to run on as a result of the thick leaf cover. There is a section of the trail here that is raised above the boggy ground by a boardwalk. From this western end you can also cross into Petts Wood which begins near St Paul's Cray Road and runs south from there.

Roughly in the centre of Scadbury Park is Moat

A rolling farm paddock in the northeast of Scadbury Park.

House: the ruins of an old manor surrounded, as the name suggests, by a swamp. This is a 100m deviation away from the Acorn Trail if you feel like having a gander.

The east of the park is characterised by rolling hills (some quite sharp) and a mixture of wood (with some huge trees) and farmland. There is a shortcut option here for the Acorn Trail and you can also follow the LOOP signs further east towards Sidcup Place (by crossing the A20).

The trails that the Acorn Loop follows are generally the main, more developed ones. But there are plenty more paths to keep you entertained if you fancy an explore.

GETTING THERE ▶

Rail: Sidcup National Rail Station (1.7mi N, Southeastern service); Chiselhurst National Rail Station (1.9mi SW, Southeastern).

Bus: 61, 160, 269, 273, B14, R1, R11 & N136.

👍 ▶ A popular spot for local walkers and runners that boasts a good loop through woods and farms, with hills thrown in for good measure.

👎 ▶ Not the greatest way-marking in London and no toilets.

MUST KNOW ▶

Circumference: 2.5mi (4km)

Surfaces: Dirt, gravel and boardwalk.

Terrain: Flat to rolling hills.

Toilets: None.

Weather Warnings: Trails can become boggy and slippery in wet weather.

Traffic Warnings: None.

Times: Best avoided after dark.

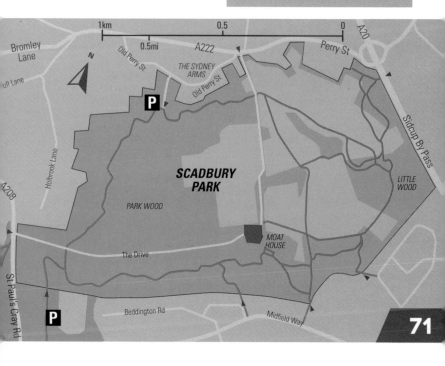

PETTS WOOD

4.0mi / 6.4k

One half beautiful woods and one half farm fields over rolling hills.

LOCATION▶ Chiselhurst, Bromley (BR7) (13mi SE of central London)

INFO▶ A series of green spaces defined by Chiselhurst in the north, St Paul's Cray Road/ Orpington Road east, Petts Wood suburb south, and Jubilee Country Park west. Two train lines dissect the area, with crossings of two footbridges in the southeast and two foot tunnels in the northwest.

The hills are high enough to open up some stunning views and also to get the legs and lungs pumping. Some of the trails in the southern end of the wood can be boggy even at the best of times. There are also maps at various key spots throughout the area.

A great feature of Petts Wood is a way-marked 4mi loop that incorporates parts of Jubilee Country Park, surrounding suburban streets, farmland, and, of course, the wood itself. It starts at the Jubilee Country Park car park on Tent Peg Lane (off Crest View Drive) and runs north from there in a clockwise direction.

Alternatively the LOOP provides a nice way-marked route through the woods, connecting Scadbury Park to Jubilee Country Park.

GETTING THERE▶

Rail: Petts Wood National Rail Station (0.8mi S, Southeastern service).

Bus: 61, 162, 273, R2 & R3.

▶ Wonderful variety of wood, heath, and rolling farmland.

▶ Okay signage but not amazing.

SEE MAP NEXT SPREAD▶

MUST KNOW▶

Circumference: 4.0mi (6.4km)

Surfaces: Dirt, gravel and sealed.

Terrain: Rolling hills.

Weather Warnings: Trails can become very boggy/slippery when wet.

Traffic Warnings: Take care when crossing the several roads around the woods and when on narrow lanes.

Toilets: None.

Times: Best avoided after dark.

A trail through the farm sections of Petts Wood.

JUBILEE COUNTRY PARK

An irregular-shaped, but flat, park offering a mix of woods, flowering meadows and many trails.

LOCATION ▶ Southborough, Bromley (BR1) (13.3mi SE of central London)

INFO ▶ This nature reserve is 25ha of woods, hedgerows, and grassy fields that bloom with wildflowers in the spring and summer.

The Jubilee Nature Trail is a good starting point for getting to know the park. It is 2mi around, if you manage to follow the way-markers (that are a bit irregular). The trail is roughly a figure-of-eight with one small loop (near the Tent Peg Lane car park) and a much larger sporadically shaped loop that starts by heading west and north from the car park.

The small loop runs clockwise and the larger runs anti-clockwise. And if you do get lost, its never too far before you hit a gate out into the surrounding suburbs, which is the signal to retrace your steps to the main trail. There are also many maps along the way.

GETTING THERE ▶

Rail: Petts Wood National Rail Station (0.3mi SE, Southeastern service).

Bus: 208, R3, R7, N47.

👍 ▶ A popular spot with a nice mix of surfaces and scenery.

👎 ▶ The park and trails are a little under-kept.

SEE MAP OVER PAGE ▶

Jubilee Country Park.

MUST KNOW ▶

Circumference: 2.0mi (3.2km)

Surfaces: Dirt, gravel and grass.

Terrain: Flat.

Weather Warnings: Trails can become boggy and slippery in wet weather.

Traffic Warnings: Watch for cyclists.

Toilets: None.

Times: Best avoided after dark.

SOUTHEAST HOTSPOTS

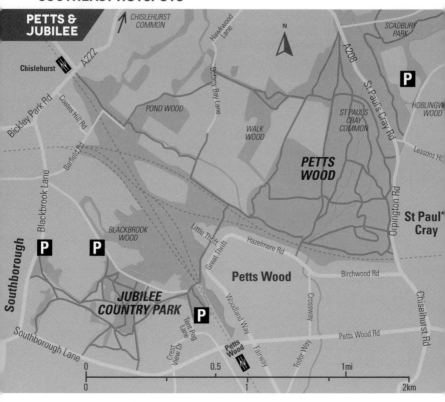

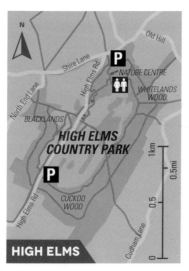

High Elms Country Park.

HIGH ELMS COUNTRY PARK

2.3mi / 3.6k

A popular nature reserve over rolling hills, encircled by sublime country-side.

LOCATION ▶ Farnborough, Bromley (BR6) (15.7mi SE of central London)

INFO ▶ From the visitor centre, near the corner of Shire Lane and High Elms Road, the High Elms Trail completes a nice loop of the park in 2.3mi (3.6km).

It starts running south through formal gardens before reaching the golf course. It then runs past the clubhouse and crosses High Elms Road (take care) where it crosses another golf fairway. The trail then runs south again through woods and grass fields before heading back across the road. Pass the car park and enter the woods that circumnavigate the golf course, eventually returning you to the visitor centre.

There are blue, numbered way-markers along the trail but it does pay to study the map at the start (near the car park) or pick up a paper map from the visitor centre.

Also from the visitor centre you can pick up a flyer for the longer High Elms Round Trail (4.5mi). This ventures further into the country-side and definitely requires a map as there are no way-markers. It passes through the village of Downe from where its just 500m further south to Charles Darwin's House on Luxted Road (look for the brown signs to "Down House").

Back in the park itself there is another looped trail that runs a little wider than the High Elms Trail. This provides a great secondary option if you want more after doing the smaller 2.3mi loop.

GETTING THERE ▶

Rail: Chelsfield National Rail Station (2.0mi northeast, Southeastern service).

Bus: 358, 402, R1, R5, R8, R10, & R11.

👍 **THUMBS UP ▶** A popular, family-friendly location.

👎 **THUMBS DOWN ▶** Running on the busy, narrow lanes is a no-go.

◀ SEE MAP OPPOSITE

MUST KNOW ▶

Circumference: 2.3mi (3.6km)

Surfaces: Dirt and grass.

Terrain: Undulating hills.

Traffic Warnings: Golf balls, golf carts and vehicles on the surrounding country lanes.

Weather Warnings: Some sections of trail can become boggy.

Times: Open at all times (although the car park may be closed).

Toilets: At the main car park and inside the visitor centre.

CONNECTING THE WOODS OF CROYDON

8.25mi / **13.25**k

Like many outer-London suburbs, this part of Croydon abounds in woodland trails. Connecting them in one run can be a challenge, so for this hotspot we make use of the fourth section of the way-marked LOOP pathway.

LOCATION ▶ Coney Hall, Bromley, BR4 (12.3mi S of central London)

INFO ▶ The LOOP is extremely well-signposted, so you shouldn't have too much trouble just following the way-markers. However, here are the instructions in case of the odd missing sign (which does happen occasionally, as well as signs being turned around!).

Starting at West Wickham Common in Coney Hall, look for the LOOP signs (green with a blue flying kestrel) which will lead you eastward through Threehalfpenny Wood. It then heads north through Kennel Wood to reach the suburb of Upper Shirley. From here the path turns south to climb up Addington Hill, where you're greeted with wonderful views (spot Windsor Castle on a clear day).

From here, carry on south to Heathfield Farm and Bramley Bank Nature Reserve, and then cross into Littleheath Woods where the LOOP joins the 66mi Vanguard Way (a trail that runs from Croydon all the way south to Newhaven on the coast—popular amongst those with ultra running tendencies).

After running through the suburb of Selsdon, you'll enter Selsdon Wood, which has 81ha of wood and meadow networked by a spider's web of trails—ideal for adding on distance.

After Selsdon Wood the LOOP trail continues south to Kings Wood where you can either carry on to Upper Warlingham & Whyteleafe National Rail Stations (1.6mi further SW) or you've got a couple of alternatives for heading back to Coney Hall.

The northern option follows Kingswood Lane/Way north, then turns left on to Old Farleigh Road, left at the A2022 and then a quick right on to Upper Selsdon Road, which takes you to Croham Hurst (on your right). Croham Hurst is 34ha of woodland and from here you can connect northeast into Addington Hills (via Coombe Wood). Follow the LOOP signage back to the start at Coney Hall (this is 8.4mi or 13.5km from Kings Wood).

The southern alternative from Kings Wood is 7.5mi (12km). Follow the LOOP back to Old Farleigh Road, turn right to reach Littlepark Wood. Head east through this wood and carry on to Greatpark Wood. Cross Farleigh Court Road and head northeast through Farleigh Green and then north to Frylands Wood. Follow Featherbed Lane to reach the A2022, turn right and head back to the start at Coney Hall (using the footpath on the north side of the road).

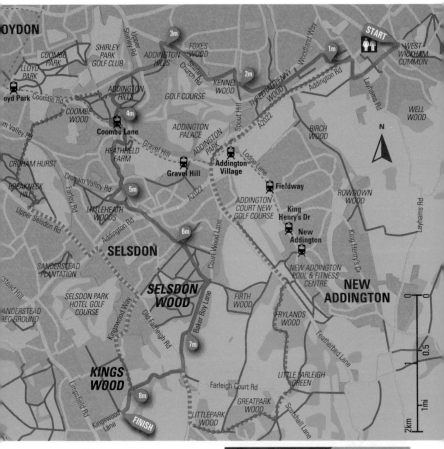

GETTING THERE ▶

Rail: Hayes National Rail Station (0.2mi N, Southeastern service).

Bus: 119, 138, 246, 314, & 353.

👍 ▶ LOOP signage connects green spaces that could otherwise be missed.

📷 ▶ Except for the tram line and spread out National Rail stations, it can be difficult for non-locals to get here on public transport.

MUST KNOW ▶

Point–to–point: 8.25mi (13.25km)

Surface: Mud and sealed.

Terrain: Hilly.

Weather Warnings: Wood trails will be muddy when wet.

Traffic Warnings: Many road crossings and narrow lanes.

Times: Open at all times (not recommended after dark).

Toilets: Croydon Road (Coney Hall).

SOUTH NORWOOD COUNTRY PARK

1.85mi / 3k

Backing on to the Croydon athletics track, this rejuvenating green space makes for a likeable jogging spot.

LOCATION ▸ South Norwood, Croydon (SE25) (9.1mi S of central London)

INFO ▸ Once a sewerage treatment plot, South Norwood Country Park has undergone

quite the transformation. Sure it looks scrappy (a.k.a. naturally unruly), with shrubs and wild grasslands, but it's becoming an important nature reserve with nice looped trails.

A good starting point is the visitor centre car park at the end of Adams Way (which is off Albert Rd), just north of the athletics track. From here run east next to the tram tracks and then turn left just before reaching a large grass sports field. This will take you on the main looped trail around the park, running just north of the park's lake and wetland.

On the way back turn right to cross over the tram tracks and enter the small cut-off section beyond

Below: Themed signage for the bird sanctuary near South Norwood Country Park. **Right:** South Norwood Country Park.

the tracks. Loop back to the car park from here, completing a 1.8mi loop.

There are many nearby options for adding on. You can follow the Waterlink Way north as it passes through the park. You can also follow the footpath south over the tram tracks at Arena Station, past the driving range and into Long Lane Wood and the grass expanse of Ashburton Playing Fields. Croydon Arena is open weekdays only, typically from 9am to 9pm (times vary).

GETTING THERE ▶

Rail: Both Elmers End (Southeastern service) & Birkbeck (Southern) National Rail Stations are within a few hundred metres of the park.

Tram: Elmers End, Arena, & Harrington Rd.

Bus: 54, 130, 197, 289, 312, 354, 356, 367 & 410.

👍▶ Easy to know your way around after the first loop. Plus the nearby rail and tram connections make access via public transport ideal for a running hotspot so far from the city centre.

👎▶ Still showing some signs of its unpleasant past as a sewerage treatment centre.

79

CRYSTAL PALACE PARK

2.05mi / **3.3**k

A hilly park with a variety of running surfaces, a prodigious history (particularly in running), and excellent training facilities.

LOCATION ▶ Crystal Palace, Bromley, SE19 (7mi S of central London)

INFO ▶ Crystal Palace is named after the 560m-long iron and glass structure that was moved here from Hyde Park following the 1851 Great Exhibition (but burnt down in 1936). Now the key landmark is the Eiffel Tower-like BBC transmitter (219m tall), which can be seen from all over London.

BBC Transmitter, Crystal Palace Park.

For runners, the hill that this tower sits atop is home to a lovely park with, as you'd expect, plenty of hilly trails plus great facilities. It's something of a spiritual home for London athletics being one of the first stadiums in the UK to get an all-weather track and having hosted numerous world class athletics meets and, with them, running records.

The park's northwestern end (near the tower) is the site of the old palace and has several Italian-style terraces providing great views. This end of the park is rather scrappy, as it awaits development (there is talk of a modern replica of the original palace being built), and can be accessed either by looping around the park's perimeter or by coming straight up the central stairs from the sports centre.

The Crystal Palace National Sports Centre houses a 50m pool, gym, sports facilities, an indoor sprinting track, and, of course, the outdoor floodlit athletics track. The centre is typically open from 7am to 9pm weekdays and 9am to 5pm weekends (at a charge) but it's future is uncertain and could succumb to park developments.

Just northeast of the sports centre is a large outdoor concert venue with a beautiful patch of lawn ideal for hill strides. Behind the stage is a lake and a hedged maze (not your usual running terrain, but good for a time filler).

The park's southeast end is your best option for flatter running with a large playing field and the Lower Lake, which has beautiful gardens, life-sized dinosaurs sculptures and a host of paved and limestone trails—the best in the park. Toilets, drinking fountains and a cafe can be found at the Thicket Road entrance.

A full loop on the park's perimeter trail is 2.05mi, with many additional internal trails.

Options | To run further afield, simply follow the Green Chain Walk signs either east towards Beckenham or north towards Dulwich Wood.

GETTING THERE▶

Rail: The Crystal Palace National Rail Station (Southern & London Overground services) is directly at the southwest entrance to the park.

Bus: 3, 122, 157, 202, 227, 249, 322, 358, 363, 410, 417, 432, 450, 931, N2, N3, N63, & N137.

👍▶ Hills, history (including dinosaurs and athletics), views, and facilities.

👎▶ The northwestern end of the park (including parts of the sports centre) are a little worse for wear and there is still uncertainty over the future of this iconic and beautiful park.

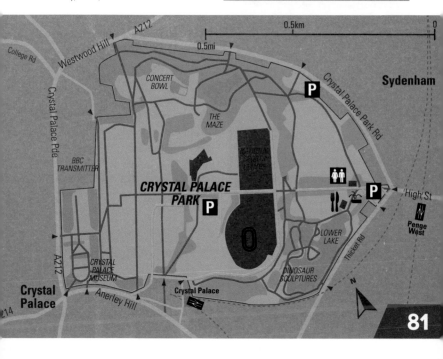

81

DULWICH PARK & WOODS

1.4mi / 2.25k

A well-presented park with a boating lake, sports grounds, large trees, and beautiful gardens. It provides two main loop options and also has a woodland nearby to explore.

LOCATION ▶ Dulwich Village, Southwark, SE21 (5.8mi S of central London)

INFO ▶ Dulwich Park's main looped path is wide and sealed, and also has a bridle path on its inside, giving you the option of getting off the hard surface. This limestone loop is just over a mile long (1670m) so if you minus 60-odd metres it can provide the ideal loop for mile intervals or a tempo run.

On the perimeter of the park is a single dirt trail—perfect for a change of scenery and a soft running surface (1.4mi around). There are other trails through the park's interior and many grassy fields for stride outs or barefoot running. The park also features a cafe, sports fields/courts, and outdoor gym equipment.

Sydenham Hill Wood | From the Roseberry Gate Entrance, in the southeast corner of Dulwich Park, it's only 400m further east along Dulwich Common (A205) to Sydenham Hill Wood. This, and the neighbouring Dulwich Wood, is one of the last remaining sections of the Great North Wood that once stretched from Deptford to Selhurst. It was also home to a railway that connected Crystal Palace to Nunhead—the remains of which can still be seen.

The wood starts off with a 400m gentle climb along a dead-straight, tree-lined lane. It then reaches an elongated loop where you have a choice of tracks, both of which finish in the same spot and can be connected into Dulwich Wood to the west. Following the trail through Dulwich Wood you will exit on Low Cross Wood Lane (this is about 1.4mi from Roseberry Gate). Here turn right and then right again onto College Road, where it's a one-mile jog back north to Dulwich Park. On the way you'll pass the Dulwich College athletics track, but it is not open to the public.

It is approx. 2.4mi (3.9km) from Roseberry Gate through the woods and back to the College Road entrance of Dulwich Park and 3.1mi (5k) for the full loop back to Roseberry Gate (via the College Road entrance).

Cox's Walk, Sydenham Hill Wood.

GETTING THERE ▶

Rail: West Dulwich (Southeastern service, 0.6mi SW) & North Dulwich (Southern service, 0.6mi N) National Rail Stations.

Bus: 176, 185, 197, P4 & P13.

👍 ▶ A mixture of surfaces, a handy one-mile loop, and a nearby wood to explore.

👎 ▶ If it weren't for the nearby options, this park would become too small too fast.

MUST KNOW ▶

Circumference: 1.4mi (2.25km) on the Dulwich Park jogging track.

Surface: Sealed, dirt, grass.

Terrain: Flat (with hills in the wood).

Weather Warnings: Keep to the sealed paths after rain.

Traffic Warnings: A busy road between the park and the wood.

Times: Open 7:30am to around dusk (4:30pm in December and 9:30pm in June).

Toilets: Near the main car park (western gate) and another near the cafe (in the park's centre).

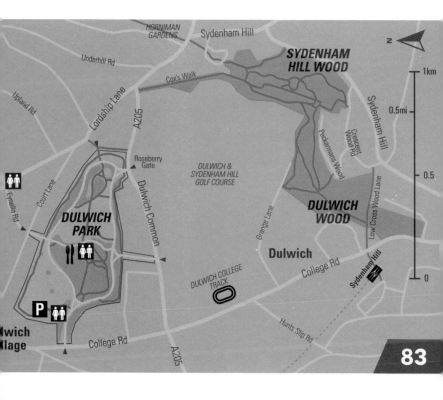

PECKHAM RYE PARK & NUNHEAD CEMETERY

1.6mi / 2.6k

A collection of sports fields and formal gardens near the colourful neighbourhood of Peckham. Plus the bonus side option of the wooded Nunhead Cemetery—slightly spooky but still great for running.

LOCATION ▸ Peckham, Southwark, SE15 (5mi S of central London)

INFO ▸ Peckham Rye Park is in the south with Peckham Rye Common in the north. Both are largely flat, however, running in the common is entirely on grass or the single dirt tracks that circumnavigate it, whereas the park has many

sealed paths and at times in summer has a marked out 400m grass athletics track.

The complete circuit of the park and the common is 1.6mi, with the park in particular providing other options in its interior around gardens, playgrounds and beside a lake. The trees in the park also make it the more sheltered option if weather conditions aren't so flash.

Nunhead Cemetery | If trees are what you're after, jog the 600m from Peckham Rye Park's east side (corner of Homestall Rd and Peckham Rye) to the fascinating and historically significant Nunhead Cemetery (opened in 1840).

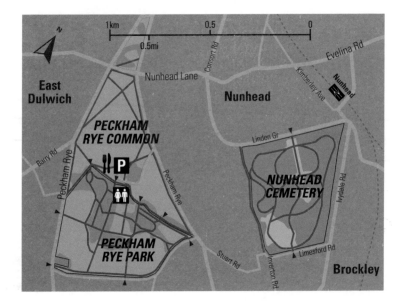

Peckham Rye Park.

Nunhead Cemetery.

Nunhead is the second largest Victorian cemetery in London. It has a rolling hill on its western
side, one wide trail around its circumference
(approx. one mile long) and several intersecting
the cemetery.

If it weren't for the fact that this is a burial place,
we'd recommend this spot as being ideal for
reps or fartlek sessions during summer (gets
boggy in wet weather). However, it's probably
better to maintain respect by just jogging the
cemetery and taking in its eerie beauty.

GETTING THERE▶

Rail: Peckham Rye National Rail Station (0.5mi
N of the common; London Overground, Thameslink, Southern & Southeastern services).

Bus: 12, 37, 63, 78, 197, 343, 363, 484, P12,
N63 & N343.

👍▶ The combo of woodland and park in close
proximity.

👎▶ Unless you're doing a very short run or
combining the cemetery with the park, you will
be running in circles.

MUST KNOW▶

Circumference: 1.6mi (2.6km) around Peckham Rye Park and Common.

Surface: Grass, sealed, dirt, gravel.

Terrain: Flat (undulating in the cemetery).

Weather Warnings: Parts of the common and
the cemetery can become boggy after rain.

Traffic Warnings: Relatively quiet suburban
streets connect to Nunhead Cemetery.

Times: Peckham Rye Park is open from 7:30am
to dusk (4:30pm in December and 9:30pm in
June; the common is always open). Nunhead
Cemetery is open from 8:30am to 4pm in winter
and 7pm in summer.

Toilets: At the northern end of Peckham
Rye Park (look for the signs).

BROCKWELL PARK

1.75mi / 2.6k

Established in 1811 (opened to the public in 1892), Brockwell Park has hills, views, soft grass trails, and an always-refreshing outdoor pool.

LOCATION ▶ Herne Hill, Lambeth, SE24 (4.4mi S of central London)

INFO ▶ The main sealed path follows the circumference of the park for a 1.75mi loop with brilliant vistas of the city and some moderate hills to make you work for it.

The interior of the park includes various sporting grounds (even a BMX track), three lagoons, a paddling pool, a walled garden, and two historical structures: Brockwell Manor and a clock tower. The remainder of the park is grass with dotted trees and several dirt/grass trails to explore through charming meadows.

The Lido is an art deco building from 1937 and boasts a 50m outdoor pool, gym (indoor), and cafe. The queues for the pool on a hot day are extremely long, so arrive early.

Options | Dulwich Park is just 1mi to the east (from the NE corner of the park follow Half Moon Lane and then Burbage Rd). The woods

Runners enjoying the popular Brockwell Park parkrun.

and fields of Tooting Bec Common are 1.5mi southwest, the ever-popular Clapham Common 1.6mi west, and the small, but still well-run by locals, Ruskin Park is 0.8mi north.

GETTING THERE ▶

Rail: Herne Hill National Rail Station (0.1mi from the NE gate; Thameslink and Southeastern services).

Bus: 2, 3, 37, 57, 68, 196, 322, 415, 432, 468, N2, N68 & X68.

👍 ▶ The hill provides some variation in terrain and the view is worth the climb.

👎 ▶ The early closing time in winter practically makes this a weekend-only option for the 8-to-5 workers.

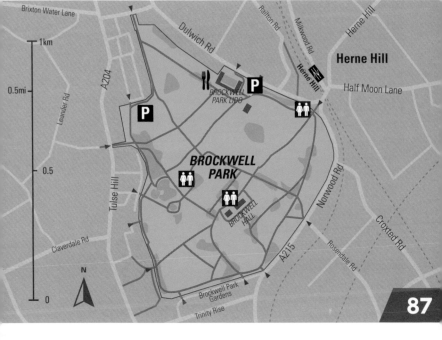

WATERLINK WAY

5.2mi / 8.3k 🔲 🏃

A way-marked trail through a mixture of suburban and green environments. A good link to other running spots or as an out-and-back long run.

LOCATION ▶ Northern start: Deptford, Greenwich (5.6mi SE of central London). **Southern start:** Lower Sydenham, Lewisham (8.3mi SE of central London).

INFO ▶ The Waterlink Way is a trail created by the Lewisham Borough Council that follows the waterways of Ravensbourne and Pool from Sydenham, north to the Thames (just west of Greenwich). Though parts of the trail are far from exceptional, it does provide a good way-marked link through southeast London to the Thames, with some nice little parks along the way.

MILE–BY–MILE ▶ Start: Creek Road. The north end of the route begins at the intersection of Copperas Street and Creek Road (just west of the bridge leading to Greenwich, which is also the bridge the Thames Path uses). From here the Waterlink Way winds south through suburban streets before crossing the A2 and passing through the elongated green space of Brookmill Park.

1.2mi: Elverson Road DLR Station. At this station the trail once again follows the footpaths of suburban streets.

1.6mi: A20 (Loampit Vale). It's a busy road so definitely use the pedestrian crossing under the bridge here. The trail then runs along the west side of the railway and re-joins the stream briefly before heading into another suburban detour.

2.4mi: Ladywell Fields. These are a series of recently upgraded parks housing sports fields, playgrounds, open grass areas, and the Ladywell Track (a good, sheltered track open 7am to 10pm weekdays and 7am to 6pm weekends and holidays). On the park pavements the council has set up a 2km running trail. When you reach the Ladywell Athletics Track be sure to take the footbridge (with the spiral on-ramps) over the railway to keep following the Waterlink Way.

3.6mi: Catford Road (near the Catford National Rail Station). The trail goes under this road, then cuts across the Halfords car park, goes under the train tracks, and enters River Pool Linear Park. As the name suggests, this is another long, thin park following the banks of the river. This green section, with many trees, lasts just over a mile and crosses the river five times. Its unbroken nature makes it a good spot for mile repeats or a fartlek session.

4.9mi: Southend Lane, Lower Sydenham. Cross over Southend Lane and follow the marked trail parallel to the tracks for another 500m to finish at Lower Sydenham National Rail Station (5.2mi from the start).

Options | From Lower Sydenham there are several extra marked trails to explore: the Beckenham Place Spur heads east into Beckenham Place Park, the Sustrans cycle route 21 heads south, and heading south to New Beckenham Station you can join the Green Chain Walk.

At the Waterlink Way's 2.3mi mark (on Algernon Rd, just north of Ladywell Fields) you're only 200m away from Hilly Fields Park (head NW on Vicar's Hill). The park has some good views and open daily 8am to dusk.

At the north end of the Waterlink Way you can obviously connect with the Thames Path on the south bank, and head either east to Greenwich or west to the centre city.

MUST KNOW ▸

Point–to–Point: 5.2mi (8.3km).

Terrain: Flat.

Surface: Sealed.

Weather Warnings: Some paths can become slippery when wet.

Traffic Warnings: This is a key cycleway so watch out for bikes.

Times: Open at all times, but caution should be taken after dark with some lonely areas.

Toilets: Brookmill Park (just N of Lewisham town centre), Ladywell Fields (near Ladywell Station), & Lewisham Town Hall (Catford).

Watch out for cyclists, especially on the narrow bridges.

GETTING THERE ▸

Rail: The trail begins just west of the Cutty Sark DLR stop and ends at Lower Sydenham National Rail Station.

Bus: Buses near Deptford include 47, 53, 177, 188, 199, 225, 453, N1, N47, & N89.

👍▸ Well sign-posted and at least two-thirds traffic-free.

👎▸ Lonely sections and busy roads to cross.

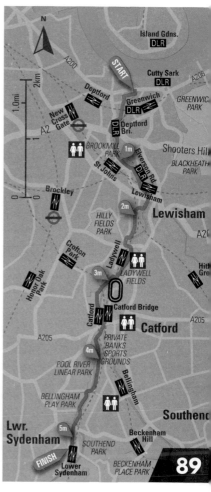

THREE COMMONS

4.8mi / 7.7k

An excellently marked loop through a cluster of superb suburban woods.

LOCATION ▶ Hayes, Bromley (BR2) (12.6mi SE of central London)

One of the many shaded and narrow roads that dissect the three commons.

Fish pond in Keston Common.

INFO ▶ Bromley calls itself the most rural of London's 32 boroughs. This route is a perfect example of why they can lay hold to the claim.

From above, the suburbs of West Wickham, Keston and Hayes, together with the surrounding dense woodlands, form a remarkable patchwork of contrasting wildlife and developed zones. This way-marked route charts a course through three of those wooded patches—making it easy to explore this otherwise maze of suburb and wood.

MILE-BY-MILE ▶ Start: Warren Road (opp. Station Hill). Begin at the clearing on the northern tip of the route. From here, head south through the woods, crossing Preston Road on the way. At 650m the outbound trail actually meets the home bound trail, so it's important to follow the signs veering left here.

0.5mi: West Common Road. Cross the road and follow the track northeast. Then veer right just before crossing Baston Road. Carry on to cross Croydon Road where there is an option to turn right, for a shortcut, otherwise veer left.

1.2mi: Commonside. Cross this road and head through Padmall Wood and Ravensbourne Open Space to Fishponds Road.

1.9mi: Fishponds Road. Cross the road and pass to the right of the large fishing pond. Then complete a small loop of Keston Common to cross over the other end of Fishponds Road. Run north through Ravensbourne Open Space and turn left into Lakes Road.

2.8mi: Lakes Road. Turn right into Keston Gardens, then take the path (303) between house numbers four and five to reach Commonside.

3mi: Commonside Again. Head north across the grass. After a short wood trail, turn left to cross Baston Road. Follow the woodland trail northwest to reach West Common Road.

3.4mi: West Common Road Again. Cross the road and continue north to also cross Croydon Road. Venture into the woods for 500m and then cross Croydon Road.

3.8mi: Croydon Road. Follow the LOOP trail signs here to reach Gates Green Road. Use the crossings at this intersection with Glebe Way to eventually turn right on Croydon Road.

4.4mi: Pole Cat Alley. After a short run on Croydon Road, turn left onto Pole Cat Alley (byway 102). This will lead you to home after a good 4.8mi.

Options | There are plenty of nearby options with the 2.5mi Ravensbourne Trail to the south (this actually overlaps some of the Three Commons). The Ravensbourne Trail starts in central Keston.

It's also possible to link several woods together north of Keston to reach Norman Park Recreation Ground. And finally, you can follow the LOOP trail signs west to Threehalfpenny Wood.

GETTING THERE▶

Rail: Hayes National Rail Station (0.2mi north, Southeastern line).

Bus: 119, 138, 146, 246, 314, & 353.

👍▶ Quality woods in pleasant suburbs.

👎▶ You need to be alert to spot both way-markers and also vehicles on the many road crossings.

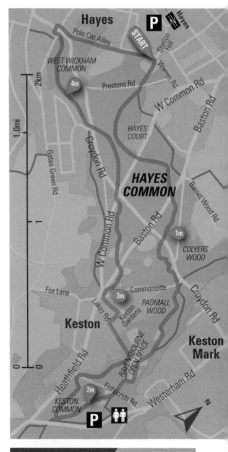

CRAY RIVERWAY

11.3mi / 18.2k

A way-marked run through marshland and woods, along old village lanes, and upon the banks of three highly contrasting rivers.

LOCATION ▶ Start: Erith, Bexley (DA8) (14.7mi E of central London)
Finish: Old Bexley, Bexley (DA5) (13.9mi SE of central London)

MUST KNOW ▶

Point–to–Point: 11.3mi (18.2km)

Terrain: Flat (with an undulating section of small hills).

Surface: Gravel, sealed, grass, & dirt.

Weather Warnings: Crayford Marsh is particularly exposed to wind.

Traffic Warnings: Take care at intersections and road crossings.

Times: Open at all times, although many lonely sections should be avoided after dark.

Toilets: Erith town centre, Crayford's Waterside Gardens, and Bexley Station.

INFO ▶ Officially this is a 10-mile (16km) trail from Erith Station to Bexley Station (or vice versa) catching the train back (it's cheap too, being all in Zone 6). However, with connections to train stations, loops and shortcuts (and add-ons), it can be either shorter or quite a lot longer.

The following route is 11.3mi long and is largely flat, although there is a climb between Hall Place and just before North Cray Road (climbing about 40m over 2mi).

MILE–BY–MILE ▶ Start: Erith Sta–tion. From here, make your way to the start of the trail via the Erith town centre. There are signposts every now and again to point the way, but here are some quick instructions:

- Take the tunnel under the A2016 and turn right onto Stonewood Rd;
- Turn right again onto Erith High St (with the Thames to your left);
- Go past the shopping centre and turn left onto Manor Rd (at the roundabout);
- Follow Manor Rd until it becomes Ray Lamb Way. Turn left towards the Erith Yacht Club and the start of the Cray Riverway (about 1.5mi from the station).

1.5mi: Thames Riverside. The trail starts on an exposed stop-bank overlooking the Crayford Marshes and the wide expanse of the tidal Thames. This gravel trail slowly bends around to the right past a few industrial eyesores. However, there are some good views of the elegant Queen Elizabeth II Bridge which spans the Thames further east.

2.4mi: Darent River. Here you leave the Thames for the much smaller Darent River, passing by the impressive Darent Flood Barrier. Running on an exposed stop bank makes for good views but the winds can be vicious.

3.3mi: Slade Green Intersection. Here is a split in the trails, with an option back to Erith to the right or to Slade Green Station (the latter will be a run of 4mi and the former 6mi running via Hazel and Slade Green Rds). Carrying on straight ahead you now get a lot more shelter thanks to a farm hedge and, shortly, the trail will leave the Darent River for the Cray River.

4.8mi: Thames Road Roundabout. The way-markers lead away from the river in order to navigate the runner through an industrial area and cross the busy roundabout on Thames Road. Rather confusingly, the signs lead you on a full loop of the roundabout before joining back up with the river from Thames Road.

4.9mi: River Cray. This section is really nice with many trees surrounding the river, with just one small stretch on suburban streets (Maiden Ln then Barnes Cray Rd) to interrupt the tranquillity before reaching Crayford town centre.

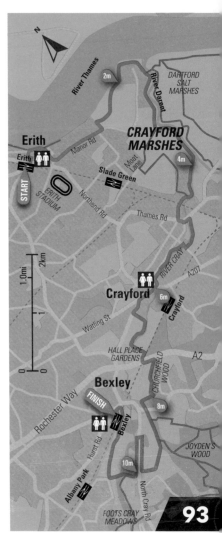

River Darent.

Hall Place.

through the edge of Churchfield Wood.

8.1mi: St Mary's Church Cemetery. After turning right you'll pass a cemetery on your right, this is the signal that St Mary's Church is coming and you need to turn left. At the time of writing there was no way-marker here, but there is an obvious intersection of trails, so instead of going straight, turn left to reach Vicarage Road.

8.25mi: Vicarage Road. Follow the small country lane opposite. With views of Joyden's Wood to your left, follow the trail right as it runs down to North Cray Road.

9.2mi: North Cray Road. This is a potentially confusing part of the Cray Riverway. The signage points you north back up to the roundabout (700m) and back south again on the other side of the road in order to use the crossing on this busy dual carriageway.

10mi: Water Lane. Turn right here, off North Cray Road. Once reunited with the River Cray, you're also reunited with the "B" route. From here, if you want to carry onto Foots Cray Meadows, turn left and follow the east bank of the river. (This option is 11.5mi long, but keep in mind that you'll need to get home from Cray Meadows ... somehow!) Otherwise, to catch the train from Bexley, cross the river to follow route "B".

10.4mi: Riverside Road. After following the path from the river, turn left onto Riverside Road. Then run straight up through the farm fields (still following the way-markers).

11.0mi: Bexley Cricket Club. Keep following the path past the cricket grounds (keeping to the right of the train tracks). After a few hundred metres the path heads under the tracks and exits on Bexley High Street.

11.3mi: Bexley Train Station. On High Street

5.9mi: Crayford. In the Waterside Gardens are public toilets (charge 10p). The trail passes directly through these gardens and then along London Road (directly opposite). Next take a left onto Bourne Road and another left into the large grass sports field. Run along the far tree line (following the river) until you reach the junction in the Cray Riverway at Hall Place.

6.9mi: Hall Place. At the large grounds of Hall Place Mansion the Cray Riverway splits in two. The "A" route goes south and is largely traffic free (and slightly longer), while the "B" route goes through Old Bexley township. (Finishing your run by going directly to Bexley Station is 8mi.) We'll follow route "A" but will come back along a portion of route B to Bexley Station.

So, head left across the river, following the edge of Hall Place Gardens to the rail line and the A2. Go over the tracks and under the A2 and run turn left and then a quick left again into Station Approach. The station is just up the hill (there are toilets on the platform). So ends your 11.3mi (18.2km) run. Trains typically run every half hour. Be sure to catch the correct train to Erith, not Dartford.

Options | Foots Cray Meadows is 0.6mi (1km) south of this route's southern-most point. It's popular amongst local walkers and joggers with a serene combination of meadows, woods and wetlands all over gently rolling hills. A full circumference of the park is 1.7mi (2.7k).

GETTING THERE ▶ (To Erith)
Rail: Erith National Rail Station (Southeastern service).

Bus: 99, 229, 428, 469, B12 & N89.

👍 ▶ Plenty of variety in scenery and well marked.

👎 ▶ Some sections are exposed and lonely (best to run with others).

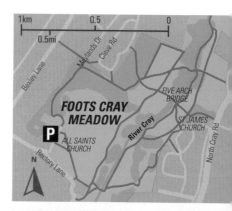

One of the many wide open spaces you'll encounter on this run.

LONDON'S GREEN CHAIN

Fifty miles of way-marked trails twist and turn their way through 300 southeast London green spaces. With so many well-marked paths, the Green Chain is perfect for composing your own favourite running loops.

GREEN CHAIN SECTIONS

1 Erith, Lesnes Abbey & Thamesmead

2 Woolwich, Oxleas & Plumstead

3 Eltham

4 Beckenham & Elmstead

5 Nunhead & Crystal Palace

From Erith in the east to Dulwich in the west, this incredible network of way-marked trails are the training grounds of choice for the majority of southeast London runners. It connects green areas that would otherwise be almost impossible to navigate between, particularly for newcomers.

The view from Oxleas Meadows.

The trails are marked with either the "G-C" or "Green Chain" signs/posts and there are frequent maps and distance guides throughout. Connections to train stations within 1mi of the trail are also signposted.

We've split the Green Chain into five distinct sections and offered suggested routes for each section.

1

Erith
Crayford
A2

Belvedere
Bexleyheath
Bexley

2mi
4km
3
A20
N
A20

Thamesmead
LESNES ABBEY

Abbey Wood
East Wickham
Welling
Blackfen
Sidcup

2

Plumstead
Falconwood

Rochester Way East
Sidcup By-Pass

OXLEAS WOOD

Beckton
Shooters Hill
Eltham Park
Chiselhurst

Woolwich

3

Charlton
Eltham
Elmstead

A2
Eltham Rd

Blackheath
Grove Park
Bromley

GREENWICH PARK

Leamouth

Greenwich
Lewisham

4

Isle of Dogs
Catford
BECKENHAM PLACE PARK
Beckenham

A2
A20

New Cross
Brockley
New Beckenham

Rotherhithe
Forest Hill

Nunhead
CRYSTAL PALACE PARK

Old Kent Rd
Peckham

ty of don

5
Dulwich
Crystal Palace

97

1. ERITH, LESNES ABBEY & THAMESMEAD

8.7mi / 14k

The eastern section of the Green Chain forms a link between the Thames and the naturally and histori-cally significant site of Lesnes Abbey. When combined with the Thames Path it makes an excellent 8.7mi loop.

LOCATION ▶ Thamesmead, Abbey Wood and Erith, Bexley (SE2, SE28, DA8, DA17) (12.5mi E of central London)

INFO ▶ Ruins are all that are left of the 12th century Lesnes Abbey, but it's the woods and heathland behind it that entice the runner to this area.

The Green Chain splits in two just south of Lesnes Abbey (in the wood) with one arm head-ing north via Southmere Lake to Thamesmead,

The beginning of the Green Chain at Thamesmead.

and the other heading east also to the Thames at Erith (via Frank's Park).

The Thamesmead route leaves Lesnes Abbey by the dead-straight raised walkway of Abbey Way. This is just under a mile long and includes foot bridges for crossing the main roads. This section, with its graffiti-riddled walls, can feel a little unsafe, particularly after dark.

You'll soon reach Southmere Lake, which can be circumnavigated (1mi around) as an extra add on. Otherwise continue up its east bank, after which the trail splits in two. Both options are of equal distance: the west route takes you to a bridge over Eastern Way, whereas east takes you under Eastern Way (the former feels the safest of the two, as the underpass is quite abandoned). The trails converge at Crossway Park from where you'll follow a series of waterways and suburban streets to the Thames.

Back at Lesnes Abbey, the route to Erith passes through Lesnes Abbey Woods which has some beautiful trees and an important patch of heather. It also has a slight rise of 30m to mix up the otherwise flat terrain. From here you'll follow the streets east to the wooded Frank's Park where it's just half a mile more to the Thames.

ROUTE ▶ To complete the full 8.7mi (14km) loop of the area (incorporating the Thames Path from Erith to Thamesmead), begin at Abbey Wood Station (if travelling by rail) or Lesnes Abbey (if travelling by car/bike). Make your way to Lesnes Abbey and follow the Green Chain east to Erith. At the Thames, head north along the highly industrial section of the riverside pathway. The factories and sewer treatment plants soon give way to the houses of Thamesmead. Look for the Green Chain sign pointing inland (it's about 1km from the start of the Thamesmead houses) and follow it back to Lesnes Abbey.

GETTING THERE▶

Rail: Abbey Wood National Rail Station (0.4mi W, Southeastern line).

Bus: B11, 229, 244, & 469.

👍▶ Nice variety of scenery and a great loop via the Thames Path.

👎▶ Some sections are lonely, particularly after dark.

MUST KNOW▶

Distance: 8.7mi (14km)

Surface: Gravel, sealed, dirt.

Terrain: A 30m rise in Lesnes Abbey Wood, otherwise flat.

Weather Warnings: Woodland trails are boggy when wet.

Traffic Warnings: Take care crossing roads.

Times: Open at all times.

Toilets: Abbey Wood Station, Lesnes Abbey, and in Lakeside Bar on the northern banks of Southmere Lake (Thamesmead).

The industrial Thames Path near Erith.

2. WOOLWICH, OXLEAS & PLUMSTEAD

10mi / 16.1k

From the Thames Barrier to Lesnes Abbey and then south to Oxleas Wood, this section of the Green Chain provides several looping options through woods, open spaces, parks, and even farmland.

LOCATION ▶ Woolwich, Shooters Hill, Oxleas, and Bostall, Greenwich (SE2, SE7, SE9, SE18) (9.8mi SE of central London)

INFO ▶ This portion of the Green Chain forms a nice triangle with the Thames Barrier (yep, the

big, funny looking silver things in the river) in the western corner, the ruins of Lesnes Abbey in the east, and the elevated Oxleas to the south.

From the river at Woolwich you'll follow a path south to Maryon Wilson Park (where the GC provides a little looping option—follow the Capital Ring signs for the most direct route) and on to Charlton Park. Here the route splits in two.

The eastern path runs past the Royal Artillery Barracks and on to Bostall Woods (running through the pleasant Plumstead and Winn's Commons). From Bostall Woods it's a mile further east to Lesnes Abbey following the GC signs or you can turn right to make your way to Oxleas Wood and Meadows via East Wickham Open Space (which has a nice 1.35mi perimeter trail) and Woodlands Farm (a taste of the countryside in the heart of London—complete with nettles and blackberry thorns, shorts wearers beware).

Back at Charlton Park, the option to the right (west) will take you past the 400-year-old Charlton House then through Hornfair Park, the wild fields of Woolwich Common, Castle Wood (look out for 18th century Severndroog Castle), and Jack Wood. The trail then opens out to the brilliant views at Oxleas Meadows where there is a cafe, toilets and drinking fountain. This makes an ideal start/finish point (with the added bonus of some cardio equipment here if the surrounding hills haven't got the heart rate up enough).

The meeting of trails at Oxleas Wood.

From Oxleas Meadows you can take an additional option north to Plumstead Common via Crown Woods Lane, passing through Shooters Hill and Shrewsbury Park on the way. This middle route creates the potential for figure-of-eight loops.

Distances:

- Thames Barrier to Charlton Park: 1.2mi (2km)
- Charlton Park to Bostal Woods: 3.5mi (5.6km)
- Charlton Park to Oxleas Meadows: 2.6mi (4.2km)
- Oxleas Meadows to Bostal Woods: 2.9mi (4.7km)
- Oxleas Meadows directly north to Plumstead Common: 1.7mi (2.7km)

ROUTES ▸ A full loop from Oxleas Meadows northeast to Bostal Woods, then west to Charlton Park, and then southeast back to Oxleas Meadows is 9mi. Add half a mile each way from the nearby Falconwood Station and you've got a perfect 10-miler.

For an even longer loop head out to Thamesmead, past Bostal Woods, and follow the Thames Path back west to Woolwich. From there follow the Green Chain to Oxleas Meadows.

GETTING THERE ▸

Rail: Falconwood National Rail Station (0.5mi S, Southeastern service).

Bus: B15, B16, 89, N89, 244, & 486.

👍 ▸ An incredible array of green spaces this far into suburbia.

👎 ▸ The number of alternative routes (with many GC signs) can be confusing.

MUST KNOW ▸

Distance: 10.0mi (16.1km)

Surface: Gravel, grass, sealed, & dirt.

Terrain: Undulating to hilly (from the Thames all the way up to 130m above sea level at Shooters Hill).

Weather Warnings: Oxleas Wood is super boggy when wet.

Traffic Warnings: Take extreme care crossing roads (use traffic lights).

Times: Open at all times.

Toilets: Maryon Wilson Park (Woolwich), Charlton House, Oxleas Meadows, Bostall Woods, & Plumstead Common.

Waist-high grass on the path through Woodlands Farm.

3. ELTHAM

7.2mi / 11.5k 🏞️ 🌿 🏢 ❗ 🏃 🧭

Laid out as a large figure-of-eight, this section of the Green Chain can either be run as two smaller loops or one large loop. It's great for viewing open parklands, pleasant suburbs, a small sampling of woodland, and even a palace.

LOCATION▶ Falconwood, Eltham, Mottingham, and Avery Hill, Greenwich (SE9) (10.3mi SE of central London)

ROUTE & INFO▶ South of Oxleas Meadows the Green Chain dissects into two paths through Shepherdleas Wood. These paths follow each side of Eltham Warren Golf Course to eventually meet again in the tree-lined fields of Avery Hill Park (which is ideal for exploring further).

This northern loop is approximately 2.9mi around (4.6km). A perfect access point is the Falconwood Station, which is just a few metres off the trail.

Moving south again from Avery Hill Park, the lower loop heads west through suburban streets (watch for the maze of GC signage as you cross the busy roundabout on Footscray Road), past Eltham Palace, along the suburban farm environment of King John's Walk, and to The Tarn.

The Tarn is a quaint formal park with a lake (which you do a loop around), an old ice well (where ice was stored before the days of fridges), and toilets. The park is closed after dusk and before 9am but is easy to avoid since the GC entry and exit points are almost right next to each other.

The trail then follows streets and the odd park through New Eltham and back into Avery Hill Park. This southern loop is approximately 4.5mi (7.2km) and is easily accessed from Mottingham or New Eltham Stations (which again are just metres from the trail).

This section of the Green Chain is ideal for running as a full loop or figure-of-eight of 7.2mi (11.5km). To carry on following GC signage further southwest, look for the main sign (and intersection of trails) on King John's Walk. To the north, from Oxleas Wood, you have three options of following the GC either northwest, north and northeast.

GETTING THERE▶

Rail: Falconwood, New Eltham & Mottingham National Rail Stations are both just off the trail (Southeastern service).

Bus: For Falconwood: B15 & B16; For Mottingham: 124, 126 &161.

👍▶ A pleasant neighbourhood with plenty of parks and open spaces.

👎▶ A couple of hard-to-follow dog legs, particularly at the Footscray Road roundabout, through The Tarn, and at New Eltham Sports Ground.

Early autumn in Shepherdleas Wood.

4. BECKENHAM & ELMSTEAD

10.1mi / 16.2k

Wood carving in Marvels Wood.

Incorporating ancient woods, rolling suburban streets, and tree-lined walkways, the Beckenham and Elmstead section of the GC will keep you visually and aerobically engaged.

LOCATION ▶ Grove Park, Elmstead, Downham, and Beckenham; Boroughs of Lewisham, Greenwich and Bromley (SE12, SE9, SE6, BR1) (9.3mi SE of central London)

ROUTE & INFO ▶ With a car park, toilets, a cafe, and a nearby train station (in Grove Park), Chinbrook Meadows makes the ideal starting point for completing a figure-of-eight around this section of the Green Chain.

The eastern loop is 3.2mi (5.1km) and heads north from Chinbrook Meadows along the banks of the River Quaggy before following a narrow, fenced-in path between sports fields. Due to the enclosed nature of this path it can feel a little unsafe at times, even just for the close proximity of the nettles and blackberry.

The signs will lead you, via streets, east then south around Eltham College (the GC has an intersection here with an option to carry running east). After Eltham College you'll cross Mottingham Sports Ground and Marvels Wood (with a bit of uphill work to throw into the mix as well). Marvels Wood becomes Elmstead Wood where you'll meet the rail line. Follow this northwest and downhill back to the Meadows.

The western loop is bigger at 6.9mi (11.1km). It heads north again along the River Quaggy, but turns west (left) via Marvels and then again via Coopers Lanes. After crossing the tracks it continues to follow suburban streets (some with nice tree-covered strips of grass in the middle of the street). You soon reach the elongated peaceful oasis that is Durham Woodland Walk.

This shaded walk spits you out near the northern entrance to Beckenham Place Park. With it's many trails and rolling terrain, this is well worth an extended explore. Follow the series of fields and woods to the park's southeast gate. Here cross over the tracks at Crab Hill and begin your journey east back towards Chinbrook Meadows.

Follow undulating suburban roads to Sunridge Park Golf Course, where you'll run on a path leading over the tracks to Elmstead Wood and then back north to Chinbrook Meadows.

Options | From Elmstead Wood you can follow the GC signs southeast toward Chiselhurst. Elmstead Wood itself has a great 1.25mi (2km) loop (follow the butterfly symbol).

GETTING THERE ▸

Rail: Grove Park National Rail Station (0.3mi W, Southeastern service).

Bus: 124, 126, 261, 273, 284, & N136.

👍 ▸ Several pockets of lush woodland, including the tranquil Downham Woodland Walk, all over undulating terrain.

👎 ▸ Some spots can be unsafe after dark (in particular, the enclosed and wooded pathways).

MUST KNOW ▸

Circumference: 10.1mi (16.2km)

Surface: Sealed, gravel, grass, dirt.

Terrain: Undulating to hilly (a lowest point of 27m at Beckenham Place Park and high point of 83m at Marvels Wood).

Weather Warnings: Wooded sections can be boggy when wet and look out for nettle/blueberry on paths in summer.

Traffic Warnings: Take care crossing roads (use traffic lights/crossings).

Times: Open at all times (but bring company if running after dark).

Toilets: Chinbrook Meadows (Grove Park), Downham, & Beckenham Place Park Golf Course.

Green Chain path over rail lines near Elmstead Wood.

5. CRYSTAL PALACE & NUNHEAD

8.5mi / 13.7k

Hills, cemeteries, woods, and parks are the order of the day on this point-to-point run through the heart of south London.

LOCATION ▶ New Beckenham, Sydenham, and Nunhead; Boroughs of Lewisham, Southwark and Bromley (start BR3; finish SE15) (start 4.7mi & finish 8.4mi SE of central London)

ROUTE & INFO ▶ From New Beckenham Station follow the GC signs west on Lennard Road, from which you'll make two diversions into surrounding parks (keep your eye out to spot the GC signs—especially for the small paths between houses). Each time,

you'll make your way back to Lennard Road. Then cross the tracks to reach Penge High Street (A234), via Station and Kingswood Roads.

From the A234 you'll enter Crystal Palace Park and be directed past the lake to the Crystal Palace Station. This is the 2.9mi (4.7km) mark of the run and you have the option of ending your run here or turning back for New Beckenham Station, otherwise keep following the GC signs.

Run along the Crystal Palace terraces to exit the park at Westwood Gate. Here you have two options, the best of which is to turn right and run through Sydenham Wells Park (which even includes a sensory garden if you feel like a break

Horniman Gardens

to smell the roses).

Upon exiting the park you'll merge with the alternative route and run around Crescent Wood Road, then dive down into Sydenham Hill Wood. Through this lovely wood, follow the old train line until you reach another split in the GC paths. One heads left to a dead end at Dulwich Park (if you choose to end your journey here, West Dulwich Station is a half-mile southwest of Old College Gate), and the one we'll follow turns right toward Nunhead.

The next green space you'll reach is the Horniman Gardens where you can catch some great views from the bandstand (there are also toilets and a cafe here) before running on to the first of several cemeteries with Camberwell Old Cemetery. Afterwards the trail splits in two yet again: left just avoids the steps, so to get the glutes firing take the right hand option and head into Honor Oak Park (the street) and One Tree Hill (the many-treed hill).

After this short wooded section, you'll be led through Camberwell New Cemetery and then on to Nunhead Cemetery. Exiting the cemetery at its northwest gate, turn right on Linden Grove, left onto Oakdale Road to reach Nunhead Station.

Options | From Nunhead Station it's not too difficult to leave the Green Chain and find your own way back to New Beckenham Station. Run for 2mi east past Brockley Station and through Hilly Fields Park to reach Ladywell Fields. Follow the Waterlink Way all the way to Lower Sydenham Station. The next station south is New Beckenham.

This will add around 5.5mi (8.9km) to your journey, so 14mi (22.6km) all up. After Hilly Fields this route home is mostly flat.

Distances | From the start at New Beckenham

Station:

- Crystal Palace Park (gate): 2.3mi
- Sydenham Wells Park: 4mi
- Sydenham Hill Wood (exit): 5mi
- Camberwell Old Cemetery: 6mi
- Camberwell New Cemetery: 7mi
- Nunhead Cemetery (gate): 7.9mi
- Nunhead Station: 8.5mi

GETTING THERE ▶

Rail: New Beckenham and Nunhead National Rail Stations (Southeastern service).

Bus: New Beckenham: 352; Nunhead: P12 & 78.

👍 ▶ The hills will take you to some great lookout spots.

👎 ▶ Many parks and cemeteries have limited access times ... not that you'd want to be in the cemeteries after dark though!

MUST KNOW ▶

Distance: 8.5mi (13.7km) non-loop

Surface: Sealed, gravel, grass, dirt.

Terrain: Hilly (a lowest point of 23m at Nunhead Station and high point of 112m near Sydenham Hill Wood).

Weather Warnings: Sydenham Hill Wood can become very boggy.

Traffic Warnings: Take care crossing roads (use traffic lights/crossings).

Times: Crystal Palace Park open 7:30am to dusk, the Camberwell Old and New Cemeteries 8:30am (weekends 10am) to 7pm (5pm winter), and Nunhead Cemetery 8:30am to 7pm or one hour before sunset.

Toilets: Crystal Palace Park, Sydenham Wells Park, Horniman Gardens, & Dulwich Park.

107

SOUTHWEST HOTSPOTS

SOUTHWEST ROUTES

CLAPHAM COMMON

2.8mi / 4.5k

One of the most popular London spots for running, this is a large park with tree-lined paths, open playing fields, and many trails to tread.

LOCATION ▶ Clapham, Lambeth, SW4 (4mi SW of central London)

INFO ▶ Clapham Common dates back to 1086 (with mentions in the Domesday Book) and is an irregular-shaped park (forming a rough triangle) intersected by main roads that effectively cut off some of its corners. However, the main section of the park is easily large enough to keep you entertained for an easy run or tempo session or even some barefoot strides on the grass. There are also various fitness stations ideal for calisthenics and strength work.

The common offers several trail options: Firstly, you can keep to the perimeter and run along the sidewalks of the roads that surround and intersect the park. A full circumference of the common, including the smaller sections of park cut off by intersecting roads, is 2.8mi (4.5km).

Clapham Common is just as inviting when covered in white rather than its usual grass green.

Clapham Common offers wide, open grass fields bordered by mature, leafy trees.

Secondly, you can keep to the main sealed paths within the common. These tend to radiate to and from the central bandstand (built in 1890).

Finally, you can explore the many single dirt trails all over the park that have been worn in (particularly just inside the perimeter). The paths surrounding the ponds and pockets of woodland also provide some interesting route options.

GETTING THERE ▶

Rail: Clapham Common & Clapham South Tube Stations are on the NE & S corners of the common respectively (both Northern Line). Clapham High Street (London Overground, 0.5mi NE), Clapham Junction (London Overground, Southern, & South West services, 0.5mi NW).

Bus: 35, 37, 50, 88, 137, 155, 249, 322, 345, 355, 417, 690, G1, N35, N137, & N155.

👍 ▶ Large expanse of easy running terrain.

👎 ▶ The intersecting roads.

MUST KNOW ▶

Circumference: 2.8mi (4.5km)

Surface: Sealed, grass and dirt.

Terrain: Flat.

Weather Warnings: Grass and dirt tracks are not ideal after rain.

Traffic Warnings: Take extreme care when crossing the streets that dissect the park.

Times: Open at all times.

Toilets: On the eastern side of the common (near the playground) and in three cafes (near the NE corner on Rookery Rd, next to the bandstand, and in the S next to the tennis courts).

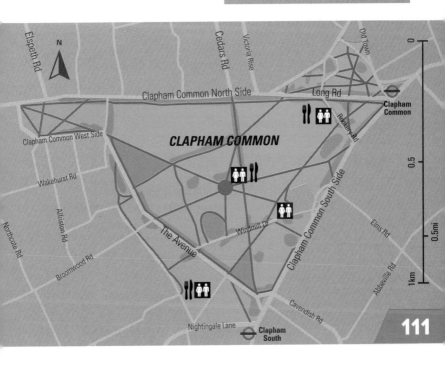

TOOTING BEC COMMON

3.9mi / 6.3k

At 92ha (221ac) this is Wandsworth's largest green space. Despite its irregular shape, it offers plenty of running routes.

LOCATION ▶ Tooting Bec, Wandsworth, SW12 (6.0mi S of central London)

INFO ▶ Tooting Bec Common is a green space that has resisted the squeeze of suburbia, maintaining an inviting mix of large tracts of woodland, grass fields, and a lake. Civilisation has left its mark on the common, however, with two rail lines and three roads dissecting it.

The northern section has the two rail lines cutting through it, creating two triangles of grass and scattered trees. This section has several dirt trails running east-west and a sealed trail on either side of it heading south to meet Bedford Hill (the road).

Crossing over Bedford Hill, the common widens and has far more trees with a thick wooded section on the park's eastern side stretching all the way south to Tooting Bec Road. West of the train line is a mix of formal parkland, sports fields, and pockets of woodland. There are many trails to choose from here—take your pick of running on sealed, dirt, or grass pathways.

South of Tooting Bec Road is a small woodland that surrounds the Tooting Bec Athletics Track (open 8am to 9pm weekdays & 7pm weekends). A full circumference of this southern-most section (below Tooting Bec Rd) is 1.5km (just short of a mile) when following the perimeter footpath.

It's possible to complete a perimeter run of the entire common (including a figure-of-eight around the southernmost section). Much of the route avoids running directly next to roads and is 3.9mi (6.3km) long, involving four road crossings (there are tunnels under the rail lines). There's also one sealed cycle/pedestrian path that runs the entire length of the common and is one mile long (but not good for reps as it crosses two roads).

There is a cafe just north of the central lake (near Hilbury Rd) and an outdoor 90m swimming pool at Tooting Bec Lido (open May to September).

GETTING THERE ▶

Rail: Tooting Bec Tube Station (0.3mi W; Northern line), and Balham Tube & National Rail Station (0.4mi NW; Northern line & Southern service).

Bus: 50, 249, 250, 315, 319, & G1.

👍 ▶ A deceptively large perimeter trail.

👎 ▶ Road crossings.

MUST KNOW ▶

Weather Warnings: Dirt trails can be muddy after rain.

Traffic Warnings: There are three roads in the common so take care when crossing.

Times: Open at all times.

Toilets: Near Doctor Johnson Ave (SE corner of the park) & at the cafe near Hilbury Rd.

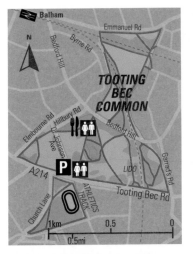

Balham

N

Emmanuel Rd

Byrne Rd

Bedford Hill

TOOTING
BEC
COMMON

Elmbourne Rd

Hillbury Rd

Dr Johnson Ave

Bedford Hill

Garrad's Rd

🍴 👥

A214

P 🚻👥

LIDO

Tooting Bec Rd

Church Lane

ATHLETICS
TRACK

1km   0.5   0

0.5mi

Wandsworth Common

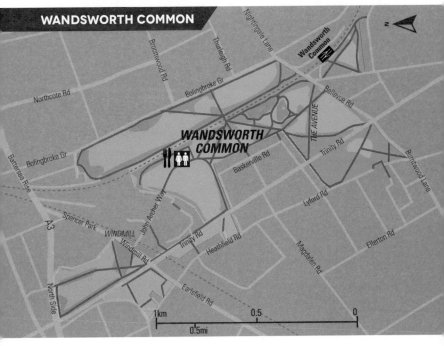

WANDSWORTH COMMON

Nightingale Lane

Wandsworth
Common

N

Broomwood Rd

Thurleigh Rd

Bellevue Rd

Northcote Rd

Bolingbroke Gr

THE AVENUE

Trinity Rd

Burntwood Lane

**WANDSWORTH
COMMON**

🍴 👥

Baskerville Rd

Battersea Rise

Bolingbroke Gr

Lyford Rd

Spencer Park

A3

WINDMILL

John Archer Way

Trinity Rd

Heathfield Rd

Magdalen Rd

Ellerton Rd

Windmill Rd

North Side

Earlsfield Rd

1km   0.5   0

0.5mi

WANDSWORTH COMMON

5.2mi / 8.4k

◀ **SEE MAP**
PREVIOUS PAGE

A disjointed park with surprisingly good running loops and plenty of beautiful trees.

LOCATION ▶ Wandsworth, SW18 & SW11 (5.1mi SW of central London)

INFO ▶ Much like nearby Tooting Bec Common, Wandsworth has an irregular shape, being split into 10 separate sections by dissecting roads and railway lines. However, this actually helps to lengthen the distances possible in the park by completing perimeter loops around each section.

In the north is a small slither of park (grass and trees) that is just over 1km around (spot the 1830s windmill in the trees). Moving south of here (either via Trinity Rd or John Archer Way) you reach the common's main sporting grounds with the tennis centre, cricket ground, and toilets and cafe.

Moving south again is the more formal parkland area of tree-lined avenues, ponds, gardens, and open grass fields. The running is brilliant through the network of trails here.

East of the tracks (there are crossings either just south of the cafe or down at Bellevue Rd) is an elongated grassy area lined with trees. There are some off-road running options here and a full perimeter loop of this section is 1.6mi (2.6km).

The are two extra little pockets of common to explore in its southern end. One, the wooded section west of Trinity Rd (well worth exploring)

and, two, the triangular section near the train station.

A full tour of the common, which includes loops of each individual section of parkland, should be about 5.2mi (8.4km). But have fun exploring and making your own loops. Combine Wandsworth with Tooting Bec and Clapham Commons for a classic southwest London long run.

GETTING THERE ▶

Rail: Wandsworth Common National Rail Station (Southern service; S corner of the park).

Bus: G1, 49, 77, 219, 319, & 337.

👍 ▶ Easy to create loops and put together a longish run in a smallish space.

👎 ▶ You've got to stay alert at the road crossings.

MUST KNOW ▶

Circumference: 5.2mi (8.4km)

Surface: Sealed, grass and dirt.

Terrain: Almost flat.

Weather Warnings: Dirt tracks in the wooded sections can become muddy.

Traffic Warnings: There are two road crossings you need to make, so take care.

Times: Open at all times.

Toilets: Near the tennis courts and cafe.

STREATHAM COMMON

2.4mi / 3.8k

SEE MAP
OVER PAGE ▶

A small park on the side of a hill with a few hidden surprises that make this a worthwhile running destination.

LOCATION ▶ Streatham, Lambeth, SW16 (6.6mi S of central London)

INFO ▶ Including Norwood Grove Recreational Ground this is another irregular shaped south London green space. With four distinct sections this time.

Norwood Grove in the southeast offers incredible views south and has a sloping grass hill. Dirt trails run around its perimeter and there is a sealed trail leading directly up, from Covington Way, to the formal gardens surrounding Norwood Grove Mansion. This path forms part of the Capital Ring trail that can take you either east to Crystal Palace or up over the hill into Streatham Common.

In the northeast corner of the common is a pocket of woodland with dirt trails to explore. Just south of this, and connecting Streatham Common to Norwood Grove, is The Rookery—an area of formal gardens open from 7:30am to dusk. There are nice sealed trails here and also a cafe and toilets near the entrance (on Streatham Common South).

From here the main part of the common stretches down the hill to Streatham High Road. It has a mixture of open grass fields and woods with a couple of sealed trails and plenty of nice soft grass to do hill repeats on.

A circumference loop of the common is 2.4mi (3.8km), including passing through The Rookery and around Norwood Grove. It does require a little bit of self-navigation through the wood atop of the hill however. This perimeter route encounters a total of 56m vertical gain—enough to get the lungs paying their keep.

GETTING THERE ▶

Rail: Streatham (Thameslink & Southern services; 0.2mi N) & Streatham Common National Rail Stations (Southern; 0.4mi W).

Bus: 50, 60, 109, 133, 159, 249, 250, 255, 417, G1, P13, N109, & N137.

👍 ▶ Hills, views, and variety.

👎 ▶ Tricky to navigate for first timers.

MUST KNOW ▶

Circumference: 2.4mi (3.8km)

Surface: Sealed, grass, and dirt.

Terrain: Hilly.

Weather Warnings: Grass and dirt trails become slippery when wet/icy.

Traffic Warnings: There is one road crossing on Streatham Common South.

Times: Open at all times except The Rookery (7:30am to 15mins before dusk).

Toilets: Near The Rookery.

SOUTHWEST HOTSPOTS

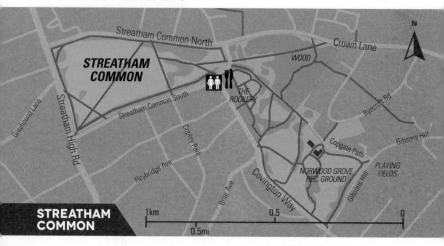

Streatham Common North
Crown Lane
WOOD
STREATHAM COMMON
THE ROOKERY
Streatham Common South
Streatham High Rd
Greyhound Lane
Copley Park
Ryecroft Rd
Gibsons Hill
Copgate Path
Heybridge Ave
Briar Ave
Covington Way
NORWOOD GROVE REC. GROUND
Gibsons Hill
PLAYING FIELDS

1km   0.5   0
0.5mi

N

STREATHAM COMMON

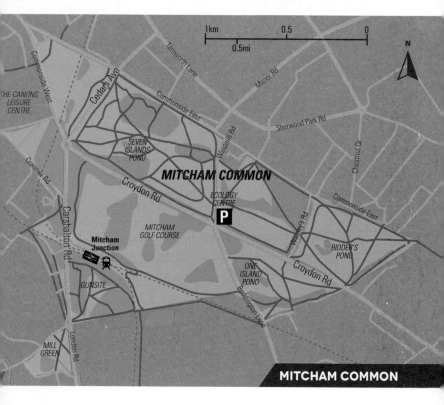

1km   0.5   0
0.5mi

N

Commonside West
THE CANONS LEISURE CENTRE
Cedar's Ave
Tamworth Lane
Manor Rd
Commonside East
Sherwood Park Rd
SEVEN ISLANDS POND
Windmill Rd
MITCHAM COMMON
Chestnut Gr
Cranmer Rd
Croydon Rd
ECOLOGY CENTRE
P
Commonside East
Carshalton Rd
Mitcham Junction
MITCHAM GOLF COURSE
Warley's Rd
BIDDER'S POND
GUNSITE
ONE ISLAND POND
Croydon Rd
Beddington Lane
MILL GREEN
London Rd

MITCHAM COMMON

MITCHAM COMMON

3.4mi / 5.5k

A nature reserve slowly emerging from its rubbish-tip-gravel-quarry past, on the way to becoming a superb off-road running destination.

LOCATION ▶ Mitcham, Merton, CR4 (9.1mi S of central London)

INFO ▶ Mitcham Common's 182ha (460ac) of green space is hugely varied. It has rolling hills (formed from mounds of domestic waste), woods, heath, grassland, and a golf course. The common is also dissected by several roads (in particular Croydon Rd and Windmill Rd/ Beddington Ln) and rail lines—segmenting the common into five distinct parts.

North of Croydon Road and west of Windmill Road is the largest section of open common featuring the Seven Islands Pond (which was once a gravel quarry) as well as pockets of woodland, heathland, and grass. There's also the first of the rolling man-made hills, plus trails galore.

South of Croydon Road is the golf course and, although you should avoid running on fairways and greens, there is a small single trail around the tree-lined course.

Heading south again, beyond the rail tracks, is the old WWII anti-aircraft gun site (from which this section gets its name) and Mill Green. Gun Site in particular is nice, with a mix of wood and heath and some cool trails to explore, but it is a little bit tricky to get to relative to the common's other sections. For access, use either the footbridge at the southern tip of the golf course (beyond the tram lines) or Carshalton Road.

Just east of the golf course (across Beddington Ln) is One Island Pond, where the feature attraction is a pond ... with an island. Seriously though, there is a nice hill here, ideal for cross country or trail race training, plus more open grass spaces and thickets of wood.

North of there (across Croydon Rd) is Bidder's Pond, which, on top of having a pond (with no islands this time), has hills and the now familiar combo of wood and grassland.

There are plenty of trails throughout the common, and you'll have fun exploring routes with the help of several maps dotted around. A perimeter loop, minus the sections south of the tracks, is 3.4mi (5.5km).

GETTING THERE ▶

Rail: Mitcham Junction National Rail Station (Southern, Thameslink & Tramlink).

Bus: 118, 127, 152, 255, 264, 270, 355, 455, 463, S1, & N133.

👍 ▶ Rolling terrain and plenty of trails.

👎 ▶ Crossing roads and rail lines and the complete absence of public toilets.

MUST KNOW ▶

Traffic Warnings: Take care crossing the several roads and tram tracks.

Times: Open at all times (take care after dark).

117

FARTHING DOWNS & HAPPY VALLEY PARK

6.7mi / 10.8k

The southern-most point of any of London's boroughs, these neighbouring green spaces offer the runner an enticing mix of nature, history and hilly trails.

LOCATION ▶ Coulsdon, Croydon, CR5 (15.7mi S of central London)

INFO ▶ Farthing Downs is predominantly open grassland, which holds extra special significance for being a Roman archaeological site and for also housing several Saxon tumuli (a mound of earth over a burial site). The running here is either on Ditches Lane that follows the ridge line north to south, cutting the downs in two, or on one of the many gravel or grass trails that run parallel to the road. Enjoy the views towards the city.

MUST KNOW ▶

Circumference: 6.7mi (10.8km)

Surface: Gravel, dirt, grass, & sealed.

Terrain: Undulating to hilly.

Weather Warnings: Low lying and woodland trails can become boggy.

Traffic Warnings: Take care when running on nearby narrow roads.

Times: Open at all times (not recommended after dark).

Toilets: Farthing Downs car park.

Heading east, across the valley, you'll come to the largely wooded New Hill. Again, there are trails-a-plenty to explore here, including a perimeter loop that skirts around the several grazing fields.

To the south is Happy Valley Park which has the same chalk grassland as Farthing Downs and large pockets of ancient woodland. The wildflowers are so abundant here that up to 40 species can be found in one single square metre of meadow. For those keen to slow down and inspect the flora, one of Britain's rarest flowers, the greater yellow rattle, grows here. Plus, visit Devilsden Wood in spring for the bluebells.

Enough of smelling the flowers, the running through Happy Valley is close to idyllic (if you don't mind some undulations) as it spans the valley from Ditches Lane up to Old Coulsdon in the east.

A full perimeter loop of all three areas is 6.7mi (10.8k). Begin at Coulsdon South Station and run southeast past Coulsdon Memorial Ground (on your left) to enter Farthing Downs from the north. Follow the downs' western fence line before crossing Ditches Lane and doing the same along the Happy Valley Park western fence line. Then loop up around the eastern fence line of the park to connect into New Hill. Complete a perimeter loop of New Hill and head back to the station via the eastern side of Farthing Downs.

Nearby options include following the LOOP

pathway east through to Coulsdon Common (adjacent to Happy Valley), Kenley Common and Riddlesdown. North of Old Coulsdon are a string of wooded nature reserves worth exploring beginning with Dollypers Hill and In Wood. For those out for a long run, consider heading west into Surrey's Banstead Wood (2mi W of Coulsdon South Station), which boasts a 3mi nature trail and a 3.1mi (5k) perimeter loop. From there, and for those out for a very long run, you can keep heading northwest to Banstead Common (2.2mi further N) and on to Nonsuch Park (a further 2.3mi NW). Again, the LOOP is helpful for navigating further west.

GETTING THERE ▶

Rail: Coulsdon South (Southern Thameslink; 0.3mi N) & Coulsdon Town (Southern; 0.7mi N) National Rail Stations.

Bus: 60, 166, 404, 405, 409, 434, 463, 466 & N68.

👍 ▶ A part of London where nature dominates suburbia—makes for charming running.

👎 ▶ Aside from the LOOP, navigating to other nearby options can be tricky without a map.

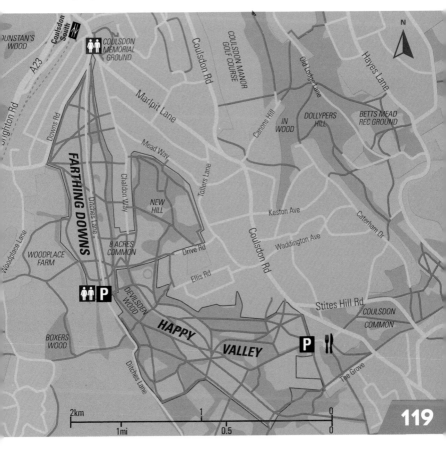

BEDDINGTON PARK

1.9mi / 3.0k

A small park with two distinct flavours and plenty of options nearby.

LOCATION ▸ Beddington, Sutton, SM6 (10.7mi S of central London)

INFO ▸ With grassy sports fields in the north and formal parklands in the south, there are two defined sections to this south London park.

The two sections are roughly cut off from each other by the River Wandle. North of the river the running is either done on the grass around the perimeter of the sports fields (with a section of single trail through the wood on the northern fence line) or on the sealed path that cuts through the centre on a diagonal and then runs south parallel to London Road.

The southern section is heavily landscaped with a boating lake, formal gardens surrounding The Grange, and several sealed and mown grass trails. There is also a small rise in this section of the park—the only noticeable hill.

One of Beddington Park's many leafy avenues.

A full loop of both sections, keeping to the edge of the grass fields in the north, is about 1.9mi (3km). If you want to avoid the grass and keep just to the main perimeter sealed paths, including using Church Road (as you go past St Mary the Virgin Church) and London Road (as you divert around The Grange), the loop is 1.7mi (2.7km). This is a good option if the grass is particularly wet.

Options | There is a connecting path in the northwest corner of the park that will take you through to Mitcham Common (1.1mi away). Also the River Wandle Trail passes along the north bank of the river through the park, so you can follow it either east towards Croydon or west to Carshalton and then north eventually all the way to the Thames (see 148 for more).

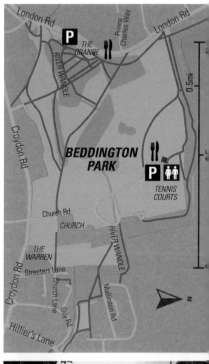

GETTING THERE ▶

Rail: Hackbridge National Rail Station (Southern & Thameslink services; 0.2mi N).

Bus: 151, 407, 410, 463, & X26.

👍 ▶ The formal parkland is a beautifully peaceful spot.

👎 ▶ No maps or signage so can be disorientating for first timers.

MUST KNOW ▶

Circumference: 1.9mi (3km)

Surface: Grass and sealed.

Terrain: Flat to undulating.

Weather Warnings: The grass sections can become boggy after heavy rain.

Traffic Warnings: None.

Times: Open at all times.

Toilets: Near the tennis courts in the north of the park.

River Wandle.

121

WIMBLEDON PARK

1.3mi / 2.1k

Perched just east of the famous tennis club and also of Wimbledon Park Golf Course (not accessible for runners) is this small but inviting park.

LOCATION ▶ Wimbledon, Merton, SW19 (6.7mi SW of central London)

INFO ▶ The park is shaped like a lowercase "q" with a large grass sports field in the north and, in the thinner southern section, tennis courts, formal gardens, a cafe, and children's play area. Just west of the cafe is the Wimbledon Park Lake, of which you only have access to a small stretch of its banks.

The large grass field has a sealed path all the way around it and also hosts the sheltered Wimbledon Park Athletics Track.

The southern section has several sealed trails, one following the park's perimeter—thus, completing a full circumference of the park on sealed paths (approx. 1.3mi, 2.1km). There are a few gates near the children's area that slow your run and you'll need to dodge the kids playing here.

Wimbledon Common is just 0.7mi from the north gate (follow the Capital Ring signs west along Wimbledon Park Rd, Bathgate Rd, and Queensmere Rd) and 1.3mi from the south gate (head southwest via Home Park Rd, Arthur Rd, Church Rd, and Wimbledon High St).

GETTING THERE ▶

Rail: Wimbledon Park Tube Station (District Line, just SE of the park).

Bus: 39, 156, 493, & N87.

👍 ▶ A lot to offer for a small park.

👎 ▶ Three or four laps are about as much as most runners' sanity levels can handle.

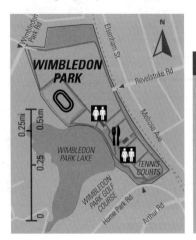

MUST KNOW ▶

Circumference: 1.3mi (2.1km)

Surface: Grass and sealed.

Terrain: Flat to undulating.

Traffic Warnings: Can be a busy park.

Times: 8am to dusk (weekends and holidays: 9am to dusk).

Toilets: Near the children's play area and at the back of the yacht club.

WIMBLEDON COMMON & PUTNEY

7.8mi / 12.5k

Being home to Thames Hare and Hounds (the oldest cross-country running club in the world, founded in 1868) it goes without saying that this huge plot of wood, grass and heath is ideal for running.

LOCATION ▶ Wimbledon, Merton and Wandsworth, SW19 & SW15 (8.1mi SW of central London)

INFO ▶ The 460ha area can be divided into two sections: Wimbledon Common itself is the largest to the south and just north of that is Putney Heath. A further 1.5mi north again, near the Thames, is the smaller Putney Lower Common (which blends into Barnes Common).

Wimbledon Common | Wimbledon Common is predominantly woodland, but also has several ponds, some beautiful clearings of heath and grass, two golf courses (technically the Royal Wimbledon is not part of the common), and sports fields.

The central focus of the common is the Wimbledon Windmill (built in 1817). Surrounding this are the museum, London Scottish Golf Course, a cafe, toilets and the info centre.

The sports fields include Richardson Evans Memorial on the west side of the common (which boasts a grass athletics track in summer and from which you can access Richmond Park) and Beverley Meads Recreation Grounds in the southern tip of the common.

The London Scottish Golf Course is accessible for runners looking for some smooth grass to run on (but stay off the greens and keep to the edge of fairways). The Royal Wimbledon Course, however, is off limits and there is a fenced pathway (affectionately labelled the "Toast Rack") that passes through its centre connecting the common south to Beverley Meads Grounds.

Much of the running in Wimbledon Common is Incredibly soft under foot.

123

SOUTHWEST HOTSPOTS

There is an abundance of trails to explore in the common. In fact the quantity of crisscrossing tracks can be overwhelming to disorientated newcomers. In a 1912 book written about the common it was said, "He does not know Wimbledon Common who is not familiar with its labyrinths of leafy glades, its tangled thickets of wild red rose, bramble, and honeysuckle" (Walter Johnson, *Wimbledon Common: Its Geology, Antiquities and Natural History*). You'll soon discover why 'labyrinth' and 'tangled' are both highly applicable descriptors (add to this the fact that maps are few and far between).

It's virtually impossible to follow a path that clings to the perimeter of the common, but there are several major paths (typically horse and mountain bike trails) that are easy to follow and make for excellent looping options. In particular, the Beverley Brook Walk (follow the deer way-markers), which begins near the Beverley Meads Grounds, heads north along the western side of the common and carries on through Richmond Park and then through Barnes and Putney Lower Commons all the way to the Thames (6.5 miles in total). Also, the Capital Ring that passes through the centre of the common (near the Windmill), from east to west, is another way-marked trail that can help provide bearings.

Surfaces are mostly dirt (and can become extremely boggy after wet weather), while some are gravel or sealed. The 16mi of horse trails in the area can make for a good running surface, but be sure to watch your step around hardened hoof marks.

Putney Heath | This is basically an extension of Wimbledon Common—once you hit the river of traffic that is the A3, you will have actually been jogging through Putney Heath for some time already. There are several subways under the A3, creating a seamless network of trails.

The heath is entirely wooded except for a few small clearings for sports fields and a dinky little suburb nestled just north of the A3. Much like Wimbledon Common, the trails are maze-like, but there is a semblance of a perimeter trail to explore. Surfaces are typically dirt and some-times gravel, grass or sealed.

A loop that combines Putney Heath and Wim-bledon Common, keeping roughly to the edges of the parks (and also passing through the Royal Wimbledon Golf Course via the fenced pathway) is approximately 7.8mi (12.5km).

GETTING THERE ▸

Rail: Wimbledon (Thameslink, South West, Tramlink & District), Southfields (District), & East Putney (District) are all within a mile or so of the Common or Putney Heath.

Bus: 14, 37, 72, 85, 93, 170, 200, 265, 424, 493, 969, & K3.

👍▸ Huge areas of untouched woodland and heath, accessible at all times.

👎▸ Can be a bit of a maze for newcomers, trails can get boggy, and it's not the safest after dark and/or by yourself.

MUST KNOW ▸

Circumference: 7.8mi (12.5km)

Surface: Dirt, gravel, & sealed.

Terrain: Rolling hills.

Weather Warnings: Dirt trails are no-go after rain.

Traffic Warnings: Use the subways to dodge the A3 and look out for golf balls when near the courses.

Times: Open at all times.

Toilets: At the Windmill.

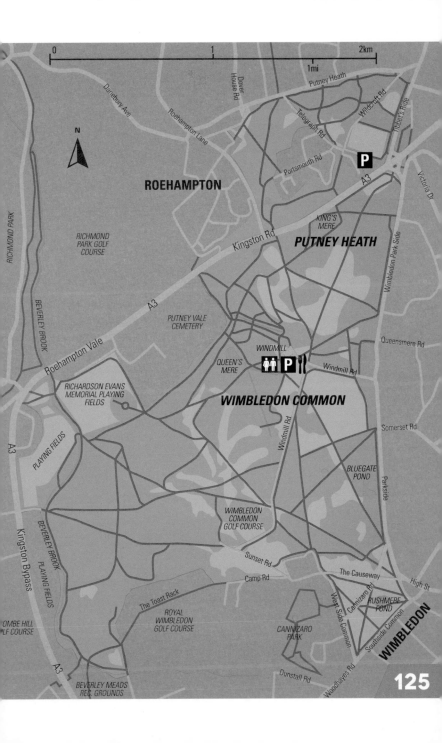

HOME PARK (HAMPTON COURT)

5mi / 8k

With many competing options nearby, this is possibly the most under-utilised running destination in London. However, this fact might be a good thing for the lucky few who do take advantage of Home Park's grassy plains, majestic rows of trees, and rare feeling of solitude.

LOCATION ▶ Kingston Upon Thames, Richmond, KT1 & KT8 (11.8mi SW of central London)

INFO ▶ Sitting next to Hampton Court Palace (and also just over the road from Bushy Park),

Home Park (as it is commonly known—Hampton Court Park if you're feeling formal) was once known as the "living larder" of King Henry VIII. And the deer he hunted still roam this enclosed piece of beautiful grassland (well, the deer's descendents anyway).

Long avenues of trees (mostly lime) break up the grass (which is also plentiful in wildflowers) and the central focus of the park is the huge stretch of water, the Palace of Versailles-inspired Long Water. At 1km long it certainly deserves its name and provides the runner with exceptional views of Hampton Court Palace (especially at sunset or sunrise) and of the water fowls that call the

The solitude of Home Park.

canal home.

There are grass and gravel trails all over the park. You can follow a perimeter circuit of 5mi (8km) that makes a diversion back into the middle of the park to run around the entire length of Long Water. If you're here in winter you can actually pass through the gates at the palace end of Long Water to enter the gardens of Hampton Court Palace, that way avoiding the 2km-diversion around the water.

There are some sealed roads and, although these are officially private, you shouldn't get in any trouble for running on them. Also, respect the private buildings dotted around the park and keep out the way of golfers (and their golf balls) when running near the course in the south of the park.

Gates to the park can be found near Kingston Bridge, Hampton Court Palace (on Hampton Court Road), and from three points along the Barge Walk, which is a continuation of the Thames Path (on the north bank). The Barge

Walk provides a good alternative to loop back along the river if you've parked at Kingston Gate.

GETTING THERE ▸

Rail: Hampton Wick Station (South West service) is just near Kingston Gate, while Hampton Court Station (South West service) is just over the Thames from Hampton Court Palace.

Bus: 111, 216, 281, 285, 411, 461, 481, 513, 515A, R68 & X26.

👍▸ Much quieter than Bushy Park but just as stunning.

👎▸ Lack of facilities like toilets and drinking fountains and the great divide of the Long Water effectively hews a full loop in two.

**SEE MAP
OVER PAGE ▸**

Hampton Court Palace.

127

HOME PARK

BUSHY PARK

DIANA FOUNTAIN

PADDOCK GATE

Hampton Court Rd

Kingston Ave

THE KING'S FIELD

Church Gr

KINGS GATE

HAMPTON WICK POND

KINGSTON AVE. GATE (WINTER ONLY)

HAMPTON COURT PALACE

DITTON AVE. GATE (WINTER ONLY)

FARM / COTTAGES (PRIVATE)

STUD HOUSE & NURSERY (PRIVATE)

THE LONG WATER

JUBILEE FOUNTAIN

OAK POND

HOME PARK

RICK POND

SURBITON PASSAGE GATE

JUBILEE GATE

BARGE WALK

Ditton Ave

GOLF COURSE

GOLF COURSE

RIVER THAMES

Portsmouth Rd

Brighton Rd

N

Summer Rd

High St

Burtenshaw Rd

1km

0.5mi

DITTON GATE

BARGE WALK

0.5

0

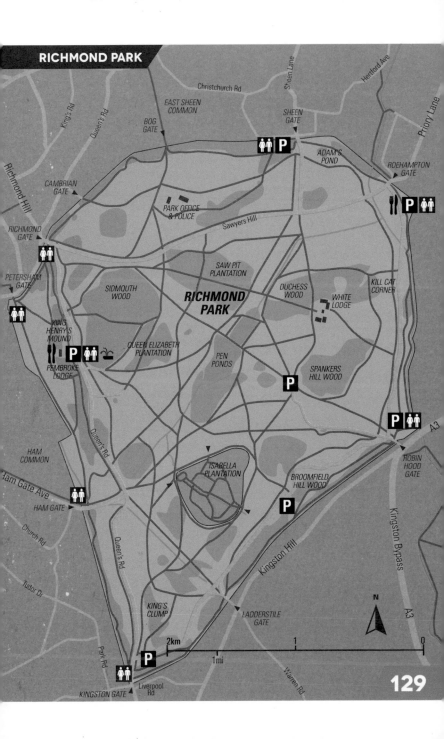

RICHMOND PARK

7.25mi / 11.7k ▦ ▦ ▦ ▦ 🏃 ❓ 🎒

The largest of London's Royal Parks, Richmond was the hunting ground for kings and queens seeking a haven from the hustle of London City. Nowadays, Richmond Park's 1000 hectares of perfect running terrain makes it the ideal haven for London runners.

LOCATION ▶ Richmond, TW10 (9.9mi SW of central London)

INFO ▶ Speak to any runner, from any part of the world, who has spent time running in London and they will rave about Richmond Park. It is simply one of the best suburban running environments in the world.

Humans have been attracted to the area since

The view from Sawyer's Hill.
Photo: Giles Bernard, The Royal Parks.

at least the Bronze Age, with a burial ground from that era on King Henry's Mound (the rise in the northwestern corner of the park). In the Middle Ages the royals began using the location for keeping deer and, in 1637, King Charles I created the park as we know it today by constructing an 8mi fence to enclose the deer. Now runners can roughly follow this fence line along the 7.25mi (11.7km) Tamsin Trail.

Various royals built hunting lodges in the park over the years, one of which interestingly was occupied by philosopher Bertrand Russell (whose grandfather, Prime Minister John Russell, was gifted the lodge from Queen Victoria).

The park's flora and fauna has immense significance with some grand oak trees dating back 750 years and, of course, several herds of non-skittish deer. However, keep at least 50m between you and the deer and avoid running with dogs from May to July (birthing) and September to October (rutting).

Apart from the circular Tamsin Trail, there are many trails and loops to explore in the park's interior. The way-marked Capital Ring trail passes from Pembroke Lodge through the central feature of the park, the waterfowl-rich Pen Ponds, and then out the east side of the park via Robin Hood Gate.

Beyond these way-marked options have fun exploring the pockets of wood (some of which are fenced and have several gates for exit and entry), garden areas (like Isabella Plantation), and rolling grass fields. Use the maps that are dotted all around the park to help you find your way.

The terrain is almost always rolling with some steeper hills in the southwest corner. The hills make for some great views.

Distances:

- Tamsin Trail: 7.25mi (11.7km)
- Southern half of Tamsin Trail (using Capital Ring to connect across—to Pembroke Lodge as opposed to Petersham Gate): 5.3mi (8.4km)
- Northern half of Tamsin Trail (using Capital Ring to connect across): 5.8mi (9.3km)
- Capital Ring Trail (gate-to-gate across the park one way): 2.5mi (4.0km)

GETTING THERE ▶

Rail: Richmond Station (District line, London Overground & South West service; 1.2mi N of Richmond Gate).

Bus: 33, 65, 72, 85, 170, 213, 265, 337, 371, 430, 493, 969, N74, K2, K3, & K4.

👍▶ Excellent running surfaces, incredible scenery, friendly wildlife, and plenty of room to explore.

👎▶ The several roads do take away some of the tranquillity of the park.

MUST KNOW ▶

Surface: Crushed limestone, dirt, grass, and some sealed sections.

Terrain: Moderate hills.

Weather Warnings: Some sections are particularly exposed to the weather.

Traffic Warnings: There are several roads through the park so do take care when crossing.

Times: Closed after dusk (opens 7:30am in winter and 7:00am in summer)

Toilets: Pembroke Lodge, Richmond Gate, Sheen Gate, Roehampton Gate, Robin Hood Gate, Kingston Gate, Ham Gate, and Petersham Gate.

◀ SEE MAP
PREVIOUS SPREAD

The grass and cinder trails of Richmond Park are extremely well-worn by London joggers.

BUSHY PARK

6.6mi / 10.7k

Bushy Park offers beautiful running surfaces.

Waterhouse Plantation.

Bushy House.

No guidebook to running in London would be complete without a thorough delve into the grassy swathe that is Bushy Park. For world record holders and first time parkrunners alike, this is London running at its glorious best.

LOCATION ▶ Teddington, Richmond, TW11 (13.1mi SW of central London)

INFO ▶ Bushy Park bares many remnants to its hugely varied history: medieval farm layouts, Tudor hunting grounds, 400-year-old water features (including canals and a water garden), and 20th century war camps.

Perhaps the most striking mark is the dead-straight Chestnut Drive, which was designed by Sir Christopher Wren and today splits the park in two—the road can be a constant flow of traffic in busy times. Wren also moved the Diana Fountain (originally commissioned by Charles I) into the large roundabout on Chestnut Drive.

Other features in the park include some rather grand royal hunting lodges, in particular Bushy House. Several wooded areas, spectacular avenues of mature trees, many lakes, and streams (including the handmade Longford River) break up the predominating grassland. Like nearby Home and Richmond Parks, you'll be accompanied by several herds of red and fallow deer. The Woodland and Water Gardens are two fenced-in areas that have restricted access times (9am to dusk), however, Woodland Gardens in particular is definitely worth running.

There are almost as many favoured loops in Bushy Park as there are regular runners, so the park does take some exploring. Start off by following the fence line trails (which sometimes become narrow single tracks) right around the park. You'll quickly discover the park's irregular-shape, especially west of Chestnut Drive. A complete circuit on the fence line is 6.6mi (10.7km), assuming you don't get lost.

After the perimeter run, try exploring the central features of lakes and plantations. There are many major thoroughfares that carve direct routes through these middle sections and also offer up a nice variety of running surfaces (some of the best grass and crushed limestone trails around).

With such a flat park, and being on soft surfaces and largely free of traffic, Bushy is the ideal place to do workouts, time trials, and tempo runs. Here are two classic routes to try.

3—Mile Tempo: Start just northeast of the Diana Fountain, on the access road to the car park (near the boating lake). Going in a clockwise direction, run north along the grass, with Chestnut Ave on your left. Run parallel to the road all the way to the northern end of the park (take care crossing the two access roads to Hawthorne Lodge). Turn right onto the gravel trail.

Follow this perimeter trail all the way east and down to Hampton Wick Royal Cricket Ground. Run on the park side of the cricket ground and then turn right to follow the perimeter trail past the playground.

Then follow the fence line left before making

your way back to Chestnut Ave (at Hampton Court Gate) where you can run next to the road back north, around the Diana Fountain, to the start location. It's 3.04mi all up if you finish where you started. So if you take off 60m or so you'll have 3mi (or add another 90m to make 5km).

The ever-popular Bushy parkrun (the founding event) follows a similar course. Also remember that the beginning and end include sections on grass—in slippery conditions this may not be ideal for faster running.

2—Mile Tempo: In the summer months, in particular, Bushy Park is the training ground to many international elite athletes. This is a common two-mile (3.2k) tempo run that they use in preparation for Diamond League events and world record attempts.

At Hampton Court Gate start on the eastern side of Chestnut Avenue and follow the trail east and then over the little footbridge, up to the playground, where you turn right and head all the way to Hampton Wick Royal Cricket Ground (run on the park side of the ground). The halfway point is exactly where you turn right next to the cricket ground.

Run around the cricket ground and then follow the park's perimeter trail almost all the way up to Chestnut Ave at Teddington Gate. The tempo run finishes after passing the first of the long rows of trees that strike off south at right angles to the trail.

OPTIONS ▶ Home Park is literally just over the road (south), the Thames Path is just a few hundred metres from Church Grove Gate (near Kingston), and the southern tip of Richmond Park is only 1.5mi away through Kingston Upon Thames. A great post-run option is Hampton Pool, heated to 28-de-

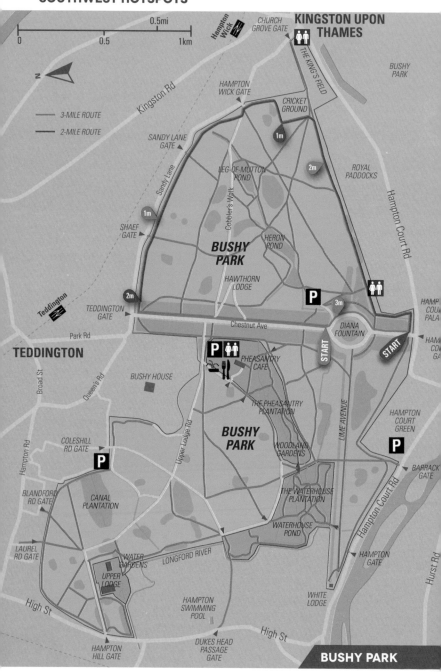

SOUTHWEST HOTSPOTS

0.5mi
0   0.5   1km

Hampton Wick

CHURCH GROVE GATE

KINGSTON UPON THAMES

N

BUSHY PARK

— 3-MILE ROUTE
— 2-MILE ROUTE

Kingston Rd

THE KING'S FIELD

HAMPTON WICK GATE

CRICKET GROUND

1m

2m

ROYAL PADDOCKS

SANDY LANE GATE

Sandy Lane

LEG-OF-MUTTON POND

Cobbler's Walk

1m

SHAEF GATE

BUSHY PARK

HERON POND

Hampton Court Rd

2m

Teddington

TEDDINGTON GATE

HAWTHORN LODGE

P

3m

HAMP COU PALA

Park Rd

Chestnut Ave

DIANA FOUNTAIN

HAM CO GA

TEDDINGTON

P

PHEASANTRY CAFÉ

START

START

Broad St

Queen's Rd

BUSHY HOUSE

THE PHEASANTRY PLANTATION

LIME AVENUE

HAMPTON COURT GREEN

Hampton Rd

COLESHILL RD GATE

P

Upper Lodge Rd

BUSHY PARK

WOODLAND GARDENS

P

BLANDFORD RD GATE

CANAL PLANTATION

THE WATERHOUSE PLANTATION

Hampton Court Rd

BARRACK GATE

LAUREL RD GATE

WATER GARDENS

LONGFORD RIVER

WATERHOUSE POND

HAMPTON GATE

UPPER LODGE

High St

HAMPTON SWIMMING POOL

WHITE LODGE

Hurst Rd

HAMPTON HILL GATE

DUKES HEAD PASSAGE GATE

High St

BUSHY PARK

grees year round (accessed via Dukes Head Passage Gate).

GETTING THERE ▸

Rail: Teddington & Hampton Wick Stations are just a few hundred metres outside the park gates N and W respectively (South West service). Hampton Court (South West service) is just over the Thames from the Hampton Court Gate.

Bus: 33, 111, 216, 281, 285, 411, 461, 481, 513, 515A, R68, R70, & X26.

👍▸ Constantly varying scenery with top-notch trails and many other runners to share the experience with.

👎▸ The western section can be disorientating. Plus, and a strong word of warning, running here can be addictive!

The deer are friendly, but are still wild, so shouldn't be approached.

CRANE PARK

4.0mi / 6.5k

This is a beautiful, long, but narrow, park that follows the River Crane under an ever-present cover of trees.

LOCATION ▶ Twickenham, Richmond , TW2 & TW13 (12.4mi W of central London)

INFO ▶ From Hounslow Rd (A314) in the west to Meadway in the east a brilliant sealed trail follows the north bank of the river, unbroken as it passes under bridges and through lovely green surrounds. This is the main route for runners on the north bank but there are several dirt track alternatives as well.

On the south bank is a limestone trail between Hounslow Rd and Great Chertsey Rd (A316). There are also two other sections of dirt trail on the south bank between Hospital Bridge Rd and Mill Rd (look for the connecting bridges across the river).

The eastern end of the park connects to Kneller Gardens—a large grassy field with a nice sealed 830m loop around it. This makes a good lollipop shaped end to your run.

So a possible route could start in the west at the A314. Run east along the limestone trail on the south bank. At Great Chertsey Rd cross to the north bank and continue running east to complete a loop of Kneller Gardens. Then come back on the north bank for a total of 4mi (6.5km).

While on this run, look out for the 25m-tall Shot Tower, which gets its name from once having produced lead shot as part of an old mill.

Running further west you'll reach Pevensey Rd Nature Reserve and follow the LOOP Trail south from Hospital Bridge Rd to reach Bushy Park (2mi away). Also following the LOOP northwest you'll hit Hounslow Heath after 1.1km from Hanworth Rd. Hanworth Park is 0.5mi southwest on Hounslow Rd. From Kneller Gardens you can carry on east by following The Duke of Northumberland's River (an offshoot from the River Crane that stretches to the Thames at Isleworth).

GETTING THERE ▶

Rail: Whitton National Rail Station (South West service; 0.5mi NW of Kneller Gardens).

Bus: 110, 111, 481, 490, 969, H22, & H25.

👍 ▶ Well made trails in a superb river park.

👎 ▶ Although it's not a problem for runners, as a result of a sewer mishap upstream, there are currently no fish in the river.

MUST KNOW ▶

Circumference: 4.0mi (6.5km)

Surface: Sealed, crushed limestone, and dirt.

Terrain: Flat.

Weather Warnings: Dirt trails can become muddy in wet weather.

Traffic Warnings: Take care crossing Meadway (use the pedestrian tunnels under other roads).

Times: 8am to dusk.

Toilets: At Kneller Gardens.

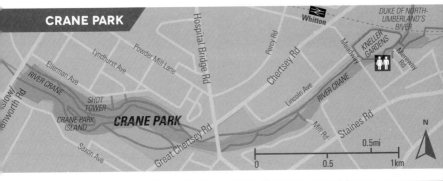

CRANE PARK

Hospital Bridge Rd
Powder Mill Lane
Lyndhurst Ave
Ellerman Ave
RIVER CRANE
SHOT TOWER
CRANE PARK ISLAND
CRANE PARK
Saxon Ave
Great Chertsey Rd
Percy Rd
Chertsey Rd
Lincoln Ave
Meadway
KNELLER GARDENS
Whitton
DUKE OF NORTH-UMBERLAND'S RIVER
Mereway Rd
RIVER CRANE
Mill Rd
Staines Rd
N

0.5mi
0   0.5   1km

Shot Tower, Crane Park.

HANWORTH PARK

FELTHAM COMMUNITY COLLEGE
Uxbridge Rd
Eastborne Rd
HANWORTH AIR PARK LEISURE CENTRE
P
P
N
Forest Rd
HANWORTH PARK HOUSE
HANWORTH PARK
Elmwood Ave
Fernside Ave
Castle Way
Park Rd
Park Rd
Hounslow Rd

0.5mi
1km   0.5   0

The wide, open grass fields of Hanworth Park.

HANWORTH PARK

1.75mi / 2.8k

Formerly a royal hunting ground, Hanworth Park became an airfield in WWII. Nowadays runners have access to a pleasant, sometimes bleak-looking, grassy plain, with wonderfully soft trails.

LOCATION ▶ Feltam, Hounslow, TW13 (14.2mi W of central London)

INFO ▶ The leisure centre car park just off Uxbridge Rd makes a good start point. From here it's simple to begin heading in a clockwise direction around the edge of the sports fields.

From the rugby club, in the south of the park, follow the sealed path up towards St George's Church. Then join the grass again to run around the meadows in the park's northwest corner.

Tucked away in the north of the park, behind a high fence and many trees, is Hanworth Park House, the old royal manor house (currently disused). This inaccessible section has the unfortunate effect of breaking up the middle of the park. So you will need to skirt around one of its fence lines or even exit the park via Forest Rd and then use Browells Lane to re-enter via the pathway just past Feltham Community College.

As you approach the leisure centre from Hanworth Park House, you'll pass an area of wild shrub land that has a few bonus trails.

Some great nearby options include Leitrim Park (500m north via Uxbridge Rd), Crane Park (just half a mile NE via Hounslow Rd), Pevensey Road Nature Reserve (opposite Crane Park also on Hounslow Rd), Hounslow Heath another 1.1km further on from Pevensey Road, and Bedfont Lakes Country Park (2mi W via High St and Bedfont Rd).

GETTING THERE ▶

Rail: Feltam National Rail Station (South West service; 0.7mi N).

Bus: 90, 111, 285, 490, H25, & X26.

👍 ▶ A large open park of grass just made for trying out barefoot running.

👎 ▶ Exposed to the elements.

MUST KNOW ▶

Circumference: 1.75mi (2.8km)

Surface: Grass (with some sealed sections).

Terrain: Flat.

Weather Warnings: After heavy rain the grass can be boggy and slippery.

Traffic Warnings: None.

Times: Open at all times.

Toilets: None (ask nicely at the leisure centre).

◀ SEE MAP
PREVIOUS PAGE

HOUNSLOW HEATH

2.5mi / 4k

A back-to-nature (read: scrappy) park with its own unique charm, plus plenty of trails.

LOCATION ▸ Hounslow, TW4 (12.5mi W of central London)

INFO ▸ Despite its rough 'n' ready appearance, the heath actually has high wildlife importance. It is said that the area is the key habitat for snakes in all of London—but don't worry, it's apparently difficult to come across one by accident.

It is mostly flat (with a few undulations) and is covered with a mixture of shrub, grass, lowland heath, wood, wetland, and meadows. There is a variety of non-sealed trails throughout, including a bridle trail of 2.1mi (3.4km) looping around the heath and a less developed perimeter trail of 2.5mi (4km).

There are maps at the main entrances, of which the car park on the corner of Frampton Rd and Staines Rd is your best option for a start/finish location. The maps come in handy because navigation can be a tricky thing amidst the dense scrub. Get to know the place initially by following the bridle trail (look for the horseshoe way-markers).

Hounslow Heath Golf Course runs seamlessly into the heath itself, so if you find yourself on a putting green, you're too far west. In saying this, the LOOP Walk cuts through the heath and then runs directly through the golf course to meet the River Crane and so provides a great option for adding on, either south to Crane Park (1.1km via Simpson and Hanworth Rds) or north to Cranford Park (3mi via River Crane predominantly).

GETTING THERE ▸

Rail: Hounslow National Rail Station (South West service; 0.9mi W).

Bus: 110, 111, 116, 117, 235, 237, 423, H26, & H28.

👍 ▸ Unique running environment with connections to some other top runs.

👎 ▸ Feels a little maze-like at times.

▸ **SEE MAP
NEXT PAGE**

MUST KNOW ▸

Circumference: 2.5mi (4km)

Surface: Crushed limestone, grass & dirt.

Terrain: Flat.

Weather Warnings: Some trails can become muddy after rain.

Traffic Warnings: None (except golfers if you stray out of the heath).

Times: Open at all times but feels rather unsafe after dark.

Toilets: None.

SOUTHWEST HOTSPOTS

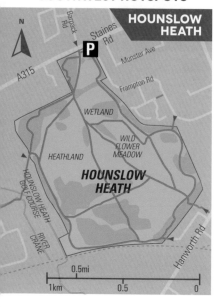

HOUNSLOW HEATH

Barrack Rd
Staines Rd
A315
Munster Ave
Frampton Rd

WETLAND

WILD FLOWER MEADOW

HEATHLAND

HOUNSLOW HEATH

HOUNSLOW HEATH GOLF COURSE

RIVER CRANE

Hanworth Rd

0.5mi

1km   0.5   0

Bedfont Lakes Country Park.

BEDFONT LAKES COUNTRY PARK

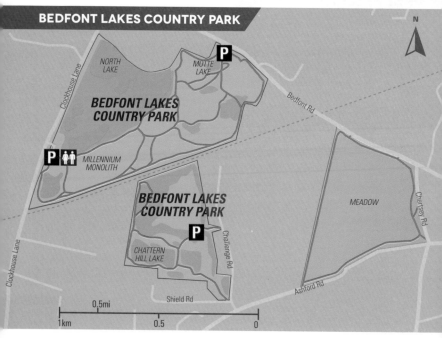

Clockhouse Lane

NORTH LAKE

MOTTE LAKE

BEDFONT LAKES COUNTRY PARK

Bedfont Rd

MILLENNIUM MONOLITH

BEDFONT LAKES COUNTRY PARK

MEADOW

Chertsey Rd

CHATTERN HILL LAKE

Challenge Rd

Clockhouse Lane

Shield Rd

Ashford Rd

0.5mi

1km   0.5   0

BEDFONT LAKES COUNTRY PARK

2mi / 3.2k

◀ **SEE MAP OPPOSITE**

73 hectares of nature reserve just waiting for runners to leave their footprints on its well kept trails and rolling hills.

LOCATION ▶ Bedfont, Hounslow, TW14 (15.9mi W of central London)

INFO ▶ The park is officially divided into two, however, the smaller southern section is on the other side of the tracks and, with no direct access to it, this review will focus on the bigger and more popular northern section.

The main attractions of the park are the six lakes. Unfortunately you can't complete a loop around the larger lake (there are commercial properties blocking the north banks) but there are plenty of trails amongst its grassy and wooded east and south banks.

Whether you're starting from Bedfont Road or Clockhouse Lane, the best way to get to know the park is to follow the perimeter trail for one loop (2mi). Then try crisscrossing through the centre of that loop and up to the top of the small hills for the view.

It's easy enough to put together 3-4mi within the park, but to mix it up a little there are several public meadows nearby. One in particular is just 0.5mi away heading east on Bedfont Rd. You'll find the meadow behind a hedge row and it boasts an exceptional sealed/limestone loop of 1.3mi (2.1km). From the southwest corner of

this meadow (on Ashford Rd) it's only another 500m heading west to the southern section Bedfont Lakes.

In Bedfont Lakes Park itself there is an orienteering course. You can download a map for the course at www.hounslow.info.

GETTING THERE ▶

Rail: Ashford (1.1mi SW) & Feltham (1.9mi E) National Rail Stations (both on the South West service).

Bus: 116 & H26.

👍 ▶ A family-friendly nature reserve.

👎 ▶ Not the spot you'd hunt out to complete a weekend long run—it's little.

MUST KNOW ▶

Circumference: 2mi (3.2km)

Surface: Crushed limestone, gravel & grass.

Terrain: Undulating.

Weather Warnings: None.

Traffic Warnings: If venturing out of the park take care on the narrow 40mph roads.

Times: Open daily (except Christmas) 8am to dusk.

Toilets: At the Clockhouse Lane car park.

TAMSIN TRAIL

7.25mi / 11.7k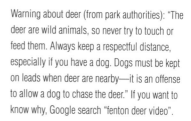

This 7.25mi trail is the perfect introduction to the perfect running destination of Richmond Park.

LOCATION ▶ Start/Finish: Pembroke Lodge, Richmond, TW10 (9.9mi SW of central London)

INFO ▶ The Tamsin Trail roughly follows Richmond Park's perimeter and can be started at any point. This description begins and ends at Pembroke Lodge, which has a car park, cafe, drinking fountain, and toilets—making it the ideal base from which to explore the park.

The meandering Tamsin Trail.

Warning about deer (from park authorities): "The deer are wild animals, so never try to touch or feed them. Always keep a respectful distance, especially if you have a dog. Dogs must be kept on leads when deer are nearby—it is an offense to allow a dog to chase the deer." If you want to know why, Google search "fenton deer video".

MILE–BY–MILE ▶ Start: From Pembroke Lodge, and going clockwise, find the paved trail heading towards the Richmond Gate entrance. Look for the blue arrows that mark the Tamsin Trail.

0.6mi: Richmond Gate. As you come to each intersecting road, look for the continuation of the trail opposite, always marked with the blue arrow. The trail keeps reasonably close to the park boundary and is largely flat over the first half, with a barely noticeable descent.

2mi: Sheen Gate. Most of this section is nestled amongst the trees that line the park boundary. These trees have recently been trimmed and thinned to keep your view of the park nice and open—making the trail much safer for solo runners.

2.5mi: Roehampton Gate. There are toilets, a cafe, and even bike hire just past this park entrance.

3.8mi: Robin Hood Gate. At the 3.5mi point (just before Robin Hood Gate) you will begin to climb up Broomfield Hill. The climb lasts about a mile all up. From the summit (58m, compared to the lows of 9m the course encounters at the

2.8mi mark) you'll head down, winding through oak trees and pockets of grassland.

4.9mi: Ladderstile Gate. This is a pedestrian-only entrance way and also marks the beginning of the descent.

5.6mi: Kingston Gate. The trail makes a 90-degree right (north) turn here.

6.4mi: Ham Gate Pond. After the final road crossing, before returning to Pembroke Lodge, the Tamsin Trail splits in two. Take the right hand option closest to the road as this will provide the most direct route home. Oh, and there's one more little climb.

7.25mi: Pembroke Lodge. Grab an ice cream or a coffee from the cafe as your reward.

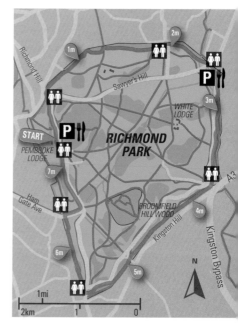

The deer of Richmond Park. Photo: Giles Barnard, The Royal Parks.

SOUTHWEST ROUTES

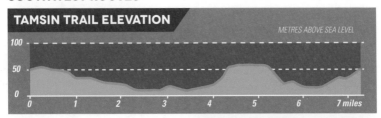

TAMSIN TRAIL ELEVATION

METRES ABOVE SEA LEVEL

100

50

0

0   1   2   3   4   5   6   7 miles

Warm Down | The walled gardens of Pembroke Lodge make for a great little warm down jog/walk. And while here, be sure to check out the little surprise view at King Henry's Mound.

Options | Explore the centre of the park, head to the nearby Thames Path (accessible from Richmond and Petersham Gates), or follow the Beverley Brook Walk east into Wimbledon Common or north to Barnes Common and the Thames.

GETTING THERE ▸

Rail: Richmond Tube & National Rail Station (District, London Overground & South West services) is 1.2mi N of Richmond Gate (where you can start the run instead).

Bus: 65 & 371.

👍 ▸ A beautiful park and an easy-to-follow trail. And of course, close ups of wild deer.

👎 ▸ Is it even possible to find fault with this? I suppose sometimes it might be rainy or cold, but, if not, be thankful you're in running paradise.

MUST KNOW ▸

Distance: 7.25mi (11.7km)

Surface: Crushed limestone, dirt, and some sealed sections.

Terrain: Moderate hills.

Traffic Warning: There are several roads through the park so take care when crossing these.

Weather Warning: Some sections are exposed to the weather.

Time Restrictions: Closed after dusk (open 7:30am in winter and 7:00am in summer).

Toilets: Pembroke Lodge & also at Richmond, Sheen, Roehampton, Robin Hood, Kingston, & Ham Gates.

Broomfield Hill Wood.

BEVERLEY BROOK

8.0mi / 13k

A great way-marked trail that gives you a taster for Wimbledon Common, Richmond Park, Barnes Common, and the Thames Path. Catch the train home or double back for a solid 16-miler.

LOCATION ▶ Start: New Malden Station, Croydon, Kingston, KT3 (10.8mi SW of central London)
Finish: Putney Station, Wandsworth, SW15 (5.6mi SW of central London)

INFO ▶ Rather than run in circles in Richmond Park or get lost in Wimbledon Common, follow this way-marked trail through sections of both to eventually emerge on to the Thames.

The signage for this walk is generally good (look for the deer icon) but it still pays to carry a map (or smart phone).

MILE–BY–MILE ▶ Start: New Malden Station. Exit the station right (onto Coombe Rd), then right onto Cambridge Ave, follow it to its end. Cross Malden Golf Course, go under the A3, and swing left to make your way to Beverley Ave and the start of Wimbledon Common.

1.2mi: Wimbledon Common. The trail clings to the right hand bank of Beverley Brook till you emerge from the common at the Kingston University sports fields. Cross the brook here and use the pedestrian bridge to cross the A3 and enter Richmond Park.

Beverley Brook, Wimbledon Common.

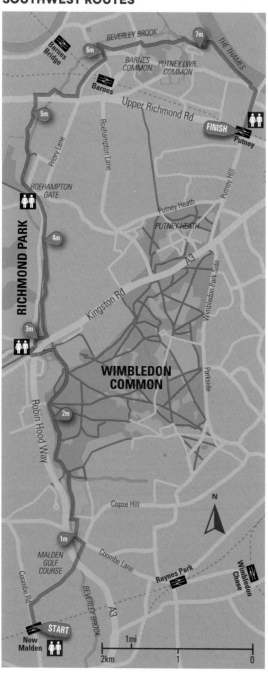

3mi: Richmond Park. While the Tamsin Trail runs closer to the road, the Beverley Brook trail clings to the brook (so it is possible to use the Tamsin Trail as far as Roehampton Gate if you prefer its surface).

4.4mi: Palewell Playing Fields. The trail makes a right turn into these playing fields. Run through the allotments and turn right when you hit Hertford Ave—follow it to its end.

5.1mi: Upper Richmond Road. Turn right here, then left for a quick detour around the crescent-shaped Priests Bridge, back to Upper Richmond, and then left down Vine Road. Take care on this narrow road, cross over the two rail tracks and then head straight into Barnes Common.

5.9mi: Barnes Common. The trail makes a little dog leg up to the western end of the common before turning right and heading due east, through a network of trails, to the Thames.

7.1mi: The Thames. Turn right at the river and follow the Thames Path all the way to Putney Bridge. Turn right to run up Putney High Street to Putney Station, completing your 8mi run.

Options | To make it a 6mi run, turn right onto Station Rd when you exit Vine Rd. This will take you to Barnes Station.

Once at Putney Station, if you feel like you'd rather run home (and are not keen to retrace your steps), carry straight on, running south along Putney High St (which becomes Putney Hill). You'll reach Putney Heath on your right—use the trail in here that runs parallel to the road. Cross under the A3 and then take the main trail directly to the Windmill in Wimbledon Common.

Pass by the Windmill and continue following the main route south (parallel to the bridle track). When you cross the golf course, bear right and head straight down to Beverley Brook. Turn left and follow the signage back home. If you don't get lost, this run will total 13.5mi (21.7km).

GETTING THERE ▸

The South West rail service provides the connection between the start and finish locations. From Putney Station, head east to Clapham Junction and transfer to the south bound service to New Malden.

👍 ▸ Passes through some truly wonderful green spaces.

👎 ▸ Running through Richmond Park can leave you wondering why you didn't just do your entire run in there.

Beverley Brook enjoying some Richmond Park sunshine.

MUST KNOW ▸

Distance: 8.0mi (13km)

Surface: Sealed, dirt, grass, & gravel.

Terrain: Flat to undulating.

Weather Warning: Wimbledon Common in particular becomes boggy when wet.

Traffic Warning: There are multiple road crossings, so take care.

Times: Richmond Park is closed after dusk (opens 7:30am in winter, 7:00am in summer).

Toilets: New Malden Station, Robin Hood Gate (Richmond Park), Roehampton Gate (Richmond Park), & Putney Station.

THE WANDLE TRAIL

13.7mi **/ 22.0**k

A 14-mile run visiting wonderful green spaces, but falls short on the navigation factor—without a map it's a way-marker treasure hunt.

LOCATION ▶ Start: East Croydon Station, Croydon, CR90, (10.6mi S of central London)

Finish: Wandsworth Town Station, Wandsworth, SW18 (5.0mi SW of central London)

INFO ▶ The Wandle River was once labelled the "hardest working river in England". And amongst the rejuvenating woodlands and pleasant riverside parks, it still displays some rusty remnants of the many mills and factories that once worked on it.

This way-marked trail (look for the water mill icon) has been constructed to roughly follow the river from East Croydon Station all the way north to the Thames at Wandsworth Town Station. You can enter and exit the trail at any point and it also makes a useful connection between parks. Particular highlights along the way are Morden Hall Park and Beddington Park (see 120), which are great for adding on.

There are maps dotted along the trail, but the inconsistency in way-marking is a real problem. Unlike the Green Chain or LOOP trails, which have way-markers every few hundred metres, this trail is rather irregular in its markings. It also doesn't help that the trail is sometimes erratic in its route by attempting to take in as many green spaces as possible.

MILE-BY-MILE ▶ Start: East Croydon Station. Turn right out of the station to head west along George Street.

The Wandle provides yet another tranquil London waterside trail.

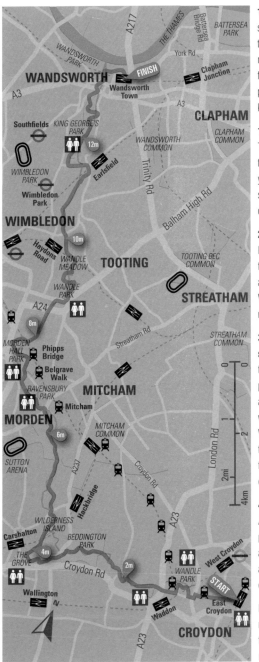

1mi: Wandle Park. You'll skim along the side of this small, but recently renovated, park. And if you feel like some extra, the main promenade is just under a kilometre around.

1.5mi: Waddon Ponds. The trail runs straight by this small park, but again, if you have the time, it's worth spending a few minutes doing a loop.

2.5mi: Beddington Park. A large park with sports fields, formal parkland and generally a beautiful setting for the Wandle and runner alike to meander their way through.

3.7mi: The Grove, Car–shalton. You'll run right through the centre of this pleasant park, past its ponds, and next to the canal that will link you back up to the Wandle. (You can skip out this detour if you like and take the signposted shortcut direct to Wilderness Island.)

4.3mi: Wilderness Island. As its name suggests, this patch of wetland/wood is accessed by bridge only, and can make a nice circular detour.

For much of the next few miles the trail follows the banks of the river, occasionally

149

SOUTHWEST ROUTES

diving into surrounding streets, and then rejoining the Wandle before long.

6.4mi: Ravensbury Park. A mill was in operation in this park right up until the middle of the last century. You'll see its remnants.

7mi: Morden Hall Park. Arched bridges, bird-rich wetlands, grassy meadows, and avenues of old trees are some of the features that may entice you to explore this park more. (To head home from here, take the tram from Phipps Bridge, this is 7.4mi from East Croydon).

9mi: Wandle Park, Colliers Wood. Another "Wandle Park", smaller than the first, and there is also close access to Colliers Wood Tube Station nearby (connect to the Southern service at Balham Station).

11.6mi: King George's Park. A series of sports fields, with the Wandle winding its way just to the east.

13.3mi: The Spit. This little island overlooking the Thames marks the end of the Wandle River. Swing a right (east) along Smuggler's Way to reach Wandsworth Town Station. If you've managed to stay on course you will have just finished a run of 13.7mi (22km). Nice work.

GETTING THERE ▶

Rail: Being a point-to-point run, easily the best mode of transport is rail. Start at the East Croydon National Rail Station (Southern & Thameslink services, & London Tramlink) & finish at Wandsworth Town Station (South West service). Take the South West to Clapham Junction then the Southern to East Croydon.

👍 ▶ Passes through some beautiful sections of south London.

👎 ▶ The lack of way-markers.

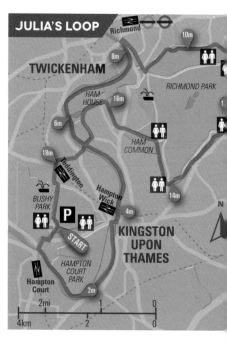

JULIA BLEASDALE'S LOOP

19.2mi / 31k ☐ ▦ ▦ 🏃 🏃 ❓ ☯

◀ SEE MAP
OPPOSITE

*This is the sort of long run that will
get you really fit. It has beautiful
scenery, a few hills, many drink and
toilet stops on the way, and oodles
of traffic-free trails. If it helped Julia
reach double top-eight at the
Olympics, it'll help all of us achieve
our personal running goals.*

LOCATION ▶ Diana Fountain, Bushy Park,
Teddington, Richmond, TW11 (13.1mi SW of
central London)

INFO ▶ Ideal for serious marathon or half
marathon training, Julia has designed this run in
order to take in the incredible parks of Richmond
and Bushy and to also spend a lot of time
following the banks of the Thames.

The benefit of doing the loop around Richmond
Park is that you can cut the run short if needed.
To do this, when you enter the park through
Richmond Gate, instead of turning left and following the Tamsin Trail clockwise, turn right to
follow it anti-clockwise, past Pembroke Lodge,
and direct to Ham Gate (leaving the park).

MILE-BY-MILE ▶ Start: Diana
Fountain, Bushy Park. From the car park head
south following Chestnut Avenue out of the park.
Turn right onto Hampton Court Road and then
left to follow the Barge Walk on the north bank
of the Thames.

3.5mi: Kingston Bridge. Cross the river here
and take the stairs down to the Thames Path and
follow it north.

8.25mi: Richmond Bridge. After following
the Thames Path all the way along this beautiful
stretch of river, head up to street level (Richmond
Rd). Turn right here, then right again onto Hill
Street. Veer left on Hill Rise, which becomes
Richmond Hill. Enjoy the views as you approach
Richmond Park.

9.0mi: Richmond Gate, Richmond Park.
Enter the park and immediately turn left to follow
the Tamsin Trail all the way around the park
(clockwise) to Ham Gate.

15.0mi: Ham Gate, Richmond Park. Leave
the park via this tree-lined road. Cross Petersham Road and run over Ham Common to turn
right onto the long, straight walkway leading to

Thames Path heading towards
Richmond (just past Ham House).

151

SOUTHWEST ROUTES

Looking southwest from Richmond Hill.

Ham House (this path is just after St Michael's Convent).

16.2mi: Ham House. Just before the path reaches the grounds of Ham House, look for the small path to your left (near the plant nursery). Follow it till Ham Street. Cross this street and follow Riverside Drive all the way around.

17.2mi: The Thames. When the parkland on your right hand side turns to houses, turn right down the path leading to the Thames. Use the two old footbridges to cross to the Teddington side of the river.

17.5mi: Ferry Road, Teddington. Follow Ferry Road as it becomes High Street. Then look for the left turn onto Park Road which will lead you back to Bushy Park.

18.5mi: Bushy Park. Run parallel to Chestnut Avenue all the way to the Diana Fountain (19.2mi later). Be sure to treat yourself to a nice recovery drink after your huge run.

GETTING THERE ▶

Rail: Teddington & Hampton Wick Stations are just a few hundred metres outside the park gates N and W respectively (South West service). Hampton Court (South West service) is just over the Thames from the Hampton Court Gate.

Bus: 33, 111, 216, 281, 285, 411, 461, 481, 513, 515A, R68, R70, & X26.

👍 ▶ A truly superb long run with options to cut it short if need be.

👎 ▶ Not being a way-marked trail, take extra care to have the directions memorised/printed out or to carry a map—getting lost on a long run like this is not a good idea.

TWO PALACES AND A CANAL

8.5mi / 13.7k [!] ▦ ⊟ 🏃 ⧖

A great 8.5mi west London run that takes in the spectacular and, at the same time, tranquil grounds of two palaces, finishing with a beautiful stretch of tree-lined canal towpath.

LOCATION ▶ Syon House car park, Brentford, Hounslow, TW7 (9.4mi W of central London)

INFO ▶ The current home of the Duke of Northumberland, the grand Syon Park is nestled on the banks of the Thames and makes a perfect starting point for this scenic medium-length run.

The other key attraction on this run is Osterley Park, which has plenty of adding on options and boasts another impressive palace. Then, not to be outdone by the grandeur of the nearby palaces, the serenity of the River Brent (Grand Union Canal) provides the perfect journey back to the start at Syon Park (there are toilets here and a cafe for post-run refreshments).

MILE–BY–MILE ▶ **Start: Syon House.**
Head west (right when facing the garden centre) to pass by the impressive front lawn of Syon House (completed in 1550).

0.5mi: Park Road. Out of Syon Park grounds follow these instructions for making your way to Osterley Park:

- Turn left onto Park Rd and then right onto Mill Plat, run to its end;
- At Twickenham Rd turn right and make a quick left up Linkfield Rd, run to its end;
- At London Rd turn left and use the crossing to then head up College Rd and veer left onto Ridgeway Rd;
- Before reaching the A4, turn left onto Church Rd, run to its end;
- Turn right on Thornbury and follow it all the way to Osterley Park.

2.5mi: Osterley Park. Open daily from 8am to 7:30pm (or 6pm in the winter, the gardens

The first of the palaces (and the starting point for this run), Syon House.

Osterley Park House.

153

Grand Union Canal at dusk.

Osterley Park Farm, from Osterley Lane.

Not a bad final resting place. Grand Union Canal.

and the house itself are charged) run directly north through the park, with a small horseshoe bend near Osterley House (there are public toilets available here) and then a slight bend westward after the toilets.

3.3mi: Osterley Lane. Turn left onto this country lane that will take you over the M4. Follow lane to its end.

4.0mi: Tentelow Lane. Turn right here, then second left onto Minterne Road, and first right onto Melbury Avenue. This will take you over the canal from which you can follow the towpath to your right (heading east).

4.7mi: River Brent (Grand Union Canal). Enjoy the tranquil surrounds and the slight downhill (particularly noticeable by the number of locks you'll pass) of this wonderful towpath section. There are many parks and reserves on either side of the canal that help to maintain this sense of solitude (and they can be used for adding on). Also keep an eye out for the old iron mile markers—making this a great place to do intervals or a tempo workout.

When you start to reach apartment blocks and hotels on the banks of the canal (and the covered canal dock) it's your clue that you're nearing the end of the canal section.

8.1mi: London Road. The towpath comes to an end and leads you up to street level. Turn right here and follow the signs for the pedestrian entrance to Syon Park (about 250m west of the river).

GETTING THERE ▸

Rail: Syon Lane National Rail Station (South West service, 0.8mi NW of Syon House car park) & Osterley Tube Station (Piccadilly line, from where you can start the run at Osterley Park).

Bus: 110, 117, 195, 235, 237, 267, 481, E2, E8, H28, & N9.

👍▸ Palaces, scenic waterways, country lanes in suburbia ... you can't ask for much more.

👎▸ Two short sections through suburban streets are a little tricky to navigate but otherwise it's very easy to follow your nose.

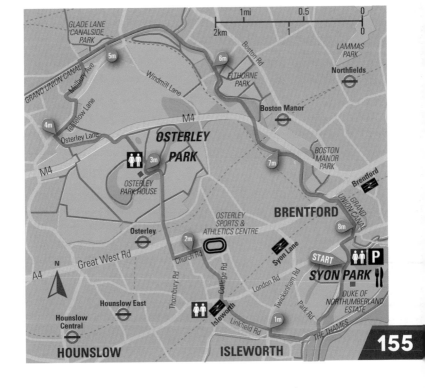

155

NORTHWEST HOTSPOTS

NORTHWEST ROUTES

HARMONDSWORTH MOOR WATERSIDE

4.2mi / 6.7k

260 acres of reclaimed land renovated by British Airways into a brilliant wildlife habitat and running terrain—ideal if you have some hours to kill at Heathrow Airport (which is just a couple of minutes down the road).

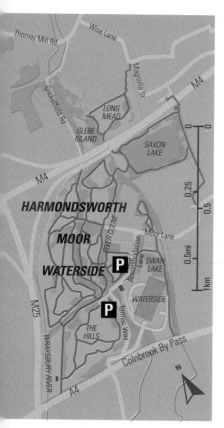

LOCATION ▶ Harmondsworth, Hillingdon, UB7 (17.2mi W of central London)

INFO ▶ This nature reserve is a great British Airways initiative that local runners and travellers passing through Heathrow should definitely utilise. It has two main rivers running through it (Wraysbury River and the River Colne, both running from south to north) and also has a large lake to the northeast. The M25 provides the western boundary to the park and the M4 passes over the park's northern section (there is a tunnel in the west and a footbridge in the east).

With so many trails in the park, it can be difficult to choose a route. And while exploring is a great way to see it, a good starting point is to do a rough perimeter loop beginning at the southern-most car park off Tarmac Way (a.k.a. Accommodation Lane).

From here run south (parallel to Tarmac Way, with the road on your left) along the grass trail all the way around this farm field (there may be livestock in here), hop over the barbed wire fence, and then turn right to follow the bridle trail north.

After crossing the next bridge turn left and run near the M25 till you reach another bridge. Instead of crossing, follow the footpath to the left, signposted to West Drayton. Head under the M4 and run along Cricketfield Road.

Cross the steel bridge on your right and then

turn right into Mill Road and right again into Wise Lane. Just as Wise Lane takes a 90-degree left, look for the entrance back into the park on your right. Follow the trail back under the M4 and then turn left to run around Saxon Lake. Finally, follow the trail back south to the car park.

This full loop is 4.2mi (6.75km) and there are many variations you can make to it. One of which is looking for a small gap in the fence on your right just after crossing the bridge on Cricketfield Road. This will take you straight back into the park, avoiding anymore streets.

The rolling hills are a major attraction of this reserve. Not only for the way they get the heart rate up, but also for the views they offer. The trails are in great condition and there are maps every so often to help point the way. The toilets, however, have been out of order for awhile.

GETTING THERE ▶

Rail: West Drayton National Rail Station (First Great Western service; 1.1mi N)

Bus: 75, 76, 77, 78, 350, 441, & U3.

👍 ▶ Hills, nature, and great limestone trails.

👎 ▶ Lack of toilets and having to jump the barbed wire fence in the southern paddock.

MUST KNOW ▶

Distance: 4.2mi (6.7km)

Surface: Crushed limestone, gravel & grass.

Terrain: Mild hills.

Weather Warnings: Some trails can become boggy.

Traffic Warnings: None.

Times: Open at all times (although vehicle gates for parking may be closed).

Toilets: None.

Saxon Lake, Harmondsworth Moor.

159

CRANFORD COUNTRY PARK

2.8mi **/ 4.5**k

A park with history, large open spaces, woodlands, wetlands and nice trails.

LOCATION ▶ Cranford, Hillingdon, TW5 & UB3 (14.2mi W of central London)

INFO ▶ The park still bears many signs of being home to a great estate, including the stables, walls and foundations of the manor house itself.

The park in the northwest, south and east is bordered by woodland areas that have various trails to explore. The remainder of the park is grassland or meadow with many mown trails. The River Crane passes along the eastern side, with two bridges providing access across it to Avenue Park.

Avenue Park is smaller and less impressive than its neighbour, but it does have a beautiful crushed limestone path running it's length and crossing into Cranford Park. This trail is a great option for doing loops around Cranford

The soft grassy trails of Cranford Park.

Park using the bridal path along the north and western fence lines, before following the road back to Avenue Park.

Cranford park continues north of the M4 with a woodland that houses the manor house site. There is a nature trail here worth checking out.

Utilising the bridle trail around Cranford Park, Cranford Lane and Park Lane, the limestone trail on Avenue Park, and the section of park to the north of the M4 (use the two sets of subways) you can put together a nice 2.8mi loop, with still plenty more to explore—the park has maps all over it if you get lost.

Options | Check out the 20-mile Hillingdon Trail going north and the London LOOP running south and north.

GETTING THERE▸

Rail: Hayes & Harlington National Rail Station (First Great Western line; 0.7mi NW) & Hounslow West Tube Station (Piccadilly line, 1.4mi SE).

Bus: 81, 105, 111, 195, 222, E6, H28, H98, & N9.

👍▸ Wide open spaces with a splash of history.

👎▸ It's a pity there isn't just one more bridge across the River Crane for completing traffic free loops of both parks.

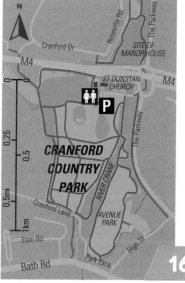
The woods dominate the northern sections of Cranford Park.

MUST KNOW▸

Weather Warnings: The grass and wooded trails may need to be avoided after rain.

Traffic Warnings: Take care when using Cranford Lane and Park Lane.

Times: Open from 9am to 8pm in summer (4pm in winter).

STOCKLEY & LAKE FARM COUNTRY PARKS

5.4mi / 8.7k ▦ ▧ ▦ ⚠ 🏃 ⏳

Two west London green spaces offering brilliant gravel and limestone trails with easy access to the Grand Union Canal.

LOCATION ▶ Hayes, Hillingdon, UB3, UB11 & UB8 (15.9mi W of central London)

INFO ▶ Looking at it from west to east, this running hotspot starts with Stockley Park—a business park and golf course with plenty of runner-friendly trails.

This park is split in two by the A408 (running north to south). In both sections, the golf course dominates the north while commercial buildings occupy most of the south (backing onto the canal). There are several sports fields and pockets of heath and woodland dotted around the golf course, particularly in the northwest.

A perimeter loop of the Stockley Park's western section, which excludes the commercial section to the south and runs over the lookout hill near the Stockley Road, is 1.4mi (2.25km). In the eastern section it's easy to put together a 2-mile loop (3.2km) around the perimeter of the golf course along well-formed trails (some of which are beautifully lined with trees).

Heading further east, over Dawley Road, is Lake Farm Country Park. This is a large space of meadow with just a few trees, a BMX track, and a mix of mown and limestone trails to break up

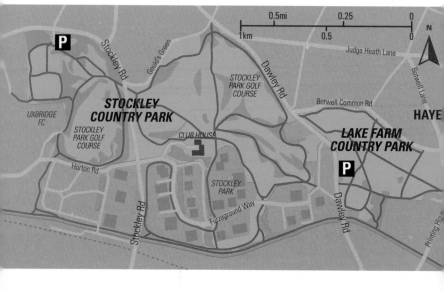

the grassland. A loop around the perimeter trails (missing out the children's play area in the east) is 1.5mi (2.4km). There are plenty of maps and signage for this park.

With the funky looking bridge over Stockley Road and by crossing Dawley Road (over to Lake Farm Park) you can run through the northern perimeter of both parks and come back along Grand Union Canal for a full loop of 5.4mi (8.7km).

GETTING THERE ▶

Rail: West Drayton (0.9mi W) & Hayes & Harlington (0.6mi S) National Rail Stations (First Great Western service).

Bus: 350, 724, 740, A10, A30, A40, U1, U3, U4, & U5.

👍 ▶ Brilliant running surfaces and great looping options with the canal nearby.

👎 ▶ Lack of signage and maps in Stockley Park and lack of public toilets.

Lake Farm Country Park.

MUST KNOW ▶

Traffic Warnings: Watch out for rogue golf balls (and carts).

Times: Open 9am to 4pm in winter and to 8pm in summer.

Toilets: None (although you can just ask nicely at the golf clubrooms).

Stockley Park trail next to one of the park's several sports fields.

HORSENDON HILL

3.5mi / 5.6k

The largest conservation site in the Borough of Ealing and a top off-road running spot.

LOCATION ▶ Perivale, Ealing, UB6 (10.3mi W of central London)

INFO ▶ This running hotspot is divided into three distinct sections. The eastern section, called Horsendon East, includes the summit of the hill itself. It offers great views and is surrounded by lush woodland. The dirt trails through here are obviously hilly with some stairs. You can also venture into the golf course to the east via several trails.

At the southern end of Horsendon East is the visitor centre and toilets. With a car park and picnic areas on the canal, this makes a good start/finish point for your run and is just 0.4mi from Perivale Tube Station.

Horsendon Lane, running north to south, separates Horsendon East from Horsendon West. This road is narrow so avoid running along it; instead, use the sealed path just east of the road.

Horsendon West is predominantly meadows separated by hedgerows with a network of mown grass paths for runners to follow. In the north are sports fields with a nice crushed limestone

Horsendon Wood.

trail. This limestone trail leads you west to the bridge over the Grand Union Canal (Paddington Branch) and to the final section of Horsendon Hill: Paradise Fields.

Paradise Fields again is predominantly grass fields with pockets of scrub and woodland. There is a main sealed trail here that takes you to the corner of Greenford Way and Greenpark Way, plus several mown grass trails. The canal tow-path can also be used for creating a loop here or for connecting back to the visitor centre.

The park has many maps on display and these maps illustrate a walking route for each of the park's three sections. These routes have way-markers so provide a good starting point for getting to know the area (although they could have used more markers). If you loop all three routes together it's about 3.5mi and leaves plenty more of the park still to explore.

GETTING THERE ▶

Rail: Perivale Tube Station (Central line; 0.4mi S) & Sudbury Town Tube Station (Piccadilly line, 0.3mi NW).

Bus: 92, 245, 297, 395, 487, & H17.

👍▶ Views, woods, hills, and the canal.

👎▶ The road can be busy and dangerous.

MUST KNOW ▶

Terrain: Flat to hilly.

Weather Warnings: Trails can be slippery when wet.

Traffic Warnings: Take care crossing Horsendon Lane.

Times: Always open (although the visitor centre car park closes at various times in the evenings).

Toilets: Visitor Centre (SE corner of the park).

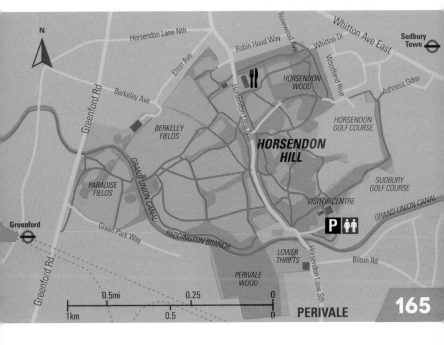

RUISLIP WOODS

9.0mi / 14.4k

The ideal weekend destination for a long run through more than 300 hectares of stunning woodland, followed by a lazy lakeside lunch.

LOCATION ▶ Ruislip, Hillingdon, HA4 (16.7mi NW of central London)

INFO ▶ The central port-of-call for any running visit to Ruislip is The Water's Edge Pub (which serves great, cheap carvery meals). There is a car park here and unfortunately the toilets at the car park were closed indefinitely at the time of writing (however, there are toilets at the Lido).

The lake itself is an old reservoir that has a sandy beach, a miniature railway, and the Millennium Walk, which roughly follows the railway around the lake and predominantly on sealed paths. The path is mildly undulating, set mostly amongst trees, easy to follow, and approx. 1.6mi (2.6km) long. It's a good warm down option or even as a spot for fartlek-style workouts.

Going beyond the lake into Park and Copse Woods you're really best just to go exploring. Run south until you hit houses, then run east, then north and west to reach Ducks Hill Road. Then run south again to the lake. If you keep roughly to the perimeter it's a tick over 5mi (8km) for the loop.

Over the road in Mad Bess' Wood it's easy to follow a perimeter trail that should equate to about 1.5mi (2.5km). The way-marked Hillingdon Trail also passes directly through here (east-to-west), which provides another option.

Further west in Bayhurst Wood, the Hillingdon Trail is again an option taking a slightly roundabout course through the park. Otherwise utilise the perimeter trail of this roughly circular wood (1.2mi or 2km). Don't be afraid to

The reservoir in Ruislip Woods.

also venture up the hill into the wood's centre to get the lungs going.

Combine all three perimeter loops (plus connections between them) and you'll easily get through eight or nine miles. Add some miles for exploring (a.k.a. getting lost) and for looping around the lake and your weekend long run is easily taken care of.

GETTING THERE ▶

Rail: Ruislip Tube Station (Piccadilly & Metropolitan lines; 1mi S).

Bus: 331 & H13.

👍▶ Stunning woods centred on a sparkling lake.

👎▶ Might want to bring a change of clothes for the pub—this run can be a muddy one.

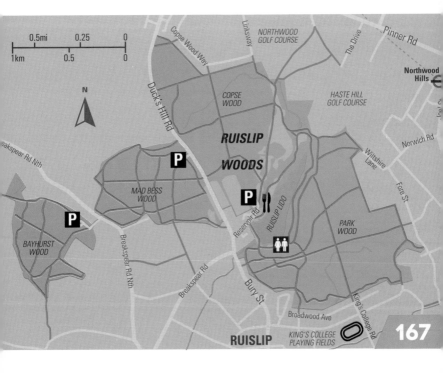

RUISLIP

KING'S COLLEGE
PLAYING FIELDS

FRYENT COUNTRY PARK

2.3mi / 3.7k

A dose of English countryside on a hill right, smack bang, in the middle of suburban London.

LOCATION ▶ Kingsbury, Brent, NW9 (9.1mi NW of central London)

INFO ▶ The park is 100 hectares (250 acres) and is predominantly grass fields sectioned off by hedgerows. Each field has a perimeter grass trail mown into it and many trails crisscrossing and connecting the fields.

The steepest parts of the park are in the south, which has wooded trails leading up to the summit. Here a tranquil pond, park benches and a stellar view of Wembley Stadium greet puffing runners.

The Capital Ring passes directly across the park and following its way-markers can help introduce you to the park. However, the best way to view the park for first timers is to do the 2.3mi (3.7km) Fryent Park Circular Walk.

This walk starts from the central car park (halfway along Fryent Way), heads west along the edge of the woodland, and then, just before exiting the wood, turns a hard left up to the summit (climbing 20m in 200m). From here it runs downhill and east through the woods to Fryent Way.

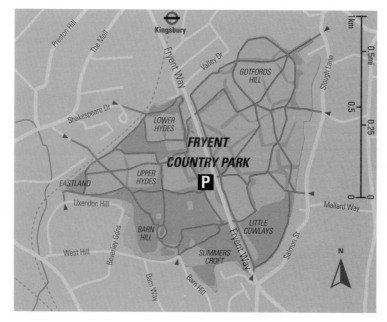

The route skirts along the side of the woods before zigzagging along hedgerows to the northeast corner of the park. Here it turns a hard left to head west and back to Fryent Way.

Now back on the west side of Fryent Way there is the spooky overgrown trail called Hell Lane (or Eldestrete). You'll be pleased to know that you don't follow this trail, but rather run parallel to it (in a southerly direction) back to the car park.

The older map at the car park (nearest the wood) illustrates the route well. There are also way-markers for this route but they're not hugely reliable.

GETTING THERE ▶

Rail: Kingsbury Tube Station (Jubilee line; 0.5mi N).

Bus: 206 & 644.

👍▶ A nice taster of the countryside, just without the cows and what the cows leave behind.

👎▶ The Circular Walk is missing three or four way-markers, plus there are no toilets.

MUST KNOW ▶

Circumference: 2.3mi (3.7km)

Surface: Dirt & grass.

Terrain: Undulating to hilly.

Weather Warnings: Trails can become slippery when wet.

Traffic Warnings: Take care crossing Fryent Way.

Times: Open at all times, take care after dark (run with others).

Toilets: None.

Fryent Country Park has that feeling of being in the countryside.

CANONS PARK

1.9mi / 3.1k

Former estate grounds, this park offers formal gardens and woodland walks and plenty in between ... and all in a relatively compact space.

LOCATION ▶ Stanmore, Harrow, HA8 (11.1mi NW of central London)

INFO ▶ After decades of decline, a £1 million facelift in 2006 returned this estate to something of its former grandeur—a grandeur that is just waiting for runners to experience.

The park begins with a 500m-long tree-lined pathway that stretches from Marsh Lane to the park's northwest corner (take care crossing Howberry Rd). Here you'll find a small woodland area with a dirt trail heading in both directions. And if you head in a more central direction you'll reach the toilets, an historic walled garden, the temple, and the manor house itself (now a school just outside the park).

The rest of the park is grass with long lines of trees and grassy trails. You can create a loop of the park by following the sealed trail that runs south along the park's western side. Then follow the dirt trail north through the strip of woodland on the eastern side. Finally connect back through the northern woodland walk. If you combine this loop with an out-and-back on the walkway to Marsh Lane it's 1.9mi. The park is open 8am to dusk.

For something extra, make the short journey southeast to the smaller Chandos Recreation Ground featuring sports fields and a nice looped trail.

GETTING THERE ▶

Rail: Canons Park Tube Station (Jubilee line; SE corner of the park).

Bus: 79, 142, 186, & 340.

👍 ▶ A good blend of sealed and dirt trails.

👎 ▶ Not many other options except for running up and down on the grass.

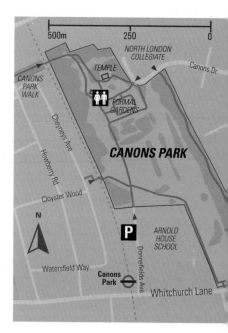

On top of the parks surrounding the River Brent (see 196) and those surrounding the Grand Union Canal (see 204), the Borough of Ealing boasts a collection of smaller parks suitable for short easy jogs or speed sessions.

1. Southall Park

Southall, Ealing, UB1 (11.3mi W of central London)

Southall Park is predominantly formal parkland with plenty of grass and trees—all over nice, rolling undulations.

The main running route is the 0.8mi perimeter trail (1.3km), which is sealed except for one section in the south on crushed limestone. There are also helpful distance markers ideal for workouts. Open 7:30am to just after dusk.

The park is only half a mile north of the Grand Union Canal (follow Green Drive, on the eastern boundary of the park, south to the pedestrian path over the rail lines) and 1mi from Brent River Park (head east along Bridge Road, A4020).

Rail: Southall National Rail Station (Heathrow Connect & First Great Western lines; 0.3mi SW).

Bus: 195, 207, 427, 607, & N207.

2. Walpole & Lammas Parks

Ealing, W13 (8.8mi W of central London)

Nestled back from any main roads, these two parks are brilliantly presented and have two incredible sealed loops.

With Pitshanger Manor and gardens dominating its northeast corner, the bulk of Walpole Park is a large grass field with many trees and a pond, all connected by a series of sealed trails. The perimeter loop is 0.95mi (1.5km).

At Walpole's south gate is the entrance to Lammas Park (there is also Lammas Enclosure directly opposite but this doesn't really offer much unless you're playing pétanque). Lammas is similar to its neighbour except that it has a much larger grass field in the south. Like

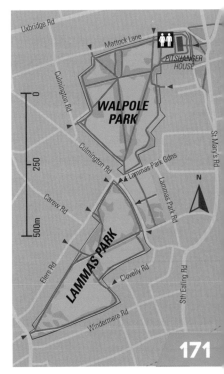

171

NORTHWEST HOTSPOTS

Walpole it has a great perimeter trail, which has 100m markers and totals 1mi (1.6km), and several other sealed trails.

The 100m connection between the parks (crossing a quiet intersection) creates a 2mi figure-of-eight. Both parks are open 7:30am to 5:30pm in winter or 10pm in summer.

Rail: Ealing Broadway Station (Heathrow Connect, First Great Western, District, & Central lines; 0.4 NE) & Northfields Tube Station (Piccadilly line; 0.2mi S).

Bus: 65, E2, E3, & N11.

3. Ealing Common
Ealing, W5 (7.7mi W of central London)

This is a compact park dissected by several roads, thus breaking up any attempts to run loops. However, its western section (west of Gunnersbury Ave) has a good 0.95mi loop, which is mostly on soft grass (or pavement if you want to be closer to the road). Add an extra 80m to make the loop a full mile. Also, by not crossing Warwick Avenue, it's easy to construct traffic-free 1km loops with the help from a GPS.

The small eastern section (across Gunnersbury Ave—take care when crossing) is not really worth visiting, except for using the toilets in the northeast corner (costs 20p) and for catching the Tube. The park also has two drinking fountains and is just 0.5mi N of Gunnersbury Park.

Rail: Ealing Common Tube Station (District & Piccadilly lines).

Bus: 65, 83, 112, 207, 226, 297, 427, 607, E1, E7, E8, E9, E10, E11, N7, N11 & N207.

4. Hanger Hill Park & Fox Wood
Hanger Hill, Ealing, W5 (8.8mi W of central London)

Hanger Hill Park occupies a small hilly green space and features a semi-formal parkland with a sealed trail around its circumference. It also has a pitch and putt golf course with access for running on its perimeter grass trail.

Just west of Hanger Hill is Fox Wood, which is mostly a sports field but on its northern edge has a nice patch of dense woodland over hilly terrain (with stairs). Use Fox Lane, which separates the parks, to complete a 1.4mi (2.2km) figure-of-eight loop of the two perimeters (running around the outside of the sports field in Fox Wood and running the complete woodland loop).

Combine these parks (which are both open at all times) with nearby Pitshanger Park and Hanger Hill Wood (on the western side of Hanger Lane—use the crossing near Hillcrest Rd).

Rail: Hanger Hill Tube Station (Central line; 0.4mi N)

Bus: 83, 112, & 226.

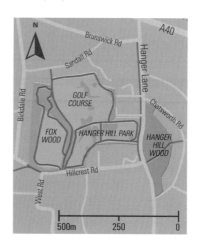

CHISWICK HOUSE GARDENS

1.25mi / 2k ▦ 🔲 🔲 🏃 ❓ ⧗

A small, but stunning, park with beautiful gardens and paths galore.

LOCATION ▶ Chiswick, Hounslow, W4
(6.6mi W of central London)

INFO ▶ With its grand vistas, towering trees, impressive flower gardens, a long mirror-like lake, and architectural surprises, this park has inspired parks all over the world, including New York's Central Park and Blenheim Palace. And much like Central Park, this is a great (if much smaller) haven for runners.

It has a perimeter trail that is exactly 2km (1.25mi), assuming you complete the loop by going out the Rustic House Gate and back in just 100m later via Duke's Avenue Gate (this avoids the walled gardens). Start with this loop and then you can easily fill in another mile or two in the interior's long straight avenues, lakeside paths, wooded trails, and formal gardens. Plus, you're only 400m from the Thames (via Grantham Rd), where you can explore the many large grass sports fields sitting on the river's north bank.

Chiswick House itself can be visited (charged) and the cafe is open daily from 8:30am.

GETTING THERE ▶

Rail: Chiswick National Rail Station (South West line; 0.3mi SW).

Bus: 190 & E3.

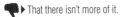 ▶ One of the top free gardens in London.

▶ That there isn't more of it.

MUST KNOW ▶

Weather Warnings: Dirt trails slippery when wet.

Times: Open daily 7am to dusk.

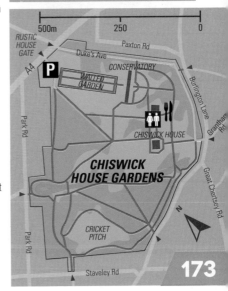

173

GUNNERSBURY PARK

2.4mi / 3.9k ⚠ 🏃 ⏳

This park consists of two old mansions and sports grounds, of which the grounds are great but the estate houses a little worse for wear.

LOCATION ▶ Gunnersbury, Hounslow, W5 (7.8mi W of central London)

If you want to run on soft green grass, Gunnersbury Park is the perfect destination.

The two mansions are in the northeast of the park and are surrounded by a network of sealed trails. There are toilets and a cafe just northwest of the mansions.

Moving in an anti-clockwise direction from the toilets you'll reach a large lake with trails right around it. By going round the top of the lake (the northern end) you can join a trail that almost perfectly follows the circumference of the park, starting with a quick in-and-out around the walled Capel Manor College and Gunnersbury Nursery.

Further west is the huge sports field. The perimeter trail goes all the way around and has some nice cover from trees, particularly in the southern corner where there is a small wood and another lake.

The eastern fence line is dominated by large trees bordering smaller grass fields. The sealed trail through here is uneven in places, so watch your step, and there are some single dirt tracks for a bit of variety. There are even some old ruins, a Gothic tower, and, as you approach the palace again, a secret garden if you're feeling particularly explorative.

In the centre of the park is a pitch and putt golf course, off limits to non-golfers, and a sealed trail that runs north-south creating a good option for figure-of-eight loops of the park. The full perimeter loop is about 2.4mi and one loop of the western field (not going all the way around the southern lake) is approx. 1.6mi.

GETTING THERE ▸

Rail: Acton Town Tube Station (District & Piccadilly lines; 0.3mi NE).

Bus: 440, E3, H91, & N11.

👍▸ Wide grass expanse on one side and twisting trails on the other.

👎▸ The state of the buildings can make the park seem a little eerie.

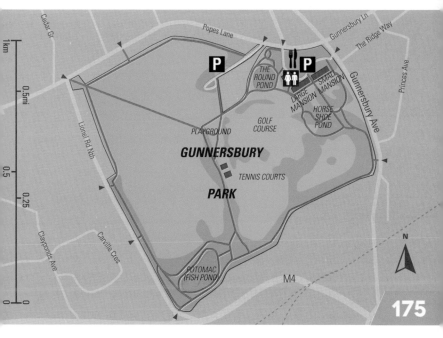

WORMWOOD SCRUBS PARK

2.4mi / 3.9k ⚠ 🚉 🌾 🏃 ❓

A vast sweep of grass fields with thickets of woodland dotted around it. Plus a cool baby sister park next door.

LOCATION ▶ White City, Hammersmith and Fulham, W12 (5.7mi NW of central London)

INFO ▶ At 80 hectares (200 acres) the park is cut in two by Scrubs Lane and the railway line (both of which run north-south), with the much smaller eastern section called Little Wormwood Scrubs. Known by locals as the "The Scrubs", this park interestingly hosted part of the 1908 Olympic Marathon course, en route from Windsor Castle to the nearby Olympic Stadium at White City (now the BBC).

The trails in the main section of the park include: a perimeter trail that is a mixture of sealed bike path, brick foot path, grass, and dirt surfaces; short single trails winding through the pockets of wood; and grass trails crisscrossing the park's interior. Following the perimeter trails you should be able to do a nice 2.4-mile loop.

Little Wormwood Scrubs can be accessed by turning off Scrubs Lane into Mitre Way. This road takes you under the railway where the park entrance is straight ahead (if you're on foot). The park has a 960m sealed loop that could well be extended slightly for some 1km reps. Thanks to a recent refurbishment, this is certainly the nicer of the two parks.

To the south of the main park is the Linford Christie Stadium (named after the famous sprinter whose club, Thames Valley Harriers, is based here) that has an outdoor 400m synthetic track. Another option to explore is the nearby Paddington Arm of the Grand Union Canal (just to the north via Scrubs Lane).

GETTING THERE ▶

Rail: East Acton Tube Station (Central line, 0.2mi SW).

Bus: 7, 70, 72, 220, 228, 272, 283, & N7.

👍 ▶ Large open space with a great track and access to the Grand Union Canal.

👎 ▶ Being so open and flat, it's a rather desolate looking park—especially when the weather is grim.

MUST KNOW ▶

Circumference: 2.4mi (3.85km) not including Little Wormwood Scrubs.

Surface: Sealed, cobbles (brick), & grass.

Terrain: Flat.

Weather Warnings: A little on the exposed side.

Traffic Warnings: Watch for cyclists on the bike path and take care crossing over to Little Scrubs.

Times: Open at all times.

Toilets: Little Wormwood Scrubs.

The Scrubs looking mighty inviting in the summer sun.

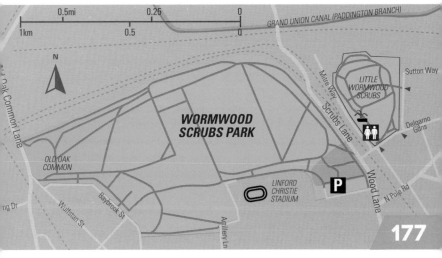

GRAND UNION CANAL (PADDINGTON BRANCH)

0.5mi   0.25   0
1km   0.5   0

N

Oak Common Lane

LITTLE WORMWOOD SCRUBS

Sutton Way

Mitre Way

Scrubs Lane

WORMWOOD SCRUBS PARK

Delgarno Gdns

OLD OAK COMMON

Baybrook St

LINFORD CHRISTIE STADIUM

P

Wood Lane

N Pole Rd

ng Dr

Wulfstan St

Artillery Ln

MUSWELL HILL PLAYING FIELDS & SURROUNDS

4.0mi / 6.5k

A collection of woods, a sports ground, and a cemetery that can be connected for some nice, largely off-road, running.

LOCATION ▶ Finchley, Barnet & Haringey, N10 (7.4mi N of central London)

INFO ▶ Coldfall Wood is the southern most point in the area and is nestled behind a row of houses. It has many trails through its beautifully open wood. It's a favourite spot for local dog walkers and families.

Moving north, Muswell Hill Playing Fields is a long and flat grass park mostly used for football but has also undergone some renovations in its northern end, with playgrounds and public toilets.

West of Coldfall Woods and the sports ground is Islington & St Pancras Cemetery. This is a large cemetery with a mix of old sites covered in trees and new open plots. The two main gates are Finchley High Road in the west and Coppetts Road in the east. You can access the cemetery on foot at anytime via the turnstile gates, but be sure to always be respectful.

Heading further north again, the North Circular Road (A406) separates you from the two extra wooded sections: Glebelands in the west, which connects to North Finchley Road, and Coppetts Wood in the east, which joins Colney Hatch Lane.

The beauty of all these spots is that you can loop them all together. Start at Coldfall Wood, then venture through Muswell Hill Playing Fields and into the cemetery by the Coppetts Road Gate. Exit the cemetery onto Finchley High Road. Turn right (north) to cross over the North Circular then look for the path to your right (near the Lido) to take you through Glebelands. Head up to Summers Lane and then into Coppetts Wood via Porters Way. Exit onto Colney Hatch Lane and head south back to Muswell Hill Sports Ground and Coldfall Wood. It's around 4mi all up.

MUST KNOW ▶

Circumference: 4mi (6.5km)

Surface: Dirt, sealed, grass and gravel.

Terrain: Undulating to hilly.

Weather Warnings: The woodland trails can become muddy in wet weather.

Traffic Warnings: Some road crossings between parks and woods.

Times: Open at all times (use the turnstile gates in the cemetery after open hours).

Toilets: Available during open hours at the northeast gate of St Pancras & Islington Cemetery (Coppetts Road Gate).

GETTING THERE ▶

Rail: New Southgate National Rail Station (Great

Northern) & East Finchley Tube Station (Northern line), both about 1mi away.

Bus: 43, 102, 134, 232, 234, 263, 299, 382, & 603.

👍▶ The whole spectrum of woods, sports fields, and even cemeteries—all equally runnable.

👎▶ Navigating the connections, due to fences and main roads, between each section takes some getting used to.

Coldfall Wood.

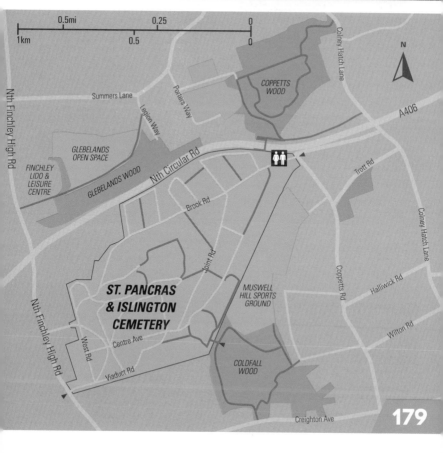

0.5mi   0.25   0
1km   0.5   0

Nth Finchley High Rd

Summers Lane

Porters Way

Legion Way

COPPETTS WOOD

Colney Hatch Lane

N

A406

GLEBELANDS OPEN SPACE

FINCHLEY LIDO & LEISURE CENTRE

GLEBELANDS WOOD

Nth Circular Rd

🚻

Trott Rd

Brook Rd

Joint Rd

ST. PANCRAS & ISLINGTON CEMETERY

MUSWELL HILL SPORTS GROUND

Coppetts Rd

Colney Hatch Lane

Halliwick Rd

Wilton Rd

Nth Finchley High Rd

West Rd

Centre Ave

Viaduct Rd

COLDFALL WOOD

Creighton Ave

WATERLOW PARK

0.9mi / 1.5k

A little, yet stunning, park with formal gardens, great views, and a nice series of sealed trails. All just an easy stroll from Hampstead Heath.

LOCATION ▶ Highgate, Camden, N6 (4.6mi N of central London)

INFO ▶ In 1889 the park was bequeathed to the public by Sir Sidney Waterlow as a "garden for the gardenless". The irony of course is that it's less than a mile away from the massive Hampstead Heath, but runner's can still benefit from Mr Waterlow's gesture with this compact park's nice, hilly circuit of trails (possibly as part of a loop incorporating the Heath and Kenwood House grounds).

The park is perched on the side of a hill, so a few circuits will get the heart rate up. For a breather check out the formal gardens and busy cafe in the northeast (and top) of the park. Running downhill from here you'll encounter tennis courts, sloping grass fields (with great views), many stunning trees, and a couple of ponds.

Though there are many trails to follow, a complete perimeter loop of the park is about 0.9mi (1.5km). Unfortunately the invitingly wooded Highgate Cemetery, which is just next-door and houses the tomb of Karl Marx, is charged for entry (and paying to go running totally defeats the purpose).

GETTING THERE ▶

Rail: Archway Tube Station (Northern line).

Bus: 143, 210, 214, 271, 603, & C11.

👍 ▶ A well-presented park with good views and lots of superb nearby options.

👎 ▶ There's no denying it, it is small.

MUST KNOW ▶

Weather Warnings: Watch the steep slopes in icy conditions.

Times: Open dawn to dusk.

HAMPSTEAD HEATH

8.0mi / 13k

A 320-hectare (790-acre) green space of woodland, heath, grass, and formal gardens, all on rolling hills with stunning city views. The ideal place for an exploration-style run.

LOCATION ▶ Highgate, Camden, N6 (4.6mi N of central London)

INFO ▶ Parliament Hill | From the athletics track in the south, the first thing you'll encounter is Parliament Hill. Rising to 98m high it's grassy slopes and tree-lined paths lead you up to the spectacular view of central London. A perfect way to get the blood pumping, before venturing further into the heath.

Hampstead Ponds | West of Parliament Hill, and moving in a clockwise direction, you'll pass through a quick section of wood to discover a series of ponds. The most northern of these is open for swimming. Like the Men's and Ladies' Ponds in the east of the heath the cost is £2 for adults and are open at either 7 or 8am year round and close between 2:30pm in winter

and 8:30pm in summer (is open only to club members in winter).

Viaduct Pond | Just to the north, the trails wind through woodland, where, at a major intersection, you'll find a working drinking fountain. Look for the Viaduct Bridge that sits on a main trail heading northwest from the Highgate Ponds.

The Vale of Health | This is a small suburb in the southwest corner of the heath (due west from the Viaduct Pond), designed to be in isolation from the busy city, completely surrounded by the park. Personally, I prefer its original name, Hatchett's Bottom—a suitable name for a weird suburb that, from our point of view, merely serves to disorientate runners.

West Heath | Heading west and across the two roads is this largely wooded section with a couple of small clearings and many single trails that you can explore through the trees. The hidden gem within West Heath is the Hill Garden that surrounds Inverforth House.

Parliament Hill looking south to the city.

181

This formal garden stands at 115m above sea level, so has wonderful views looking west, and boasts a wedding-photo-ready 800-foot pergola, which is worth a leisurely jog through (particularly if you happen to be jogging with that special someone!). The Hill Garden opens at 8:30am and closes at dusk.

Golders Hill Park | This is a fenced area (open 7:30am to dusk) connected to West Heath with a small zoo, formal gardens, sports grounds, a cafe, and toilets.

Sandy Heath | Sitting just north of West Heath, this is predominantly wooded with some clearings of heath—which is a far cry from what was once a sand and gravel pit supplying London industry. Again it has numerous trails that connect it to other parts of Hampstead Heath.

Hampstead Heath Extension | This shoots out into the suburbs to the northwest and has a string of sports fields, bordered by beautiful trees and hedgerows. The grass around here is as good you'll find anywhere for doing strides or barefoot running (in summer there is even a marked 90-metre sprinting track).

Kenwood House | The entire northeast corner of Hampstead Heath is occupied by Kenwood House and its surrounding grounds (122 acres). The grounds are open to the public, free-of-charge from 7am till dusk. There are gates to the grounds dotted along its fence line.

The house itself (which dates back to the 17th century) stands like a grand old lady over-looking a sloping green field, ornamental pond, lush woodland, and then beyond to central London. The woodland in the estate grounds are some of the most rich and mature (meaning great to run through) in Hampstead Heath.

Highgate Ponds | Along the eastern border of the Heath is a string of six ponds. Two of these are open for swimming (the second-to-top pond for women only and the second-to-bottom pond for men only). Trails surround all the ponds, providing many options for making your way back to Parliament Hill Fields in the south.

The Track | Parliament Hill Fields Athletics Track is open from 7:45am till dusk (charged).

Kenwood House dominates the northeast corner of the Heath.

Parliament Hill is a popular spot for brutal, mid-winter cross country races.

Between mid-September and mid-April, on Tuesday and Thursday nights, the track is floodlit and available for use until 8:40pm.

Orienteering | There is a fixed orienteering course in the heath. See londonorienteering.co.uk for maps.

Swimming | As well as the ponds, the outdoor (unheated) Lido is great for summer swimming (and for winter swimming for the mad and/or wetsuit clad). It costs £5.50 (or £2 early morning or evening) and open from 7am to 8:30pm (summer) and 12pm (winter).

GETTING THERE ▶

Rail: Gospel Oak & Hampstead Heath Stations (London Overground, S), Hampstead Tube Station (Northern line, NW) & Golders Green Tube Station (Northern line, SW).

Bus: 24, 46, 168, 210, 214, 268, 603, C2, C11, H2, H3, & N5.

👍 ▶ Rolling hills, muddy trails, well-kept paths, and always changing surrounds.

👎 ▶ Despite several maps at entry points, there is a general lack of signage.

MUST KNOW ▶

Circumference: 8.0mi (13km) approx.

Surface: Gravel, dirt, grass, & some sealed trails.

Terrain: Hilly—some of the best (or worst) hills in London.

Weather Warnings: Some trails become boggy in wet weather.

Traffic Warnings: Although the main section of Hampstead Heath is free of vehicles, the sections to the northwest have several intersecting roads.

Times: Golders Hill Park, the Hill Garden, the Pergola, & Kenwood Estate are closed after dusk.

Toilets: Parliament Hill Fields, near Vale of Health, Golders Hill Park, Hampstead Heath Extension, Kenwood House, & Dukes Field.

Viaduct Bridge, Hampstead Heath.

THE PARKS OF PYMMES BROOK

2.5mi / 4k

A collection of parks that follow the Pymmes Brook. A great out-and-back run with many extra trails to explore.

LOCATION ▶ Southgate, Barnet & Enfield, EN4 & N11 (8.7mi N of central London)

INFO ▶ The Pymmes Brook Trail stretches all the way from Monken Hadley Common to Lee Valley. However, because of it's faded and infrequent way-marking we cover here just the section of the trail passing through three particularly attractive and adjacent parks.

Arnos Park | This is the southern-most of the three parks and is just around the corner from both Arnos Grove Tube Station and Broomfield Park.

Starting from the park's southeastern end (at Wilmer Wy) there are open grass fields with Pymmes Creek on the southwest side and a thin strip of woodland on the other. As you move along the park in a northwest direction, paved trails follow both of its sides with additional dirt trails exploring the wood.

Further north the railway, on top of a bridge made of many brick archways, dissects the park. In one of these archways can be found toilets near the tennis courts.

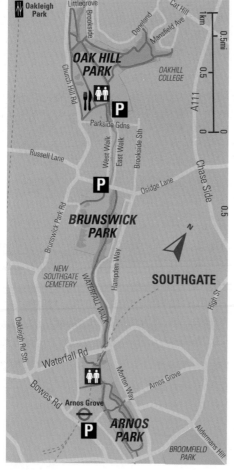

Waterfall Walk (Brunswick Park) | Heading north over Waterfall Road you'll find Waterfall Way, which is a wide sealed path next to the stream and a narrow stretch of woodland. As you head north, the surrounds open up with the addition of grass fields and more wooded areas. There are some nice grassy trails to explore here.

When you reach Osidge Lane, crossover to keep following the stream north either on East Walk or West Walk.

Oak Hill Park | Crossing over Parkside Gardens (the street) you'll find yourself in Oak Hill Park. This park spans the Oak Hill Valley, meaning it has hills on either side of the Pymmes Creek, which runs straight through its centre.

The main trail follows the creek to the far end of the park on Church Hill. However, it's worth doing a loop of the park to explore it further. Near the creek are grass fields and on the northern hills is an inviting wood filled with oaks from which the park is named (follow the short marked trails in here).

A direct point-to-point return journey through the three parks (without any extra loops or explorations) is 5mi (8k).

GETTING THERE ▶

Rail: Arnos Grove Tube Station (Piccadilly line; 0.2mi SW)

Bus: 34, 184, 232, 251, 298, 382, & N91.

👍▶ A nice collection of small, but very runnable, parks.

👎▶ It's a pity the Pymmes Brook Trail doesn't have better way-marking.

The railway arches at Arnos Park.

MUST KNOW ▶

Length: 2.5mi (4.0km) one way.

Surface: Sealed (with grass and dirt options).

Terrain: A slight slope running up from Arnos Park to Oak Hill, plus hills on the edges of Oak Hill Park.

Weather Warnings: None.

Traffic Warnings: There are two road crossings.

Times: Open at all times.

Toilets: Arnos Park and Oak Hill Park.

MONKEN HADLEY COMMON

4.6mi / 7.4k

This long stretch of woodland, with plenty of running trails to be traversed, marks the border between suburban London and the countryside to the north.

LOCATION ▶ Monken Hadley, Barnet, EN5 (12.0mi N of central London)

INFO ▶ The common begins in the west with a sports field and an open meadow and then merges into the woodland that stretches from here all the way to Cockfosters Road in the east.

The only break in this stretch of woodland is the railway line, which has just one bridge over it, so any loops of the common need to pass over it forming figure-of-eight loops.

There is a main trail that follows the southern side of the common for its full length. To the west of the tracks a loop can be easily completed near the perimeter of the common. Trails in this area are informal but reasonably easy to follow.

East of the tracks is the Hadley Wood Nature Reserve in the north and Newman's Hill in the south. Both are wooded with various trails, however, the main wide trail runs through Newman's Hill.

Further east again is Sewitt's Hill in the north, which is an open rolling field, and actually a nice change from the wooded areas. There are several trails crisscrossing this field. Southeast of there is Beech Hill Lake—a popular fishing spot surrounded by woods and nice trails. Directly north of here is a golf course inaccessible to runners.

From the lake, the common stretches east as it narrows to meet Cockfosters Road, where it is easy to connect just a few hundred metres south to the entrance way of Trent Park. And for longer runs, consider connecting to the trails along Dollis Brook and Pymmes Brook.

GETTING THERE ▶

Rail: Cockfosters Tube Station (Piccadilly

line; 0.3mi S of eastern entrance), High Barnet Tube Station (Northern line, 1.3mi S of western entrance), & New Barnet National Rail Station (Thameslink service, 0.7mi S via the footpath just west of the tracks).

Bus: 298, 384, & 399.

👍▸ Woods, meadows, hills, and a pretty lake.

👎▸ Parts of it can feel a little unsafe if running alone.

MUST KNOW ▸

Circumference: 4.6mi (7.4mi)

Surface: Dirt, sealed, gravel, & grass.

Terrain: Hilly (high point of 132m in the west drops down to 65m at the lake).

Weather Warnings: Some trails are heavily root-bound and can also become boggy.

Traffic Warnings: None.

Times: Open at all times but take care if running alone.

Toilets: None.

The meadow at the western end of Monken Hadley Common.

TRENT COUNTRY PARK

4.8mi / 7.8k

This is a popular weekend destination for picnicking families and a top running environment as well.

LOCATION ▶ Cockfosters, Enfield, EN4 (11.8mi N of central London)

INFO ▶ In previous lives, this park has been a royal hunting ground, a grand estate, a WWII prison camp, and now partly used as a university. Its undulating hills, woodlands, and open fields provide a wonderful, safe and enclosed running environment.

The ideal starting point is the carpark accessed from Cockfosters Road. To complete the 4.8mi perimeter, follow the trail heading northeast through beautiful woodland and then alongside a large farmed field. This trail reaches a series of lakes that occupy the centre of the park, just north of the Middlesex University campus.

At the lakes, swing a left up the hill on the large avenue cut through woodland to the Obelisk at the park boundary. Here you can turn left and run along the north side of the farm field you passed earlier all the way to Cockfosters Road (where there is a pedestrian access gate). To stay in the park, turn right at the Obelisk to run through Moat Wood (keep an eye out for the swampy moat).

Carry on heading east into Ride Wood. Join the bridle trail here which will take you south through more extraordinary woodland, past another farm field on your right, and then into Williams Wood. At this point you have the option

either of carrying on straight south or keeping to the perimeter of the wood by turning left.

When you near the golf course, follow the path heading due south and out of the park, to Enfield Road. Turn right here, following the road until just after Snakes Lane, where you'll enter the park again. Follow the path northwest through the fields, pockets of wood, and hedgerows up to the car park.

Alternatively, instead of exiting the park near the golf course, head southwest and skirt around the southern border of the university campus. There is a cool obstacle course here if you fancy breaking up your run with a little fun and games. Once past the campus, continue heading straight (following the tree-lined trail) and then veer north back to the main car park.

There are plenty of other trails to keep you busy in the park. Also check out the lanes and footpaths that dissect the farmland of Enfield Chase to the north and Monken Hadley Common to the west.

GETTING THERE ▸

Rail: Cockfosters Tube Station (Piccadilly line; 0.2mi S).

Bus: 121, 298, 299, 307, 377, 384, 399 & N91.

👍 ▸ A great park with a real countryside feel.

👎 ▸ Being broken up by the university, golf course, and farmland, it can be disorientating.

MUST KNOW ▸

Circumference: 4.8mi (7.8km)

Surface: Dirt, grass, gravel, & sealed.

Terrain: Rolling hills.

Weather Warnings: Some dirt trails become boggy in wet weather.

Traffic Warnings: There are cars within the park, so take care on sealed sections.

Times: 8am (8:30am on Sundays) to dusk.

Toilets: Near the main entrance.

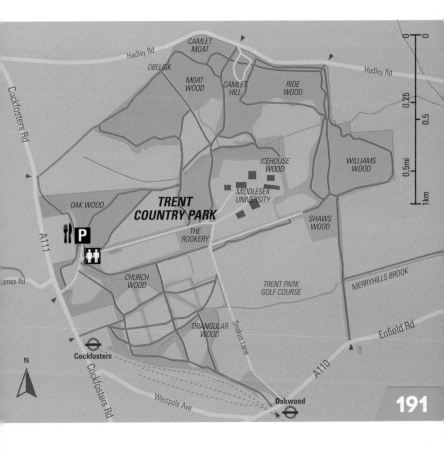

191

CELANDINE ROUTE

11mi / 17.8k

An 11mi unique green run through outer northwest London following the River Pinn. However, "river" is probably not the most appropriate noun ... it's more of a gently flowing stream.

LOCATION ▶ Start Point: Pinner Tube Station, Pinner, Harrow, HA5 (14mi NW of central London)

Finish Point: West Drayton National Rail Station, West Drayton, Hillingdon, UB7 (16.5mi W of central London)

INFO ▶ This point-to-point run requires a little navigation, for, although it is way-marked, the signposts are often missing at some intersections of trails.

In general it's a safe rule to keep as close to the River Pinn as possible and also to follow a "Public Footpath" sign if there are no other "CR" or "Celandine Route" signs to follow. It would

One of the several wooded areas you'll pass through on the Celandine Route.

also pay to carry either these text directions or a map with you. In saying this, there are seven helpful maps and info stations along the trail, which even provide rough distances to the next map.

It's possible to shorten this run by running through Ruislip to Ruislip Tube Station (approx. 4mi) or by turning left at Swakeleys Drive (after Swakeleys Park) for Hillingdon Tube Station (approx. 6.5mi). You can also add on at the end with an out-and-back venture in three directions along the beautiful Grand Union Canal.

MILE-BY-MILE ▶ Start:

Pinner Station. Run down Station Approach, turn left onto Marsh Road and then right onto West End Avenue, follow to its end.

0.5mi: West End Lane. Turn left into West End Lane and then the first right into Cranbourne Drive, where you will see the finger post marking the start of the Celandine Route: a trail passing behind the allotments. Follow the River Pinn through the wood to Cheney Street (keeping the stream on your left).

1.0mi: Cheney Street. Cross the street and follow the trail parallel to the stream, then cross High Road Eastcote, run through the cricket ground, turn left at Joel Street, and then right at the next two roundabouts. Look for the trail to your right shortly after the second roundabout.

1.6mi: Eastcote Village. Enter the

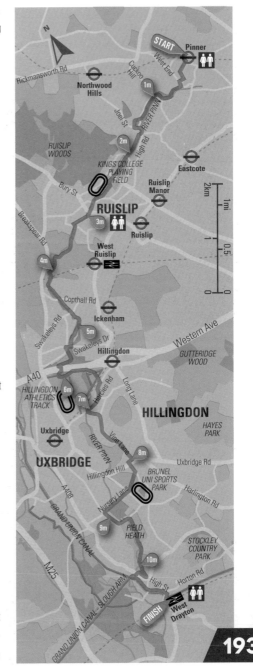

Grand Union Canal.

King's College Playing Fields Track.

tree-lined trail running on the north side of the stream. Follow this trail, crossing two streets, looking for the trail opposite on both occasions.

2.1mi: King's College Playing Field. The trail crosses the southern edge of these grass fields, which house a cool old cinder running track. Shortly after the cinder track, the trail crosses the stream to reach St Martin's Approach.

2.7mi: St Martin's Approach. Cross this road and then, shortly after, cross Pinn Way, running on to Bury Street. Cross over to follow the trail again, then cross the stream to the north bank and run on to Grasmere Avenue. (There are toilets in nearby Ruislip, 500m south along St Martin's Approach.)

3.2mi: Grasmere Avenue. Turn left here and then right down Woodville Gardens. Run to the end of the road, enter the gate, and cross the paddock. From here run on the south bank of the stream for 2mi all the way to Swakeleys Drive (passing Copthall and Swakeleys Rds).

5.2mi: Swakeleys Drive. Exiting the park, turn right, cross the road (use the crossing) and enter Warren Road. Then follow the footpath signs into the wood. This will take you around the back of the school to a footbridge that crosses the A40. Then cross the narrow strip of wood to the paddock.

5.9mi: Unmarked Fields. With the A40 and wood behind you, turn left to run parallel (east) with the A40. Cross the stream and then follow one of the more southeasterly paths to reach the rail footbridge. Cross it and run on to Hercies Road.

6.6mi: Hercies Road. Turn right and follow Hercies till you turn left on to Honey Hill. Then turn right on to Vine Lane, following it to its end at Hillingdon Hill (opposite St John the Baptist Church).

8mi: St John the Baptist Church. Cross Hillingdon Hill and then follow (the almost opposite road) Royal Lane. Turn right into the footpath that runs next to the running track. Cross Kingston Lane and follow the footpath opposite to reach Church Road.

8.9mi: Church Road. Turn left at Church Road, then left again to stay on Church Road at the roundabout. Shortly after, turn right to re-join the stream via a nice gravel path. With the stream on your right, follow this path all the way to High Street.

10.1mi: High Street. Turn right here and, after 250m, turn left to follow the tree lined path to the canal towpath. Turn left.

10.5mi: Grand Union Canal. Follow the towpath south to reach High Street once again. Run under it and then turn left to join the street and cross the canal to, finally, turn left again onto Station Approach—the end of your run at West Drayton Station 11mi later.

GETTING THERE ▶

Start: Pinner Tube Station (Metropolitan line).

Finish: West Drayton National Rail Station (First Great Western service).

👍▶ A largely green run over a variety of surfaces through sleepy west London suburbs.

👎▶ Lack of way-markers and the rail connections can be a little tricky to workout.

MUST KNOW ▶

Distance: 11mi (17.8km) point-to-point.

Surface: Dirt, gravel, sealed, and grass.

Terrain: Net downhill (but barely noticeable) with undulations.

Weather Warning: Trails between miles one and six can be boggy.

Traffic Warning: Many street crossings—take care.

Times: Many unlit portions so best avoided after dark.

Toilets: At the two stations and in nearby Ruislip (3mi into the run).

BRENT RIVER PARK FOOTPATH

5.9mi / 9.5k

A largely traffic-free run that takes in many of Ealing's best parks.

LOCATION ▶ Start Point: Hanwell Station, Ealing, W7 (10.2mi W of central London).

Finish Point: Hanger Lane Station, Ealing, W5 (8.7mi W of central London).

INFO ▶ Brent River Park, rather than just one park, is a collection of parks and riverside walkways that follow the Brent River from Hanger Lane to Brentford. This run follows the park from Hanwell Station (so not quite as far as Brentford) all the way to Hanger Lane Station.

MILE–BY–MILE ▶ Start: Hanwell Station. Exit the station and follow Campbell Road left (west), then turn left onto Golden Manor. Follow this street under the tracks and all the way south to Uxbridge Road. Turn right. (Alternatively you can take the shortcut through Alwyne Rd Park by turning right off Golden Manor before going under the train tracks.)

Wharncliffe Viaduct, Brent River Park.

0.6mi: Hanwell Bridge. Pass over the bridge and turn right to join the trail next to the River Brent. This trail doubles as a section of the Capital Ring and of the Brent River Park Footpath (marked with the blue and yellow arrow and "BRP" logo).

Follow the trail north mostly keeping to the right of the river (the path is on the left side of the river only up to Wharncliffe Viaduct and also through the golf course).

The trail for this portion (between Uxbridge Rd and Ruislip Rd) is a mix of gravel, dirt and grass. Some sections are not clear trails (particularly the grass in Brent Lodge Park) and one or two of the way-markers are missing. If you keep close to the river, as it meanders along, you shouldn't go too wrong.

There are toilets just 100m off the trail near the

playground in Brent Lodge Park (these are open daily 10am to 5pm).

Interest: Wharncliffe Viaduct. The huge train bridge that you pass under shortly after Hanwell Bridge was built in 1837. It is said that Queen Victoria used to have her train stop here so she could check out the view.

2.4mi: Ruislip Road. This is the point where the Capital Ring and Brent River paths part, with the former going left and the latter going right. Go right and cross the road (use the crossing 50m E) and follow the trail opposite and slightly to the right.

The trail through Perivale Park occupies just a thin slice of green between the river on your left and Ruislip Road on your right. Also keep in mind that the signs for the Brent River pathways, for the remainder of the run, are less

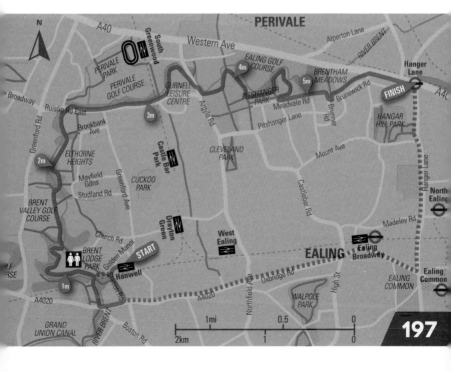

NORTHWEST ROUTES

frequent than the Capital Ring signs were.

3.0mi: Train Bridge. Just after passing under the train bridge, the trail continues to hug the banks of the river but leaves the road as it goes behind Gurnell Leisure Centre. The river and trail complete a full horseshoe bend before meeting Argyle Road.

3.5mi: Argyle Road. Cross the road and turn right, running along the footpath till you reach a dead straight walkway to your left. Follow it to an intersection of paths and make a soft left, then a hard right. Now you'll be running through the enclosed pathway across the Ealing Golf Course. Take the next left into Pitshanger Park.

4.2mi: Pitshanger Park. This park has a wonderful perimeter trail that hugs the river for much of the way. Complete an almost full lap of the park in a clockwise direction in order to exit the park at the main gate onto Meadvale Road.

4.8mi: Meadvale Road. Turn left out of the park to run to the end of Meadvale. Turn right onto Neville, then left onto Brunswick, where you need to make a quick left again at the Brent River Park Footpath sign.

Do not enter Brentham Meadows but follow the footpath around to your right. Pass by the allotments to find yourself on Lynwood Road with the busy A40 to your left.

5.5mi: The A40. Turn right at the A40, joining the footpath on the road's south side. Run up the hill to your final destination: Hanger Lane Tube Station. Well done, that's 5.9mi (9.5km) completed.

Options | It's easy to make this run a full loop. Instead of entering Hanger Lane Station, turn right on to the Northern Circular Road. Run over

One of many small bridges over the Brent River.

the hill until you reach Ealing Common. Turn right here again, onto Uxbridge Road (A4020), to run all the way back to near the start point at Hanwell Bridge. Discounting the trip to and from Hanwell Station, this full loop is 8.9mi (14.3km).

For the really keen, combine the above loop with Two Palaces and a Canal run (making a figure-of-eight circuit of almost 18mi, see p.153). Connect to the midway point of this extra loop (on the Grand Union Canal) by following the River Brent south from the A4020. The canal is only a few hundred metres from here.

GETTING THERE ▸

Start: Hanwell National Rail Station (First Great Western service towards Slough).
Finish: Hanger Lane Tube Station (Central line).

👍▸ A picturesque river connecting several quality green spaces.

👎▸ The combination of a meandering river and infrequent signage can make navigation tricky.

MUST KNOW ▸

Distance: 5.9mi (9.5km)
Surface: Gravel, dirt, grass, and sealed.
Terrain: Small undulations.
Weather Warning: Trails become muddy after rain.
Traffic Warning: Take care at road crossings.
Times: Any time, but limited lighting after dark.
Toilets: Hanwell Station, Brent Lodge Park at the 1mi mark (100m from trail, open daily 10am to 5pm), & Hanger Lane Station.

Pitshanger Park.

DOLLIS VALLEY GREENWALK

13.2mi / 21.2k 🏠 🗺️ 🏃 🏃 🎒

This way-marked walk charts a path through the bulk of the Borough of Barnet, taking in some incredible green spaces along the way. The Dollis Brook is your companion for much of this run, along with good signage and well-kept paths.

LOCATION ▶ Start Point: Edgware Station, Barnet, HA8 (10.8mi NW of central London).
Finish Point: East Finchley Station, Barnet, N2 (6.1mi N of central London).

INFO ▶ Most of this route follows the Dollis Valley Greenwalk (look for the green discs and the wooden finger posts). However, to connect easily to Tube stations we have added on an extra 2.3mi at the start (from Edgware Station) and have diverted the final section to follow the Capital Ring trail directly to East Finchley Station rather than to Hampstead Heath.

Also, there are options to cut the run in half by stopping at either Totteridge and Whetstone Station (6.9mi from start, 6.3mi from finish) or Woodside Park Station (8mi from start, 5.3mi from finish), both of which are very close to the trail and signposted.

MILE-BY-MILE ▶ Start: Edgware Station. Turn right to head north along Station Road. At the roundabout, turn right onto Penshurst Gardens and follow to its end. Use the short footpath to reach Hale Lane, turn left and

then a quick right to go up Highview Gardens. When this street makes a 90-degree turn to the left, instead turn right to reach the A41.

1.0mi: The A41. Use the footbridge to your left to cross the A41 and then follow the footpath on the northern side of the road to the right (east). Run over the M1, then under the following roundabout to come out on the east side of the A1 by turning left (north).

1.5mi: The A1. Keep to the right hand side of this road all the way up until you reach a car park set amidst the woods of Moat Mount Open Space, which is where we join the official Dollis Valley Greenwalk.

2.3mi: Moat Mount. With good way-marking the navigation should be far easier from now on. As you head northeast across this nature reserve, enjoy its woods, fields and views (a great reward for the 70m of vertical ascent you've

2mi
4km

N

OAK HILL PARK

A110
Church Hill Rd
Oakleigh Park
Oakleigh Rd Nth

w Barnet

A1003

COPPETTS WOOD

Colney Hatch Lane

Fortis Green

HIGHGATE WOOD

COLDFALL WOOD

St PANCRAS & ISLINGTON CEMETERY

FINISH

East Finchley

13m

A1

East End Rd

LYTTELTON PLAYING FIELDS

North Circular Rd

A1000

Friern Barnet Lane

Totteridge & Whetstone

DOLLIS BROOK

Woodside Park

Ballards Lane

West Finchley

Finchley Central

12m

A1

BIG WOOD

LITTLE WOOD

7m

n Barnet

6m

BARNET PLAYING FIELDS

Barnet Lane

GOLF COURSE

Totteridge Lane

Laurel Way

8m

Argyle Rd

9m

Dollis Rd

GOLF COURSE

Frith Lane

Regent's Park Rd

Hendon Lane

11m

10m

Circular Rd

DARLAND LAKE NATURE RESERVE

Mill Hill East

Holders Hill Rd

A1

Finchley Lane

HENDON PARK

HITINGS HILL EN SPACE

5m

GRANGE PLAYING FIELDS

Totteridge Common

GOLF COURSE

Devonshire Rd

ALLIANZ PARK

Great North Way

Hendon Central

4m

Hendon Wood Lane

The Ridgeway

ARRANDENE OPEN SPACE

Pursley Rd

COPTHALL PLAYING FIELDS

SUNNY HILL PARK

M1

A1

Hendo

Barnet Rd

3m

MOAT MOUNT OPEN SPACE

Marsh Lane

A1

M1

Mill Hill Broadway

Colindale

A5

arnet By Pass

A1

GOLF COURSE

2m

Hale Lane

WATLING PARK

MONTROSE REC GROUND

SCRATCHWOOD OPEN SPACE

1m

Highview Gdns

Deansbrook Rd

Burnt Oak

Stag Lane

FRYENT COUNTR PARK

Kingsbury

A41

START

Edgware

Penshurst Gdns

CHANDOS REC GROUND

Queensbury

EDGWAREBURY PARK

Edgware Way

A5

Canons Park

201

just done).

3.2mi: Hendon Wood Lane. Turn right here and, after passing a row of houses, turn left into Totteridge Fields. Follow the hedgerows past grass fields (that can display wonderful wild flowers) till you reach Dollis Brook for the first time.

4mi: Dollis Brook. Follow the brook east (past farms that may have livestock in them) before crossing to the north side of the brook at some playing fields. Continue heading east past the houses on your left until you reach Barnet Lane and Barnet Playing Fields.

5.7mi: Barnet Playing Fields. The LOOP trail heads north here up to Monken Hadley, so be sure to follow the Dollis Valley way-markers. These will lead you east and then veer to the south as the Dollis Brook bends down through Wyatts Farm and Brook Farm.

6.9mi: Totteridge Lane. Turn right here and then continue south on the trail that begins

on the opposite side of the road about 100m later. Follow the trail across the stream just before reaching Laurel Way. Cross the road and continue on to Tillingham Way. At Totteridge Lane you can instead head to Totteridge and Whetstone Tube Station (Northern line; 50m to the left) to end your run. There are also toilets 500m away (left on Totteridge Ln and left again onto High Rd).

7.8mi: Tillingham Way. Here you have two options: Left will take you past Woodside Park Tube Station (another option for finishing your run) and right is more scenic as it takes a left onto Southover and another left to be back with the brook.

8.3mi: Argyle Road. After crossing this road, the trail sticks to the right (west) of the brook and makes three quick crossings just before the impressive viaduct train bridge.

9.3mi: Viaduct. Follow Dollis Road under the bridge and then make a left turn to once again

follow the trail and creek (with the creek on your right).

10.5mi: The A1 Again. The trail passes under the A1 and soon after the Dollis Brook merges with Mutton Brook (together they form the River Brent). Follow the signs east alongside Mutton Brook (here the Dollis Valley Walk joins the Capital Ring Trail). At the junction of the two brooks there are toilets 600m to the west along Bell Lane.

11.2mi: Finchley Road. Cross the road and continue following the trail as it soon swaps from the north of the creek to the south. (Keep an eye out for the 16-foot statue nicknamed the "Naked Lady" or, by locals, "Dirty Gertie".)

11.6mi: Addison Way. Turn left onto this street and be aware that Dollis Valley Greenwalk swings a right shortly after. Instead of following this route to Hampstead Heath, we want to carry on straight, following the Capital Ring signage, to our rail connection at East Finchley (it is also possible to carry on to Hampstead Heath and catch trains from Golders Green). Pay attention to the Capital Ring way-markers as the trail dives in and out of parks and suburban streets (there are toilets in the last park, Lyttelton Playing Fields).

12.6mi: Norrice Lea. At this street turn left, cross Lyttelton Road, turn right, and then immediately left into Vivian Way. Follow the Capital Ring signage via Vivian Way, Deansway (left), Edmunds Walk (right), to reach East Finchley Station and the end of your run, 13.2mi later.

GETTING THERE ▶

Start: Edgware Tube Station (Northern line, Edgware branch).
Finish: East Finchley Tube Station (Northern line, High Barnet branch).

👍▶ An excellently marked trail that passes through stunning parks and woods.

👎▶ A lack of toilets on the trail and the start connection from Edgware is not particularly scenic.

MUST KNOW ▶

Distance: 13.2mi (21.2km)

Surface: Mostly sealed & dirt (some gravel & grass).

Terrain: Mild undulations to hilly.

Weather Warning: Dirt trails scattered throughout the run can become very boggy.

Traffic Warning: Many road crossings.

Times: Open at all times but some sections are not recommended after dark.

Toilets: High Road (Totteridge), Bell Lane (Hendon), & Lyttelton Playing Fields.

The impressive arches of Dollis Brook Viaduct.

GRAND UNION CANAL: PADDINGTON BRANCH

14mi / 22.5k

More than a half marathon of uninterrupted towpath stretching from Little Venice almost all the way west to Heathrow. Easy to navigate and a bucket list running accomplishment.

LOCATION ▶ Start Point: Paddington Station, Westminster, W2 (2.8mi W of central London).
Finish Point: Hayes & Harlington Station, Hillingdon, UB3 (14.3mi W of central London).

ROUTE & INFO ▶ From Paddington Station make your way northwest to the canal junction of Little Venice (follow the pedestrian signs). Once there head to your left (west) to begin following the Paddington Branch of the Grand Union Canal.

From this point on the navigation really couldn't be easier. Just keep following the towpath that clings to the south bank of the canal all the way till it joins the Grand Union Canal proper in Hayes.

Terraced housing perched on the banks of the canal.

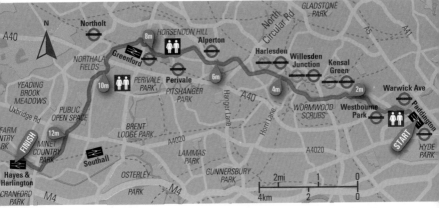

The first few miles are quite industrial and lonely at times. However, the surrounding greenery becomes more prominent the further west you head.

One green spot in particular makes a good pit stop location just past the halfway mark. At 7.4mi you'll come to Horsendon Hill, the visitor centre is just over the canal (look for it just past the golf course) and has toilets and commands a nice view of the canal. If you fancy calling it a day at this point, Perivale Tube Station is just a half mile south via Horsendon Lane.

Just shy of 10mi you'll pass Marnham Fields on your left (east) and the recently developed Northala Fields over the canal on your right (west). Both are worth a look if you fancy a detour.

At 13.2mi (by the time you've completed a half marathon) the canal meets the actual Grand Union Canal. Turn right (west) here and follow the Grand Union under three bridges and at the fourth, go up the stairs to Station Road, and turn left to run to your destination at Hayes & Harlington Station. Well done, 14mi in the bank.

GETTING THERE (RAIL)▸

Start: Paddington Station (Bakerloo, District,

Circle, Hammersmith & City, First Great Western, Heathrow Connect, & Heathrow Express).
Finish: Hayes & Harlington National Rail Station (First Great Western service).

👍▸ Navigation couldn't be easier.

👎▸ Parts of the canal can be lonely and industrial (take a friend or two).

MUST KNOW▸

Distance: 14mi (22.5km)

Surface: Sealed, crushed limestone, cobbles, & gravel.

Terrain: Flat.

Weather Warning: Towpaths can become slippery when wet/icy.

Traffic Warning: Be considerate of other canal users, particularly cyclist around bridges.

Times: Open at all times (take company after dark).

Toilets: Paddington Station (charged, also have showers), Little Venice, Little Wormwood Scrubs, Horsendon Hill Visitor Centre, Oldfield Lane (Greenford, 1mi east via Ruislip Rd), & Hayes & Harlington Station.

NORTHEAST ROUTES

NORTHEAST HOTSPOTS

BROOMFIELD PARK

1.2mi / 1.9k [ ] [ ] [ ] [ ] [ ]

An open, community-orientated park with three distinct sections and a total perimeter trail of 1.2mi.

LOCATION ▸ Palmers Green, Enfield, N13 (8.4mi N of central London)

INFO ▸ Of its three sections, the western end of Broomfield Park is a large grass field occupying a slight slope with scattered trees. A 0.8-mile paved trail follows its circumference The middle section is a walled formal garden with a bandstand and four ponds with many wide paved trails.

The eastern section is a sports field with a great looped trail (a combo of sealed and crushed limestone) ideal for workouts. It's 820m around if you follow the inside trail on the north side, so running it twice and subtracting 30m gives a nice 1mi loop. Occasionally a grass athletics track is marked out on the field.

The park is open 8am (8:30am Sundays and holidays) to dusk.

Options | The Pymmes Brook Trail connects west into Arnos Park and also east towards Lee Valley. However, the old signage for this way-marked trail is hit or miss nowadays.

Grovelands Park is just 1mi north via Old Park Road and Fox Hill. Do a loop of this before following the A111 northwest to Cat Hill. Turn left and then left again onto Church Hill where you can follow the parks of Oak Hill, Brunswick,

and Arnos back to Broomfield—a total run of 8.3mi (13.5km).

GETTING THERE ▸

Rail: Palmers Green National Rail Station (Great Northern service).

Bus: 34, 102, 121, 232, 299, 329, W6, N29 & N91.

👍 ▸ A good perimeter trail with other internal options.

👎 ▸ Unless combined with other nearby parks, can get too small fast.

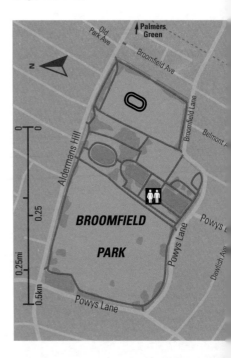

GROVELANDS PARK

1.7mi / 2.7k [info] [grass] [wood] [run] [time]

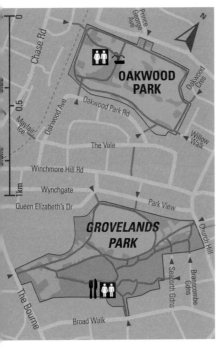

or 4.8km). This section of the park slopes west to east dropping 20m.

Finally, the woodland in the southeast is relatively open with many trails, including a lovely stretch of raised boardwalk.

By running from the park's southwest gate (on The Bourne) to the northeast gate (on Church Hill) and back again, looping around the lake on the way out and the playing fields on the way back, you'll run 1.7mi (2.7km).

The park is open 8am (8:30am Sundays and holidays) to dusk.

Options | Broomfield Park (1.0mi S), Pymmes Brook (1.2mi SW), and Oakwood Park (0.4mi N). Oakwood has an excellent 1.3mi (2.1km) loop, many grass trails through meadows, toilets, and an impressive avenue of poplars.

GETTING THERE ▶

Rail: Southgate Tube Station (Piccadilly line; 0.4mi NW) or Winchmore Hill National Rail Station (Great Northern line; 0.4mi E)

Bus: 121, 125, 298, 299, 377, 382, W6, W9, & N91.

👍 ▶ Good spot for speed workouts, a nice wood and lake, and many options nearby.

👎 ▶ Can leave you asking for more.

A great suburban park boasting variety in both terrain and scenery.

LOCATION ▶ Southgate, Enfield, N14 (9.8mi N of central London)

INFO ▶ The park effectively has three main sections: In the south the tree-lined boating lake has a sealed path around it that is 0.54mi (870m) long.

Just north of the lake is the main grass playing field, which also has a sealed path around its circumference (0.75mi, so four loops makes 3mi

HACKNEY MARSH & SURROUNDS

4.3mi / 7.0k

One large recreation ground surrounded by unique wildlife areas and two rivers—making for endless traffic-free running options.

LOCATION ▸ Homerton, Hackney, E9 (5.7mi NE of central London)

INFO ▸ This running hotspot is comprised of the large open grass sports field of Hackney Marsh in the middle, the filter bed nature reserves to the north, and Wick Woodland to the south. They are all connected by the dual waterways of River Lea and the River Lee Navigation. The car park in the southeast corner of Hackney Marsh makes the ideal starting point as there are

toilets here (in the centre, open 8am to 6pm).

Hackney Marsh | The flat grass sports fields are lined with trees that shelter the two rivers running either side of the park.

A sealed path follows the river down the park's eastern side, which also makes for a great workout spot being sheltered amidst the trees and just over a mile long. This path also connects into Olympic Park to the south. On the west side of the park you'll either need to follow the Navigation towpath or run on the grass. In total, the park is 2.2mi around.

Waterworks Nature Reserve & Middlesex Filter Beds | These filter beds were built in the

Hackney Marsh (looking south to Queen Elizabeth Olympic Park).

1850s to provide clean drinking water, prompted by a cholera outbreak. Nowadays, with the huge reservoirs upstream making these redundant, they're nature reserves and provide some interesting running environments.

The basins are full of vegetation but the paths atop of the old ponds are frequented by walkers, nature lovers and joggers. Exploring them can easily add another mile or two to your run. Access Waterworks Reserve via a bridge at the northern end of Hackney Marsh. The reserves are open from 8am to 6pm (7pm weekends).

Wick Woodland | Follow the Lea Navigation south to reach this regenerating wood. It is just under a mile around and although the trails get a bit boggy there are plenty of them to enjoy.

A full loop of the perimeter of all these adjacent options will get you through 4.3mi—add on more by exploring the parks further or by following the River Lee north or south. Also be sure to check out Walthamstow Marshes (0.1mi N), Victoria Park (0.7mi SW), and of course Queen Elizabeth Olympic Park (0.3mi S).

GETTING THERE▶

Rail: Leyton Tube Station (Central line; 1.2mi NE) & Hackney Wick Rail Station (London Overground, 1mi S).

Bus: 236, 276, 308, W14 W15, & N26.

👍▶ Plenty of wildlife and countless nearby options for adding on.

👎▶ The filter beds are nice, but can be a little maze-like with limited entrance ways.

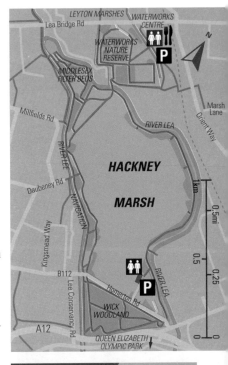

EPPING FOREST

15mi / 24k

At 2400ha (6000ac), the uber long Epping Forest is essentially London's largest running environment. At its widest point it is just 2mi across, but from tip-to-toe (beyond Epping to Ilford) it's a whopping 16mi—plenty to keep you fit.

LOCATION ▶ Boroughs of Waltham Forest, Redbridge, and out beyond London (the southernmost point of the forest is 8.0mi NE of central London)

INFO ▶ The forest is widest up near the M25 and then narrows as it winds through suburbs,

A perfectly undulating Epping Forest trail.

crossing under or over several roads before reaching Wanstead.

In 1878, a groundbreaking parliamentary act reserved the forest for public use and recreation. In fact, in 1882, Queen Victoria visited the forest and said, "It gives me the greatest satisfaction to dedicate this beautiful forest to the use and enjoyment of my people for all time."

The forest is predominantly woodland and is renowned for its ancient oak, beech and hornbeam trees. There are also pockets of heath, swamp, grassland and many ponds. Wildlife is in plentiful supply with squirrels, foxes and rabbits everywhere, and you may even be lucky enough to spot some deer.

Due to clay-based soil, most of the trails are boggy practically year round. However, within the forest there are 30 miles of gravel tracks that offer better drainage. In particular, the Green Ride, running north to south, is an immaculate (in most sections) gravel path made for Queen Victoria's visit in 1882 (although she never got round to using it).

Loops | The Corporation of London has provided four way-marked looped trails. These include:

- *Oak Trail* (approx. 6.6mi, starting at Theydon Bois Station);
- *Beech Trail* (2.5mi, starting at the Pillow Mounds car park on Manor Rd, just N of the visitor centre);
- *Holly Trail* (2.5mi, Bury Rd car park, 500m N

of the Chingford Station);

- *Willow Trail* (2.5mi, starting at the Connaught Water car park on Ranger's Rd, 0.9mi E of Chingford Station).

Wooden signs with coloured arrows mark the way for each of these trails. Runners can get involved with the planning for Epping Forest through their runners' forum. Search for "walking and running Epping Forest" and cityoflondon.gov.uk for info.

Long Runs | Another great way to explore the forest is to catch the train to Epping Tube Station (Central line) and run back either to Chingford Station (approx. 8mi, Greater Anglia), Highams Park Station (approx. 10mi, Greater Anglia), Snaresbrook Tube Station (approx. 12mi, Central line), or all the way to Manor Park Station (approx. 15mi, Greater Anglia).

The route from Epping to Manor Park Stations roughly follows the old Centenary Way. It is not way-marked so you do need to follow your nose/map a lot (seriously, a compass and/or GPS isn't a stupid idea as this forest is notorious for disorientating people).

From Epping Station run south via Centre Drive, then right onto Ivy Chimneys Road, and left on Theydon Road. You'll cross the M25 and then find the forest. From here aim to follow the Green Ride and other main trails that run in a southwest direction predominantly (and make a small deviation west to the visitor centre).

When doing these long journeys be prepared

Epping Forest.

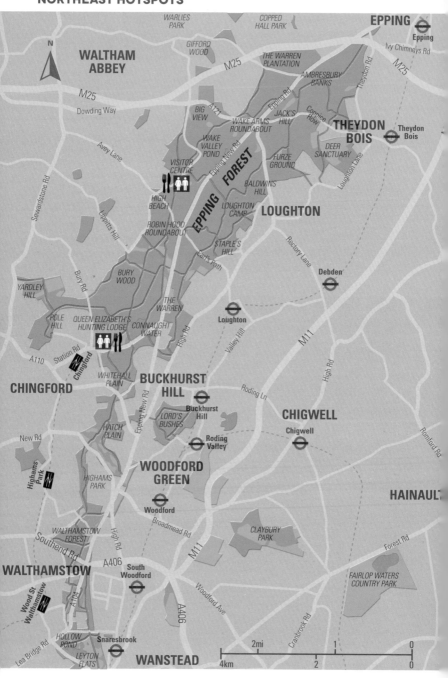

with warm clothing, food, money and water, as this can become a much longer run than planned if (read: when) you take wrong turns.

GETTING THERE ▶

Rail: Greater Anglia service to Chingford and Central Line to Epping.

Bus: Various—the 575 if the only option all the way to Epping.

👍▶ Trees, wildlife, and trails galore!

👎▶ Navigation is difficult outside of the four way-marked trails.

The distinction between swamp and trail can be a blurry one in parts of Epping Forest.

WANSTEAD FLATS & WANSTEAD PARK

6.9mi / 11k

Wanstead Flats and Wanstead Park combine to make a wonderfully diverse running spot of grass, woods, swamps, and even a cemetery.

LOCATION ▶ Wanstead, Redbridge, E12 (8.0mi NE of central London).

INFO ▶ Wanstead Flats | This is a large, flat (as you've probably guessed from the name), and predominantly open grass park with some wooded corners and ponds to keep things interesting. The park is in three sections with two roads dissecting it north to south.

There are many dirt or gravel trails to explore in Wanstead Flats. Some are dead straight, cutting through the centre of the three main sections.

Others meander amongst the trees on the park's borders. Options abound for creating your own loops or for just finding a predominantly traffic-free route north to Epping Forest or east to the cemetery/Wanstead Park.

Bush Wood lies just northeast of Wanstead Flats and is a small wooded area with several intersecting tracks. A full perimeter of the Flats (including Bush Wood) is approx. 4.7mi (7.6km). There is also the way-marked Lime Trail (1.5mi long) that loops around the western end of the Flats and Bush Wood (look for the wooden arrows).

Wanstead Park | Connecting from Bush Wood, you can enter Wanstead Park by crossing Blake

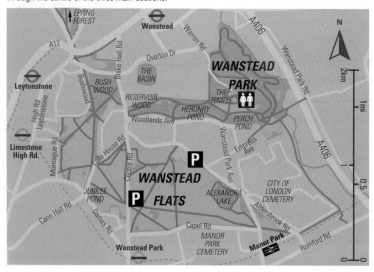

Hall Road into Reservoir Wood (look for a small gate in the fence). Here you'll be met with a series of picturesque ponds nestled amongst equally aesthetically pleasing oak trees.

Moving further east you'll find yourself in Wanstead Park. This is the site of the once impressive Wanstead Manor that had grounds of exceptional gardens and water features. Today you can still see its rough layout from satellite imagery and there are some remaining buildings, including The Temple and the Grotto, both built in the mid 1700s. There is a small cafe near Perch Pond (in the south of the park) and also toilets at The Temple (open daily until dusk).

Apart from two grass clearings, the majority of Wanstead Park is wooded and has mud trails that wind between the many man-made ponds and ornamental canals, as well as alongside the River Roding (in the east of the park). There is the 3.3mi way-marked Chestnut Trail within the Park and it's a very good way to see the main sights and not get too lost (follow the wooden signs with the arrows).

Bringing It Together | From the southeastern corner of Wanstead Park is a path that runs south, past the City of London Cemetery and the Ilford Golf Course, to Romford Road or to Aldersbrook Road (going between the tracks and the cemetery). Use this path to create a full loop of both Wanstead Park and Flats.

For a good introductory loop, start and finish at Manor Park Station and complete a clockwise loop by following the southern and then western sides of Wanstead Flats, before running through Bush Wood to connect to Reservoir Wood and Wanstead Park (loop around the northeast corner of the park), before following the path south past the cemetery to the station. This will be approx. 6.9mi (expect longer if it's your first time).

Wanstead Flats (looking south from Bush Wood).

NORTHEAST HOTSPOTS
GETTING THERE ▶

Rail: Wanstead Park Station (London Overground, S), Manor Park National Rail Station (Greater Anglia service, SE), Leytonstone Tube Station (Central line, NE), & Wanstead Tube Station (Central line, N)—all stations are within a few hundred metres of the parks.

Bus: 58, 66, 86, 101, 104, 145, 308, 474, W13, W14, W19, N8, & N55.

👍▶ A great combination of large open grass fields and woods, plus plenty of water features and historical remnants to keep us runners entertained.

👎▶ Some sections are not recommended after dark (just stay in the well-lit areas near the roads).

Meadows in Wanstead Park.

VALENTINES PARK

2.0mi **/ 3.2**k ⛭ 🔥 ⊞ 🏃 ⏳

Fifty hectares of formal parkland that includes several ponds, cricket fields, an abundance of trees, a palace, and many running trails.

LOCATION ▸ Ilford, Redbridge, IG1 (10.2mi NE of central London)

INFO ▸ This award-winning park is one of the Borough of Redbridge's flagship green spaces. It is immensely popular with local joggers, who also use it to connect with Wanstead Park (just 0.6mi W, via Bethel Ave, Cowley Rd, Exeter Gdns, and the footbridge over the North Circular).

Sealed trails circumnavigate the park except for around the two cricket fields (one on the east and the other on the west side of the park) and also the grassy Melbourne Field in the southeast. To complete a 2mi (3.2km) perimeter loop of the park you can run on the grass in these sections.

The trails through the interior are well worth your time as they circle the two large ponds, follow two streams, and run around the mansion in the north of the park (this is the original Valentines Mansion built in 1696).

There are also two cafes, one near the boating lake and another near the mansion. The park has a slight hill sloping up toward the mansion house.

GETTING THERE ▸

Rail: Gants Hill Tube Station (Central line; 0.2mi N) & Ilford National Rail Station (Greater Anglia service, 0.4mi S).

Bus: 66, 123, 128, 145, 150, 167, 179, 296, 364, 366, 396, & 462.

👍 ▸ A peaceful park with plenty of trails.

👎 ▸ The wild meadows in the northeast are unfortunately fenced off.

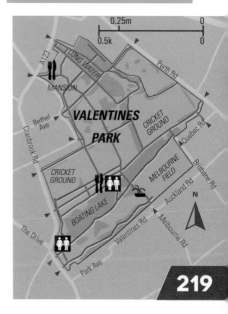

219

CLAYBURY WOODS & PARK

2.7mi / **4.3**k

Claybury Woods and Park occupy a lush hillside with abundant natural beauty and some stunning views.

LOCATION ▶ Woodford Bridge, Red-bridge, IG8 (12.4mi NE of central London)

INFO ▶ Humphrey Repton, the landscaper of Claybury Hall (built in 1791), said, "When Nature has been so bountiful of charms as in the situation of Claybury, Art can seldom greatly in-terfere without violating the genius of the place."

The park's natural beauty remains with ancient woods (that have brilliant flowering forest floors) in the northeast, a strip of meadow and grassland through the interior, and regenerating wood in the southwest.

The park drops just over 40m from north to south and the variety of trails makes for excellent running. There is a way-marked nature trail (about 2.5mi long), but your best bet is to complete a full circumference by starting at the gate on Tomswood Hill, run into Hospital Hill Wood, then follow the park's edge anti-clockwise all the way back to the start 2.7mi (4.3km) later. The gates will let you know if you make a wrong turn.

GETTING THERE ▶

Rail: Fairlop Tube Station (Central line; 0.9mi SE) & Woodford Tube Station (Central line; 1.1mi W).

Bus: 169, 275, & W14.

👍 ▶ Plentiful greenery, changing terrain and vistas.

👎 ▶ Lack of toilets and other facilities.

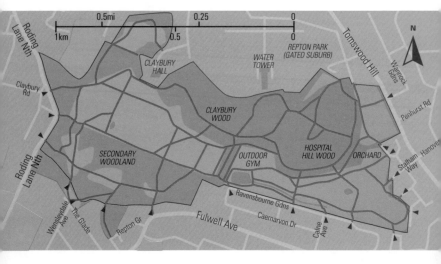

FAIRLOP WATERS COUNTRY PARK

2.9mi / 4.6k ▦ ▦ ▨ 🏃 ❓

One hundred and twenty hectares of green space with possibly the nicest limestone trail in the city.

LOCATION ▶ Fairlop, Redbridge, IG6 (12.5mi NE of central London)

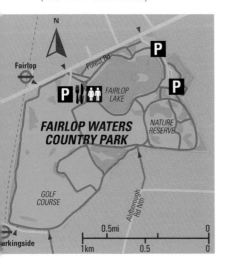

INFO ▶ This mixed-use recreational park has three main features: a golf course, a boating lake, and a nature reserve (of grass, shrubs, wetlands and some trees). All three have trails around them (although for most of the golf course you're just running on grass at the edge of the fairways) and all can be looped together for a complete perimeter run of 2.9mi (4.6km).

However, the best trail is the crushed limestone path around the lake that is 1.1mi (1.75km) long.

It wouldn't be too hard to work out a mile and use it for mile reps, utilising the extra 140m for recovery between efforts. You can also create a figure-of-eight by combining the lake loop with the nature reserve loop just south of it.

The park is open 7am to 11pm (midnight on Fridays and Saturdays). There is also a restaurant and bar near the clubhouse for post-run refreshments.

Nearby options include the huge grass football fields (just N across Forest Rd), Claybury Woods (1mi NW along Forest Rd then Tomswood Hill), and also Hainault Forest (1.8mi E along Forest Rd).

GETTING THERE ▶

Rail: Fairlop (Central line; 0.1mi W) & Barkingside Tube Stations (Central line, 0.3mi, SW).

Bus: 150, 167, 169, 247, 275, 462, & N8 (all from the roundabout at the W end of Forest Rd).

👍 ▶ Top-notch limestone loop.

👎 ▶ The lack of paths around the back of the golf course.

HAINAULT FOREST COUNTRY PARK

6.0mi / 9.7k

A classic country park with a lake, grasslands, woodlands and plenty of trails over rolling terrain.

LOCATION ▶ Hainault, Redbridge, IG7 (14.2mi NE of central London)

INFO ▶ This country park sits in a basin with hills on three sides and Romford Road (A1112) on the other. The northern hilltops are occupied by a large woodland area that houses many dirt trails and wider bridleways. A golf course marks the southern and eastern borders of the park with a thin strip of woodland (also with dirt trails) dividing the golf course from the park.

In the basin of the park is a lake surrounded by meadows and grassland. Here the central focus is the cluster of buildings, which include the visitor centre, cafe, toilets, and a children's farm. Pay and display car parking is available here and it is a good place to start and finish your run.

From the car park nearest the cafe trails spread out in all directions and it really is a case of pick and choose. To get you started there's a short loop trail around the lake and back again of just 0.8mi (1.25km). Then for something quite a lot longer head northeast along the driveway past the visitor centre to reach the golf course and follow the perimeter of the park in either direction. You have to do your own navigation through some of the less-well formed trails but a full loop of the park is about 6mi (9.7km). Otherwise the many mown grass trails heading

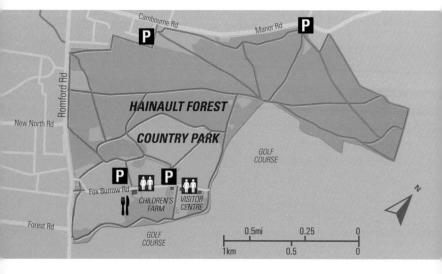

north from the car park will beckon you uphill to explore the wood. Have fun!

Navigating the park is easy. There are signposts every so often and some clear bridle trails to follow. And if you reach a road or a golf course or a fence you know you need to turn. There is also a fixed orienteering course in the park, for which you can pick up info from the visitor centre.

GETTING THERE ▶

Rail: Grange Hill Tube Station (Central line; 1.4mi W).

Bus: 150, 247, & 362.

👍 ▶ Rolling hills and varied scenery, plus a nice spot to relax at the cafe afterwards.

👎 ▶ That there isn't more of it.

MUST KNOW ▶

Circumference: 6.0mi (9.7km)

Surface: Dirt, grass, & sealed.

Terrain: Hilly.

Weather Warnings: Some woodland trails can become boggy.

Traffic Warnings: None.

Times: 7am to dusk.

The grass trails of Hainault Forest will draw you up and into the woods.

NATURE RESERVES OF HAVERING

Like many outlying London boroughs, Havering has a green belt of nature reserves on its outer borders ideal for the explorative runner.

INFO ▶ As these spots hug the M25 and are therefore out of the range of most London runners, here is a taster of what to expect from Havering's key outer nature reserves. The way-marked London LOOP links many of these parks together if you'd like to hit multiple spots in one run.

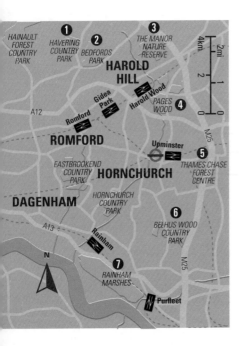

1. Havering Country Park
Havering-Atte-Bower, RM4 (16.8mi NE of central London)

Perched in the quaint village of Havering-Atte-Bower, this park is 1.7mi (2.7km) east of Hainault Forest (via the London LOOP) and just 0.6mi (1km) west of Bedfords Park.

It is predominantly woodland and meadows and features an impressive avenue of giant sequoia (tall pines imported from California). The stunning views of the surrounding countryside are the icing on the cake.

2. Bedfords Park
Havering-Atte-Bower, RM4 (17.1mi NE of central London)

With woods, scrub, grassland, lakes, and plenty of views south over London, Bedfords' many trails are rich in diversity. A full perimeter loop of the park is approx. 2.8mi (4.5km).

There are toilets and parking at the visitor centre (accessed from Broxhill Rd). A footpath connects a string of parks (Rise, Raphael and Lodge Farm Parks) south to Romford and the Romford National Rail Station (2.5mi away—take care crossing the A12).

3. The Manor Nature Reserve

Harold Hill, RM3 (18.8mi NE of central London)

In Harold Hill the LOOP passes through the open fields of Central Park from where you can run northeast to enter Hatter Woods (across Dagnam Park Dr), which is the first section of The Manor Nature Reserve.

From Hatter Woods you'll reach Dagnam Park, which has a variety of grass, dirt, and limestone trails. Further east again, is Fir Wood and the coppiced Duck Wood is in the south (which has a gravel loop and an impressive bluebells display in spring).

Parking available on Settle Road. The nearest station is Harold Wood (2mi).

4. Pages Wood

Harold Wood, RM14 (17.8mi NE of central London)

74 hectares of farm and regenerating woodland with a main perimeter figure-of-eight loop of 2.5mi (4km), with 4mi total of well-formed trails.

Use the LOOP signage to navigate the 1km to Pages Wood from Harold Wood Station. There is also parking available off Hall Lane. Just north of the park, via Lodge Lane, you'll find the smaller Harold Court Woods, and northeast you'll discover Tylers Common and Wood (here you can use the bridle bridge over the M25 to access several additional woods).

5. Thames Chase Forest Centre

Upminster, RM14 (19.6mi E of central London)

A family friendly park that straddles the M25. The western side of the park has a well-formed perimeter loop of 1.8mi (2.9km). There are toilets, refreshments and parking available at the visitor centre.

The park is 2mi east of Upminster Station

(District Tube line and c2c and Greater Anglia services). The 13ha Cranham Marsh is a few hundred metres to the west (via public footpaths off Pike Lane).

6. Belhus Wood Country Park

Aveley, RM15 (18.8mi E of central London)

The highlights of this park are the many lakes which are surrounded by woods and grassland. There are plenty of trails including a heritage trail loop and public pathways to surrounding parks and woods.

The park is open from 8am to dusk and has toilets and parking at the visitor centre (off Romford Rd).

7. Rainham Marshes

Rainham, RM13 (15.7mi E of central London)

A rather exposed section of the Thames riverside, but it has abundant bird life, exceptional views of the Queen Elizabeth II Bridge and a close up of the concrete barges used in WWII D-Day landings.

Rainham Marshes itself costs to enter (free for residents of Havering and Thurrock). However, the cycle path that follows the river (and doubles as the final section of the LOOP) provides a great link from Rainham to Purfleet National Rail Stations. This is 5.1mi (8.2km) one-way and there are toilets and parking at the Rainham Marshes Visitor Centre (1km from Purfleet Station).

EASTBROOKEND COUNTRY PARK

3.2mi / 5.2k

Nestled between the suburbs of Dagenham and Romford, this sprawling wildlife reserve is a brilliant off-road running destination.

LOCATION ▶ Dagenham, Barking & Dagenham, RM10 (14.0mi E of central London)

INFO ▶ Eastbrookend Country Park has three distinct sections, which the roads that dissect it in the shape of an upside-down "T" help to define. South of the "T" is the main section that includes The Millennium Centre, the main car

park, three large ponds, some pockets of wood, and many trails through grassy undulations.

Northwest of the "T" is Fels Fields, which again is a mixture of grassland, wood, and wetland. This has a nice looped trail around it and it also connects directly through to Central Park (which is dead flat with many sports fields and plenty of grass running to be done).

Northeast of the "T" are the lakes of Eastbrook Pond (west) and Chase Waters (east). A trail loops all the way around Chase Waters, part of

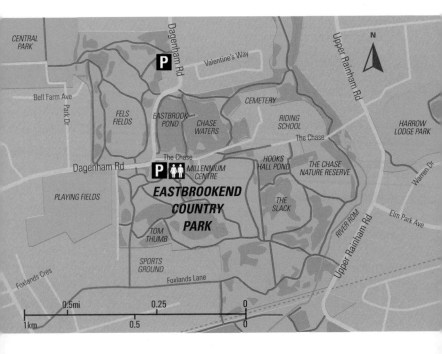

which is a beautifully soft wood chip surface.

From the northeast corner of Chase Waters, a path heads eastward connecting you, behind the cemetery and riding school, to The Chase Local Nature Reserve. This elongated park follows the River Rom north-to-south. Joining the river here, you can head south all the way to the rail lines (through the horse grazing area on poorly defined trails), of which you can follow west till you reach a footpath that leads you behind a fenced-in football field, then back north to Eastbrookend Country Park. By keeping to the perimeter of both parks (of Chase Reserve and going around all three sections of Eastbrookend Park) a full loop is approximately 3.2mi (5.2km).

Beyond this perimeter loop, each section of park has other trails to keep you busy. There is also Beam Valley Country Park just south over the tracks (use the footbridge in Chase Reserve), Central Park to the northwest (enter via Fels Fields), and Harrow Lodge Park to the east over Rainham Road (connect via The Chase footpath that carries on from Dagenham Road). So there is plenty to keep most runners entertained.

GETTING THERE ▶

Rail: Dagenham East Tube Station (District line; 0.5mi SE).

Bus: 103 & 174.

👍▸ Plenty of off-road terrain to explore with few road crossings.

👎▸ In wet weather be prepared to get muddy in Chase Reserve.

MUST KNOW ▶

Circumference: 3.2mi (5.2km)

Surface: Dirt, grass, gravel, and bark.

Terrain: Undulating.

Weather Warnings: Sections can become extremely muddy, particularly in the Chase Reserve.

Traffic Warnings: Take care crossing Dagenham Road.

Times: Open at all times.

Toilets: In The Millennium Centre.

The trail between Chase Waters and Eastbrook Pond.

227

HORNCHURCH COUNTRY PARK

2.5mi / **4.0**k

Once a key RAF base for the defence of London, this outer-city park is now home to some beautiful trails amongst regenerating woods, marshes and grasslands.

LOCATION ▶ Hornchurch, Havering, RM12 (15.8mi E of central London)

INFO ▶ The scattering of pillboxes throughout the park testifies to its importance as a former RAF base. However, now the park's importance is more about ecological protection (largely because of its marshlands that surround the Ingrebourne River) rather than the protection of London from Nazi invasion.

The park's borders are not particularly clear but are roughly defined by the houses to its north and west, the Ingrebourne River to the east, and Ingrebourne Hill Park to the south.

The best starting point is in the northern car park at the end of Squadrons Road. From here the main sealed trail heads south, parallel to the river and over several undulations, all the way to the fishing lake at the park's south end. Run around the lake, past the farmhouse and then follow the mown grass trail along the park's western border to make your way back to the car park. This full perimeter loop is 2.5mi (4km) and there are plenty of other internal trails to explore (including another central sealed trail).

Options | There is a connecting trail east over the Ingrebourne Marshes into Berwick Woods and on to Berwick Pond Road. Heading north you can follow the LOOP Walkway up the Ingrebourne River to Upminster and beyond to Harold Hill. Finally, Ingrebourne Hill Park to the south is a slightly hillier version of Hornchurch Park with a large figure-of-eight looped trail.

GETTING THERE ▶

Rail: Hornchurch Tube Station (District line; 0.8mi N).

Bus: 103, 165, 252, 256, 287, 365, & 372.

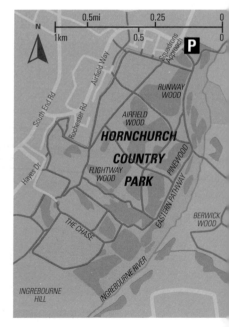

Spot the pillbox, Hornchurch Country Park.

👍▸ With the pillboxes and abundance of nature you kind of feel like you're running through a battlefield (ideal for a tempo run!).

👎▸ No maps, no signage, no toilets.

MUST KNOW ▸

Circumference: 2.5mi (4km)

Surface: Sealed, gravel, and grass.

Terrain: Undulating

Weather Warnings: This area of London is exposed to the elements and after heavy rain you'll need to stick to sealed trails.

Traffic Warnings: None.

Times: Open at all times.

Toilets: None.

MAYESBROOK PARK

2.0mi / 3.2k

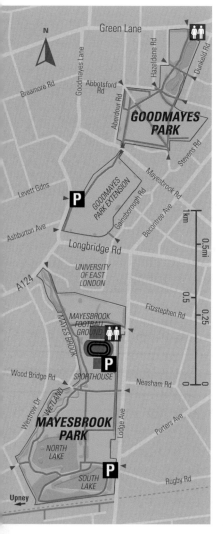

Wildlife areas, lakes, sports grounds, a climate change defence (for floods and droughts), a track, and facilities galore—this park has plenty to offer us runners.

LOCATION ▶ Dagenham, Barking & Dagenham, IG11 (10.9mi E of central London)

INFO ▶ In the north are sports fields while the south boasts the main recreational area. Between these two running attractions are the Barking and East Ham United FC Ground, a beautiful all-weather track, a sports centre, and tennis courts.

Connecting these various sections is a main sealed path running north to south, which splits in two at the recreational area. A return trip from the northern gate, with a loop at the southern end, is 2mi (3.2km).

Explore the sports field in the north and wetland, woodland, and lakes in the south. Open 6:30am to 7pm (10pm summer). Nearby options: Goodmayes (0.2mi N), Parsloes (0.6mi E), and Barking (0.9mi W) Parks.

GETTING THERE ▶

Rail: Upney Tube Station (District line; 0.3mi SW).

Bus: 5, 62, 145, 368, 387, & N15.

👍 ▶ A developing park that will get better with age.

👎 ▶ A lack of trails given the size of the park.

GOODMAYES PARK

2.5mi / 4.0k

Formal Parkland in the north and flat grass fields in the south. Combine the two to make a 2.5mi figure-of-eight fence line run.

LOCATION ▶ Goodmayes, Redbridge, IG3 (11.8mi E of central London)

INFO ▶ The southern Goodmayes Park Extension is simply a flat, grass sports field with one trail on its western side. The grass itself makes a good perimeter running surface.

The north section is a little more interesting with two lakes, rows of trees, large grassy areas and even a parkour (free running) gym. Like the

Extension, a perimeter trail around this northern section needs to be done mostly on the grass, but the sealed trails provide enough to keep you going if the ground is wet. Open 8am to dusk.

GETTING THERE ▶

Rail: Goodmayes National Rail Station (Greater Anglia line; 0.5mi NW).

Bus: 128, 150, 364, 368, & 387.

👍▶ A great traffic-free thoroughfare from which to reach Mayesbrook Park.

👎▶ The south section is a little lonely and exposed.

A leafy avenue of Goodmayes Park.

PARSLOES PARK

2.5mi / 4.0k 🏞️ 🚻 🏃 ❓

A large open swathe of sports fields and some formal parkland. Great for barefoot running on the grass.

LOCATION ▶ Dagenham, Barking & Dagenham, RM9 (12.3mi E of central London)

INFO ▶ This huge sports field provides the runner with a wonderful grass expanse that is 2.5mi around (including a section on sealed trails in the formal parkland area in the south-west corner). Given the grassy surface, you may even like to ditch the shoes and go barefoot.

The lake in the formal parkland area has a nice sealed loop that is 0.4mi (640m) long. So 2.5 laps makes a mile and five laps makes 2mi—ideal for a workout, particularly as this is the most sheltered section of the park (which is otherwise highly exposed to the elements).

There are also several sealed paths dissecting the park and in the west one section of grass field has been left to grow wild with some nice mown trails through it. Finally, a small warning: the park can feel unpopulated at times and it may not be safe after dark if alone. Open at all times.

GETTING THERE ▶

Rail: Becontree Tube Station (District line; SW corner of the park).

Bus: 62, 145, & 364.

👍 ▶ It's huge, relative to other nearby parks.

👎 ▶ It's also exposed to the elements, dead flat, and lacking trails.

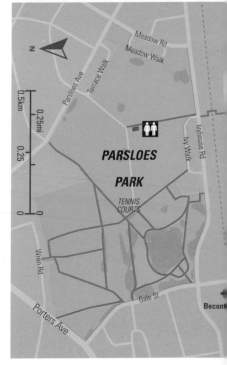

BARKING PARK

1.25mi / 2.0k

A beautiful park and popular east London running hotspot.

LOCATION ▸ Barking, Barking & Dagenham, IG1 (9.7mi E of central London)

INFO ▸ The northern boundary of the park features the 920m-long lake that almost stretches all the way from Ilford Lane in the west to South Park Drive in the east. A sealed trail follows the lake's southern banks and then continues via tree-lined avenues all the way around the remaining edges of the park. This main trail creates a loop of 1.25mi (2km)—ideal for workouts or time trials.

There are several other sealed trails throughout the park, in particular, one that dissects the park north to south, providing a good option for figure-of-eight loops.

In the west are formal gardens accompanied by grand old trees. The remainder of the park includes grass sports fields, tennis courts, a splash park, and a cafe in the centre. The park is open 6:30am to 7pm (10pm in summer).

GETTING THERE ▸

Rail: Barking Tube/National Rail Station (Hammersmith & City, District, c2c & London Overground; 0.3mi SW).

Bus: 5, 62, 145, 169, 366, 387, EL1, EL2, N15.

👍 ▸ With the long lake, open grass fields, and abundant trees it feels like a mini Hyde Park.

👎 ▸ Not enough of it.

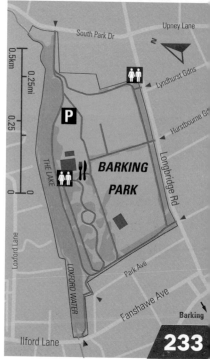

233

GREENWAY PATH

4.8mi / 7.7k

The banks of a sewer are here transformed into a 5mi raised corridor for traversing east London on foot.

LOCATION ▶ Stratford to Beckton, Newham, E3 to E6 (5.1mi E of central London)

INFO ▶ The Greenway is a huge stretch of pedestrian pathway spanning almost all the way from Victoria Park to the Royal Docks.

It begins just east of the A12 with access from Wick Lane and Dace Road. 200m along the Greenway you will go over your first waterway (the towpaths of the River Lea may well tempt you to make an early diversion) and you will also pass in to Olympic Park at this point.

At 800m (0.5mi) you'll reach View Tube—a visitor centre designed from recycled shipping containers to be a viewing platform of the Queen

Elizabeth Olympic Park. Being dubbed the place for "a view, a brew, and a loo", it makes a good early stop if nature calls.

It is at View Tube that, due to rail works, you must make a diversion under the railway line to Marshgate Lane and on to High Street before finding your way back up to the eastward part of the Greenway. (This diversion was current at the time of publication.)

At just over a mile in, you'll be back on the Greenway heading east. The going is straight forward here (aside from several road crossings that have pedestrian signals) until you meet the second and final diversion on the Greenway that goes under the A13.

Exiting the Greenway here you'll turn right, cross Roman Road, use the crossings to go under the A13, then turn left to use the crossings again on Woolwich Manor Way, and then follow the A13 east for 100m before turning right on to the Greenway again. The Greenway comes to an end 1km later.

The Greenway is popular with walkers and commuters but the eastern end is certainly the most quiet. So run with others after dark. A great feature of the path is that every time it crosses a street it provides distances in metres to the next street, which is useful for gauging your pace and knowing exactly how tired you should feel.

Options | The Greenway provides access to Beckton District Park (S), Memorial Recreation Ground (S—see details below), West Ham

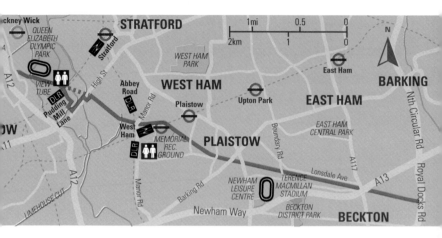

Park (N), east London canals, Queen Elizabeth Olympic Park (including an athletics track opening in 2016), Victoria Park (NW), and Terence Macmillan Stadium (S).

Memorial Recreation Ground hugs the south bank of the Greenway (2mi from its western end) and is predominantly made up of football and rugby grounds but also has some nice trails to pound. A full loop of the park's perimeter is 1.1mi (1.8km).

GETTING THERE (WEST) ▸

Rail: Hackney Wick Rail Station (London Overground line; 0.5 N), & Pudding Mill Lane DLR Station (near View Tube).

Bus: 276, 339, & 488.

👍 ▸ Forget public transport, this is the ideal runner's highway through east London.

👎 ▸ Can feel unsafe after dark.

QUEEN ELIZABETH OLYMPIC PARK

3.6mi / 5.8k

The great remnant of the 2012 Olympics, this park has almost everything for the runner: trails, facilities galore, and an impressive array of canals and parks close by.

LOCATION ▶ Stratford, Newham, E15 (5.8mi NE of central London)

INFO ▶ Touted as London's newest park, it is similar in overall size to Hyde Park. However, much of that space is dominated by the glorious stadia left over from the Games (and of course the bizarre ArcelorMittal Orbit). The parklands that surround these structures have, as a result, a rather disjointed nature.

The threads that tie it all together are the waterways: River Lea (which flows straight down the middle from the north) and then Old River Lea,

City Mill River and Waterworks River (which all branch off from the River Lea in the south).

The River Lea section is more about the tranquillity of wild flowers and wetlands, all traversed by many trails. The southern end has the bigger playgrounds, a greater number of tourist attractions, and of course the Westfield Shopping Centre on the east side and the stadium on the west side (opening permanently as the home of West Ham United and for athletics competitions in 2016). There will also be a community athletics track just south of the main stadium.

For a good taster of the park, follow the 3.6mi (5.8k) art trail. Start at Westfield (on Westfield Ave) and run directly toward the stadium via Stratford Walk. On the way, you'll pass the information point on your right where you can check out a map of the park.

The red dashed route (opposite) covers the rough course of the art trail as it runs a loop just south of the Aquatics Centre, then crosses the river to run another loop near the Orbit. After this you'll head north to the A12. Then follow mostly streets back to the north side of Westfield.

For adding on, consider heading north on the River Lea, the Greenway (south)

and Limehouse Cut (south), and Victoria Park (west). For some cross training be sure to check out the London Aquatics Centre, Copper Box Arena (with gym), and VeloPark (with velodrome, BMX track, road circuit, and 5mi of mountain bike trails).

GETTING THERE ▶

Rail: Stratford Station (DLR; Jubilee & Central lines; London Overground, Greater Anglia & c2c services) & Stratford Int'l Stations (DLR & Southeastern High Speed 1).

Bus: 25, 69, 86, 97, 104, 158, 238, 241, 257, 262, 276, 308, 339, 388, 425, 473, D8, N8 & N86.

👍▶ The perfect family destination with playground and shopping centre so close to the running terrain.

👎▶ It's not the most logical layout for creating your own running loops and watch out for congestion during major events.

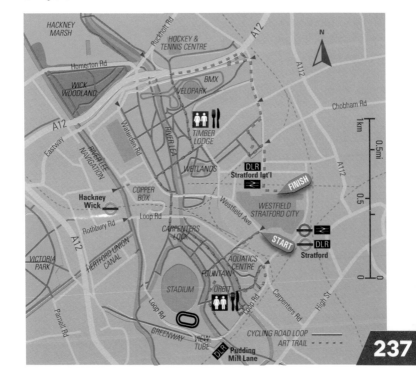

237

WEST HAM PARK

1.25mi / 2k

Before Olympic Park arrived this was northeast London's premier park. It attracts over one million visitors each year, many of whom are running.

LOCATION ▶ West Ham, Newham, E15 (6.6mi E of central London)

INFO ▶ West Ham Park is 77 acres and has a summer grass athletics track, a measured 2k circuit, and many more sealed and dirt trails—so if you can avoid the crowds of other park users there is plenty of speed work to be done here.

The park is mostly grass with pockets of gardens all over and trees doted all over. The paths are well sheltered by these trees, meaning that it is ideal for doing workouts, particularly on the 2k route that starts in the east at Main Gate (off Upton Lane) and runs anti-clockwise around the main trail that essentially follows the fence line (you hit 500m when turn left at the northern fence line on Ham Park Rd). Being such a popular park, choose quiet times to use this circuit if you're training fast.

Be sure to also make use of the single dirt tracks and the grassy areas for your running as well. The ornamental garden is worth a look but not really big enough to bother including as part of your everyday running.

GETTING THERE ▶

Rail: Plaistow Tube Station (Hammersmith & City & District lines; 0.5mi S).

Bus: 104, 238, & 325.

👍 ▶ A great measured training loop and brilliant gardens.

👎 ▶ If only it were bigger.

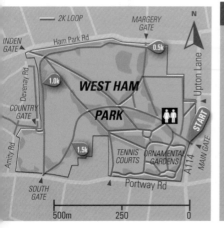

MUST KNOW ▶

Circumference: 1.25mi (2.0k)

Surface: Sealed with grass and dirt options.

Terrain: Flat.

Weather Warnings: None.

Traffic Warnings: It's a very busy park so take care if training at speed.

Times: Open 7:30am to 4:30pm (winter) or 9:30pm (summer) and various other times in spring and autumn.

Toilets: In the east (near the main gate).

LIMEHOUSE CUT

1.4mi / 2.3k

An important traffic-free connection for east London runners to and from other great running destinations.

LOCATION ▶ Start: Limehouse, Tower Hamlets, E14 (3.9mi E of central London)

Finish: Bromley-by-Bow, Tower Hamlets, E3 (5.4mi E of central London)

INFO ▶ This canal runs in a straight line—except for a little wiggle or two—from Limehouse Basin, on the banks of the Thames, to the Bow Locks on the River Lea (in the east).

From Limehouse you have options both east and west following the Thames Path and you can also heading north along Regent's Canal. From Bow you can venture north along the River Lea or into Queen Elizabeth Olympic Park and east along the Greenway. So the beauty of Limehouse Cut is the variety of options that it opens up.

Limehouse Basin.

NORTHEAST HOTSPOTS

The canal itself has a towpath on its southern bank, which is a mixture of crushed limestone and grass, making for a pleasant running surface.

An interesting feature is the award-winning floating section of the towpath as you approach the Bow Locks. This takes you through a tunnel under the A12. Also, watch your step on some of the other tunnels because, for some reason, the path has been built with cobbled speed bumps that could buckle a cyclist's wheel or trip up a distracted runner.

Finally, keep in mind that this is a quieter canal as far as pedestrians go, so not the safest after dark.

GETTING THERE ▶

Rail: Limehouse DLR/National Rail Station (c2c service).

Bus: 15, 115, 135, 277, D3, D6, D7, N15, N550, & N551.

👍▶ Excellent traffic-free access to surrounding options.

👎▶ A little lonely and watch those speed bumps.

MUST KNOW ▶

Distance (one way): 1.4mi (2.3km)

Surface: Crushed limestone, grass, & cobbles.

Terrain: Flat.

Weather Warnings: Towpaths can be a little slippery in wet/icy conditions.

Traffic Warnings: Be considerate of other pedestrians and cyclists.

Times: Open at all times.

Toilets: None.

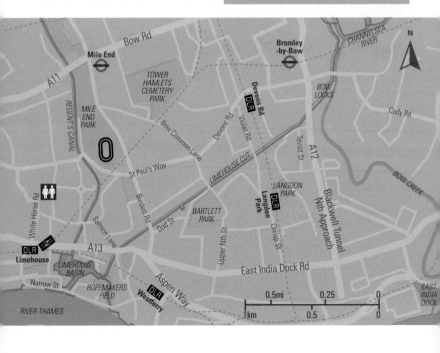

Epping Forest.

The lake at Hainault Forest Country Park.

Hainault Forest Country Park.

EAST LONDON MARITIME

6.6mi / 10.6k ⚠ 🗺 🏃 ❓ ⏳

From the industrial-turned-financial nucleus of Canary Wharf to the globally significant Royal Greenwich Observatory, this run is a great way to tick some must-see boxes and enjoy some top running environments.

LOCATION ▶ Start/Finish: Jubilee Park, Canary Wharf, Tower Hamlets, E14 (5.1mi E of central London)

INFO ▶ Songs have been written about Britain's dominance at sea and this run will take you through the heart of Britain's maritime heritage. It starts in the Canary Wharf business district, which was once a bustling port, heads south through the interior of the Isle of Dogs to Greenwich on the south bank of the Thames (via the foot tunnel). Then it comes back on a section of the 184mi Thames Path.

MILE-BY-MILE ▶ Start: Jubilee

Park. Run south to cross the impressive South Quay Footbridge, then turn left keeping to the banks of the South Dock.
Interest: This area was once the international hub of cargo shipping, but in the 1980s was given a total overhaul as a financial district. One Canada Square (at 235m) is the second tallest building in the UK, behind The Shard.

0.3mi: Millwall Docks. When you hit the adjoining waterway of Millwall Inner Dock, turn right and keep to its west bank passing under Marsh Wall and the DLR line. At 0.7mi cross the dock using the Pepper Street bridge. Turn right

and follow the dock's east bank until you reach a small park where you'll follow an underpass on your left.
Interest: The Inner and Outer Millwall Docks were opened in 1868 as ports for timber and grain and more recently were the location for filming of the James Bond instalment The World is Not Enough.

1.0mi: Mudchute. After passing under the rail line, cross East Ferry Road and enter the gate directly opposite into Mudchute Park. Head up the steps and veer right following the narrow trail south to exit the gate 250m later. Head southeast (left out of the gate) to follow the sealed trail around the Millwall Park sports fields. Exit the park near the Island Gardens Station, cross Manchester Road, continue south via the path opposite, and cross Saunders Ness Road to reach Island Gardens and the dome-topped entrance to Greenwich Foot Tunnel.
Interest: Mudchute Park occupies an area of land that was the dumping ground for mud and silt extracted from the nearby docks.

1.6mi: Thames Tunnel. The Greenwich Foot Tunnel is open at all times and has a lift and a spiral staircase to take you down (remember, that real runners only ever take the stairs!). The tunnel is 400m and ends with another lift/spiral staircase. Immediately outside the tunnel exit is the Cutty Sark. Run along the eastern (left) side of this old ship and follow the King William Walk south past the Naval College and over two roads to Greenwich Park.

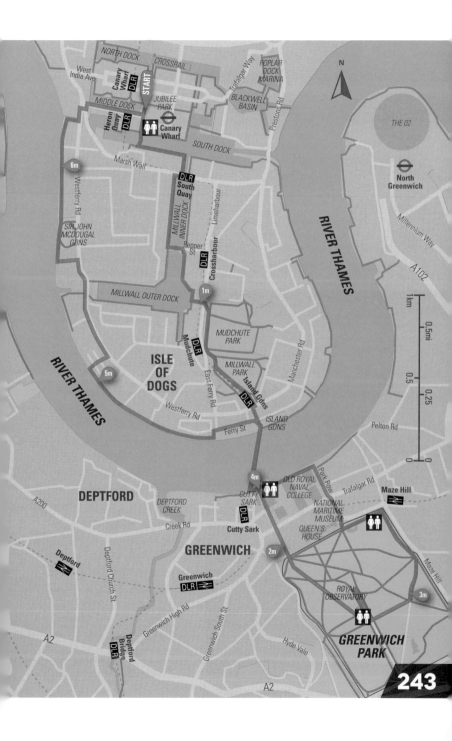

NORTH DOCK
CROSSRAIL
West India Ave
Canary Wharf **DLR**
START
Trafalgar Way
POPLAR DOCK MARINA
BLACKWELL BASIN
Prestons Rd
MIDDLE DOCK
JUBILEE PARK
Heron Quay **DLR**
Canary Wharf
SOUTH DOCK

N

THE O2

Marsh Wall
6m
Westferry Rd
DLR
South Quay
MILLWALL INNER DOCK
Limeharbour

North Greenwich

SIR JOHN MCDOUGAL GDNS

Pepper St
DLR
Crossharbour

RIVER THAMES

Millennium Way

A102

MILLWALL OUTER DOCK
1m

1km
0.5mi

5m
MUDCHUTE PARK

DLR
Mudchute

ISLE OF DOGS

MILLWALL PARK
Island Gdns
DLR

Manchester Rd

0.5

0.25

RIVER THAMES

Westferry Rd
East Ferry Rd
ISLAND GDNS

Ferry St
ISLAND GDNS

Pelton Rd

0

DEPTFORD

DEPTFORD CREEK
4m
CUTTY SARK
OLD ROYAL NAVAL COLLEGE
Park Row
Trafalgar Rd
Maze Hill

A200
Creek Rd
DLR
Cutty Sark
NATIONAL MARITIME MUSEUM
QUEEN'S HOUSE

Deptford
Deptford Church St

GREENWICH
2m

A2
Greenwich
DLR
ROYAL OBSERVATORY
3m

Greenwich High Rd
Greenwich South St
Deptford Bridge
DLR
Hyde Vale
Maze Hill

A2
GREENWICH PARK

243

NORTHEAST ROUTES

Interest: In the 19th century the Cutty Sark worked the tea trade from Asia to the UK and later the Australian wool trade (of which it holds speed records).

2.15mi: Greenwich Park. Follow the main road south through the park for 650m to head up the hill to the roundabout (there are toilets near the top of the hill on your left). Turn left at the roundabout and jog to the Royal Observatory and viewing platform.

After a few photos, retrace your steps back to the roundabout and turn left (east) following Great Cross Avenue. Pass the bandstand and veer left. Pass the Roman ruins and veer left again to

follow the trail along the boundary of the park. Head down the hill, turn left and then exit the park near the pond.

Interest: At the Observatory you can pay to stand on the ceremonial meridian line, but there is also a small line of grey bricks near the ticket booth that also marks the meridian—you can stand on this one for free.

3.55mi: Greenwich Museums. You'll exit the park onto Park Row; follow this street all the way north to the Thames. Turn left to run past the symmetrical grandeur of the Old Royal Naval College and back to the Greenwich Foot Tunnel.
Interest: The Old Royal Naval College was originally opened in 1706 as a hospital for returning injured seamen. It is said that the building was split in two to allow an unbroken view of the Thames for the Royals staying at the Queen's House.

4.3mi: Thames Path, North Bank. Upon exiting the Foot Tunnel on the north bank, look for signs marking the way west along the Thames Path (look for the acorn symbol). You'll spend the first 300m away from the river and then just over a half mile along the river's banks as it bends back towards Canary Wharf. There is one more section where the Thames Path leaves the riverbank for about a half mile before re-joining the riverside past some impressive apartment blocks.
Interest: The Isle of Dogs is called an island because of the combination of the horseshoe bend the river makes and the West India Docks stretching from one side to the other—effectively surrounding the suburb with water.

6.2mi: Canary Wharf Again. The next time the Thames Path takes you away from the river (at 6.2mi) you will come to

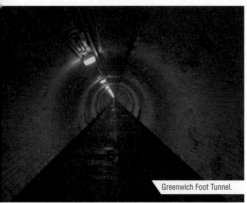
Greenwich Foot Tunnel.

Old Royal Naval College with Queen's House in the background.

a roundabout where you need to cross over two roads to turn right onto Heron Quays. This street will lead you back to Jubilee Park, 6.6mi later.

GETTING THERE ▸

Rail: Canary Wharf Tube Station (Jubilee line & DLR).

Bus: 135, 277, D3, D7, D8, & N550.

👍▸ Oodles of maritime history and some great running terrain through a diverse mix of neighbourhoods.

👎▸ Some parts of the Isle of Dogs can seem a little solitary, but it does make a nice change from the hustle and bustle of both Greenwich and Canary Wharf.

Mudchute Park, looking north to Canary Wharf.

MUST KNOW ▸

Distance: 6.6mi (10.6km)

Surface: Sealed (with some brick/cobbled sections)

Terrain: One hill and some stairs, otherwise flat.

Weather Warning: Cobbles/bricks can become slippery when wet/icy.

Traffic Warning: Some road crossings. Pedestrian traffic can be heavy during commuting hours in Canary Wharf and in the afternoons around Greenwich.

Times: Greenwich Park is open between 6am and roughly dusk (6pm in winter and 9:30pm in mid-summer).

Toilets: Canary Wharf Tube Station, Cutty Sark (charged), & Greenwich Park.

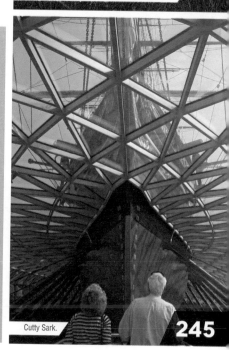
Cutty Sark.

FINSBURY PARK TO ALLY PALLY

5.2mi / **8.3**k

A tranquil, (mostly) traffic-free run with everything from palaces to parks and old railways to ancient woods.

LOCATION ▶ Start Point: Finsbury Park Station, Finsbury Park, Haringey, N4 (4.3mi N of central London).

INFO ▶ The connecting green trail between Finsbury Park and Alexandra Palace, called Parkland Walk, is a runner's treasure that could easily be missed, even by locals. It includes two sections of disused railway (closed in 1970) that is now a well-used nature trail with a solid, dry surface and even some pleasant views along the way.

The Parkland Walk serves to connect the two parks of Alexandra and Finsbury and, on this run, we will also be visiting two woods (Queen's and Highgate) that can be avoided when running after dark or in wet weather.

This run begins at 35m above sea level and reaches a peak of about 100m. However, because you spend most of the climb on the railway line, the gradient is so gentle that you barely notice it. The worst of the hills are actually the undulations through the woods (but if hills are what you're after, just do a circuit of Ally Pally Park).

MILE–BY–MILE ▶ Start: Finsbury Park Station. Turn left out of the station, cross Stroud Green Road and, just before the rail bridge, turn right into Finsbury Park.

0.1mi: Finsbury Park. Keep to the west (left) side of the park and after 500m turn left out of the park, following the footbridge over the railway. (If you need to make an early toilet stop there are bathrooms at the Finsbury Park Cafe, 150m into the centre of the park from this exit.)

0.4mi: Parkland Walk (South). You'll see the Parkland Walk sign and the start of the trail to your right. This runs for 1.7mi and there are maps signifying key distances and also information boards throughout. The gravel surface makes it dry in most weather conditions and the solid vegetation on either side creates a woodland feel rather than a thin avenue of green.

2.1mi: Highgate Streets. The old railway ends at the blocked off train tunnels in Highgate. Follow the trail left up to Holmesdale Road, turn right and then right again onto Archway Road. From here, depending whether you want to dive into the forest or stay on the road (after-dark option), you have two choices: the road route follows the Parkland Walk signs to the north section of old rail line (follow Archway Rd for another 250m then turn right onto Muswell Hill Rd) or take the more scenic route (described below) through Queen's and Highgate Woods.

2.2mi: Priory Gardens. Just 50m after joining Archway Road, turn right into Shepherds Hill and then left just before Highgate Library to run through a small wood to Priory Gardens. Turn right and follow this street for 250m before

Street art meets the Parkland Walk's southern section.

entering Queen's Wood via the footpath.

2.5mi: Queen's Wood. Follow the Capital Ring signs. At 2.65mi these signs will take you across Queen's Wood Road and then back into the wood. At 2.9mi you'll reach Muswell Hill Road (after passing the Queen's Wood Cafe). Cross over Muswell Hill, enter the iron gate into Highgate Wood and turn right, still following the Capital Ring signs.

3.1mi: Highgate Wood. At a meeting point of several paths (and the major Capital Ring signpost and monument) follow the trail to your right (however, if you turn left here there are toilets and a cafe 150m away). Following the Capital Ring trail you'll encounter a drinking fountain after another 150m (the water is good for drinking), turn left here and carry on to reach the gate, exiting the wood.

3.4mi: Muswell Hill Rd. Leave the Capital Ring trail here and turn right down the path that follows the fence line of the wood. Once back on Muswell Hill Road, turn left and keep to the left-hand footpath that takes you under the road and

on to the north section of the Parkland Walk.

3.6mi: Parkland Walk. This section of old railway is 700m long and opens up some wonderful views of the city over the top of hundreds of brick-red chimneys and roofs.

4.0mi: Muswell Hill. The Parkland Walk finishes here. Cross this street and follow the signage to Alexandra Palace (just to the right of the school). You are now in Alexandra Park. Follow the signs through to the palace and check out the view from the top.

4.5mi: Alexandra Palace. After soaking up the views of the city, carry on past the palace, through the car park on its eastern side, and then straight through the rose garden. Turn right to the palace access road where you can turn left and follow this road to the Alexandra Palace Station footbridge 5.2mi (8.3km) from the start.

Route Back to Finsbury | Rather than catch the train from Alexandra Palace, why not jog another 2.7mi (4.4km) back (downhill) to Finsbury Park? The New River Path

provides a route south from Alexandra Palace Station, but its signage is fickle unfortunately and some of the green spaces it uses were on private land or through construction areas at the time of writing. Try this route instead:

- Start on the east side of the station and run south on Station Rd to the roundabout.
- 0.3mi: Turn right onto Mayes Rd, and left at the next roundabout staying on Mayes.
- 0.5mi: At Wood Green Shopping Centre turn right on to Hornsey Park Rd.
- 0.9mi: At the end of this street, Cross Turn-pike Lane directly over to Wightman Road. Follow this road for 1.1mi (or use the traffic free Harringay Passage which runs parallel).
- 2mi: With Finsbury Park now opposite, turn left and follow Endymion Road for 250m before turning right into the park.
- 2.2mi: Run to the right hand (west) side of the park and follow it all the way to the gate at which you entered at the start of the run. Exit here and cross over to Finsbury Park Station (completing 7.9mi in total).

EXPLORING THE PARKS▶

Finsbury Park | At 46ha Finsbury Park is your

The impressive view from Ally Pally.

classic London park boasting one main wide sealed perimeter path (with bridle path either side) of 1.4mi (2.3km) and several sealed and non-sealed trails coming off it. There is also a boating lake, outdoor gym equipment, a cafe, toilets, plus a gym and a worse-for-wear athletics track. The park itself is open dawn till dusk.

Alexandra Park | Affectionately known as Ally Pally, the palace was built as "The People's Palace" in 1873 but was tragically destroyed by fire just two weeks later. It was rebuilt, only to be gutted again by fire in 1980. Nevertheless, it is now restored and plays host to many events.

The park itself is 80ha with the palace standing on a flat plateau in the north (there is also an ice skating rink, a lake, and gardens at this end). South of the palace the park falls away steeply with grass fields and pockets of trees. At its southern end are sports fields and a cemetery. There are many trails to explore and some great lactate inducing hills. Following the perimeter trails creates a 3mi (4.8km) loop of the park. The park is always open.

Queen's Wood | 21ha of grand, old oaks trees.

Named after Queen Victoria.

Highgate Wood | An ancient wood of 28ha boasting a sports field in its interior with marked out sprinting tracks in summer. The wood perimeter trails form a 1.25mi (2km) loop. Open daily 7:30am to dusk.

GETTING THERE ▶

Rail: Finsbury Park National Rail/Tube Station (Great Northern; Piccadilly & Victoria).

Bus: 4, 19, 29, 106, 141, 153, 210, 236, 253, 254, 259, 341, W3, W7, N19, N29, N253, & N279.

LEAVING THERE ▶

Rail: Alexandra Palace National Rail Station (Great Northern service).

Bus: 184 & W3.

👍 ▶ Brilliant brew of parks, woodland, suburban greenways, and city views.

👎 ▶ Its a pity the return journey doesn't match the Parkland Walk's high standards.

MUST KNOW ▶

Distance: 5.2mi (8.3km)

Surface: Sealed, dirt, & gravel.

Terrain: Some hills/undulating.

Weather Warning: Boggy trails in woods (but can also be avoided).

Traffic Warning: Street crossings.

Times: Finsbury Park and Highgate Wood both close at dusk and open at dawn and 7:30am respectively—diversion possible though.

Toilets: Finsbury Park, Highgate Wood, & Alexandra Palace.

EXPLORE THE RIVER LEA

7.7mi / 12.4k   𝓚 🐾

A flat run following a waterway and marshland with immense historical and natural significance.

LOCATION ▶ Start/Finish: North Millfields Rec Ground, Lea Bridge, Hackney, E5 (5.4mi NE of central London)

INFO ▶ The London portion of the River Lea stretches from Limehouse Basin (on the Thames) for 18mi up to Waltham Abbey (just

north of the M25). It is possible to follow the Lea for 26 miles all the way to Ware in Hertfordshire (marathon training anyone?). However, our route bites off a digestible chunk of this wonderful running environment, leaving you to venture further up or down the river on future outings.

The valley is abundant with wildlife, with otters even making their homes in the area. It has also been home to industry throughout the centuries,

The tranquil waters of the River Lea/Lee, looking southeast toward Walthamstow Marshes.

of which old cranes, locks and the many man-made river diversions all bear witness.

Confusingly, despite thousands of years of human habitation, we still can't decide whether to call the river and valley "Lee" or "Lea"—instead, both are correct.

There is a chain of huge reservoirs just east of the river, not accessible to the public. The Lea Valley Walk is way-marked with a swan symbol. And in recent years, rumours of a crocodile or other large predator have been circulating after several geese have been seen "sucked" under the water by something very large. But don't worry, none of these reports have been confirmed by authorities and as yet no runners have succumbed to this "sucking" predator.

MILE-BY-MILE ▶ Start: North Millfields Rec Ground.

There is an iron sculpture of a tree in the northeast corner of the park that marks your starting point. From here follow the towpath north (running to the left when facing the river).

0.5mi: Spring Lane. The trail leaves the river briefly to pass behind the awesome looking kids' adventure play centre. Then it connects to the river side of Springfield Park.

0.9mi: Lea Rowing Club. Keep following the left hand side of the river northwards. There is also a cafe here and a footbridge over the river in case you've got an early niggle and want to take an alternate route home.

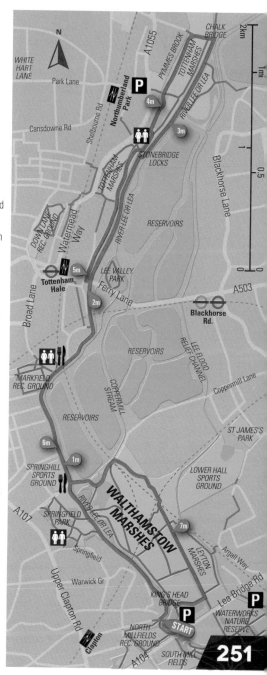

1.4mi: Markfield Recreation Ground. Continue heading along the towpath (the northern end of the park has a cafe and toilets as well as a museum and old engine house).

2.1mi: Ferry Lane. Pass under the bridge. As the river splits in two, follow the trail straight ahead that sticks to the narrow finger of land straddling between the two parallel branches of water.

2.75mi: Stonebridge Locks. Cross over the river to its eastern bank and continue heading north on the towpath.

3.1mi: Side Option. Look for a trail to your right that gives you the option of crossing a small bridge and looping around a smallish scrubland area with well-formed trails. The reserve runs parallel to the river so you will re-join the trail 400m ahead (having added on another 500m or so). Otherwise continue following the towpath.

3.5mi: Chalk Bridge. This is the northernmost point on your journey; you can carry on for many miles north along the towpath, but the scenery you'll encounter over the next few miles isn't quite so special (at least until Gunpowder Park near the M25). Instead, cross the footbridge over to the west bank, then follow the trail straight ahead for 150m to the other side of the open grassland (part of Lea Valley Regional Park). Follow the trail south along the west side of this field to take you back to the river at Stonebridge Locks where there are public toilets.

4.3mi: Tottenham Marshes. Immediately after the toilets turn right and enter Tottenham Marshes. This is another open grass field with a choice of trails. Keep to the eastern side this time, closest to the river.

4.6mi: Allotments. The marshes are now replaced with community gardens. Keep following the trail south.

5.0mi: Ferry Lane Again. The trail leads you back to Ferry Lane. Cross the road and head down to the canal path, follow it south, re-tracing your steps.

6.2mi: Lea Rowing Club Again. Instead of following the towpath, cross over the bridge and follow the path east behind the marina. 200m from the bridge turn left down the sealed road (Coppermill Lane). When you pass under the train tracks turn right on to the trail through Walthamstow Marshes (heading southeast).

6.8mi: Walthamstow Marshes. Dive under the two train tracks and continue heading south on the marshes.

7.4mi: The Home Straight. Once past the horse centre (left), take the trail to your right.

After 250m this trail comes to an end, turn right again, heading north briefly before turning left and crossing the bridge. Turn left and you'll be back at the iron tree.

OPTIONS ▶ Springfield Park | Just 0.6mi north of the start/finish point you will encounter this lovely park on the western bank of the river. It has nice gardens, good views (meaning a couple of hills) and a cafe and toilets up the top (in the White Lodge open 10am to 6pm daily).

Lee Valley Athletics Centre | These impressive training facilities (used by UK Athletics athletes) are just northwest of Pickett's Lock (1.5mi N of Chalk Bridge). It has both an outdoor and indoor track and a gym and is open for public use on weekdays 1pm to 10pm and weekends 8am to 8pm.

GETTING THERE ▶

Rail: Clapton National Rail Station (Greater Anglia line, 700m W along Southwold Road).

Bus: 48, 55, 56, 308, 393, N38, & N55.

👍 ▶ With only small, parallel diversions from the river in open green spaces, plus good signage, it is hard to get lost on this route. Traffic-free, plenty to see and options galore for adding on or turning back early.

👎 ▶ Lonely after dark.

ROYAL DOCKS & BECKTON DISTRICT PARK

7.4mi / 12k   🔲 🔲 🏃 ⛷ ❓

This run takes in the huge Royal Docks and then connects up to the famous Greenway via some equally green suburban trails.

LOCATION ▶ Start/Finish: Custom House for ExCeL DLR Station, E16 (6.9mi east of central London)

INFO ▶ The run starts at Royal Victoria Dock, which is one of three massive bodies of water constructed for shipping in the 19th century and early 20th (the Royal Albert Dock and King George V Dock lie to the east, with London City Airport separating them). Together they're the largest docks in the world and, today, provide the runner with plenty of wide waterside paths and great vistas (especially eye-catching on a still day).

This run also takes in the Jake Russell Walk to the north, the Greenway, and the long and narrow Beckton District Park, following a portion of the Capital Ring.

Royal Albert Dock, looking west toward Canary Wharf.

MILE-BY-MILE ▶ Start: Custom House for ExCeL. From the station run due south, past the ExCeL entrance, directly to the placid water of Royal Victoria Dock. Swing a right to follow the waterside path around the western end of the dock, past the water sports areas, the Crystal, and cable car (Emirates Air Line, which is a great and surprisingly inexpensive and scenic transport alternative from North Greenwich).

1.1mi: Royal Victoria Dock Bridge. Climb up the stairs of this impressively sleek footbridge (15m above water level) and make your way back to the north shore of the dock. Turn right at the base of the stairs to follow the waterside path east (passing the lengthy ExCeL Centre on your left).

1.9mi: Royal Albert Dock. Continue

following the water's edge under Connaught Bridge and then for 200m alongside the Royal Albert Dock. Once past the London Regatta Centre Boathouse, turn left to follow the path under the DLR tracks, over Royal Albert Way and to the Jake Russell Walk.

2.25mi: Jake Russell Walk. Turn right here to follow the path in a northeast direction as it crosses Stansfeld Road and Beckton District Park South (ideal for adding on with a sealed 1.1mi path around its perimeter, using the footpath along Strait Rd). Carry on to Woolwich Manor Way.

3mi: Woolwich Manor Way. Turn left here and run past the Mary Rose Mall (which has toilets if needed). Follow the footpath on the left hand side of Woolwich Manor Way up to the A13. Cross under this road and enter the Greenway on your left, just after Roman Road.

3.5mi: Greenway. Head west along this traffic free walkway until you reach Boundary Lane (the first road you'll encounter).

4.4mi Boundary Road. Turn left here and run to the street's end, entering the footpath straight ahead. Follow it until you reach the A13. Turn left to reach the footbridge and use it to run over this busy highway. Head straight south along Viking Gardens till you reach the entrance to Beckton District Park North.

5.0mi: Beckton District Park North. For

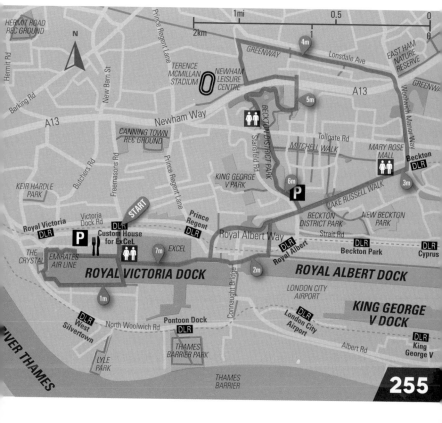

NORTHEAST ROUTES

simplicity you can just follow the Capital Ring signs from here down through the park to reach the Jake Russell Walk. However, it's worth doing a quick loop around the lake in the north section of the park before rejoining the Capital Ring trail to head south.

6.1mi: Jake Russell Walk Again. Upon reaching the junction of this walk and the Beckton District Park South, enter the walk again by turning right and crossing Stansfeld Road. Follow the path past the point at which you earlier joined it, until you pass allotments on your right. Cross Victoria Dock Road here and use the footpath to run under the DLR line and arrive back at Royal Victoria Dock.

6.7mi: Royal Victoria Dock. Turn right to run

between the ExCeL Centre and the water again. Then turn right back up to Custom House DLR station. Well done on your 7.4mi (12km) run!

OPTIONS ▶ Thames Barrier Park | From the south side of Royal Victoria Dock run south to Woolwich Road. Turn left here and then right into Thames Barrier Park.

Being set against the incredible backdrop of the giant silver structures of the Thames Barrier, the layout and gardens of this modern park are suitably unique. It has a wide perimeter path (sealed) that is exactly 1km around.

You can join back to the route above by exiting the park onto Woolwich Road. Turn right and then left onto Connaught Bridge. Use the

On a still, clear day the docks are an incredibly peaceful spot to run. Royal Victoria Dock.

footpath under the road (which starts on the right hand side and crosses under the bridge to the left). Once on the north bank, head under Connaught Bridge again to join the waterside path heading east along Royal Albert Dock.

The Docks | King George V Dock is entirely closed to the public and Royal Albert Dock is closed in the south because of the airport. But its north bank is open and incorporates a section of the Capital Ring as it connects to the Thames at North Woolwich (use the foot tunnel or free ferry to reach the south bank).

New Beckton Park | Just east of the southern section of Beckton District Park, this small park has a nice 700m loop.

GETTING THERE ▸

Rail: Take the DLR to Custom House for ExCeL (Beckton branch).

Bus: 147, 241, 325 and N551.

👍▸ The docks have a grand and unique beauty about them that is something quite special, particularly at sunset and sunrise.

👎▸ Some sections can be lonely so it's best to take company.

Beckton District Park.

MUST KNOW ▸

Distance: 7.4mi (12km)

Surface: Sealed with some cobbles.

Terrain: Flat (with stairs and undulations).

Weather Warning: None.

Traffic Warning: There are several road crossings, so do take care.

Times: Greenway open 5:30am to 7pm (winter) or 9pm (summer), take company after dark on this run.

Toilets: The ExCeL Centre, Mary Rose Mall, & Beckton District Park North (near the lake).

THAMES PATH

The River Thames is an artery that has sustained, connected and inspired Londoners ever since humans first set up camp on its banks.

In west London it is alive with canal boats and pleasure craft and is surrounded by thousands of trees and grand old parks. The centre of London presents a Thames that at times harks back to a Dickens novel and then screams out 21st century. Finally, the tidal vastness of the river's east section creates wide-sweeping views amongst the remnants of an empire built on the sea—an empire that called this river home.

The 184mi that makes up the Thames Path stretches from the Cotswolds almost to the sea in the east and is way-marked the entire way by an acorn symbol. The path makes up a huge chunk of the yearly mileage of most London runners by providing its own looping options (via the many bridges across the Thames) and also providing a link between parks. What follows are several route ideas for getting you started.

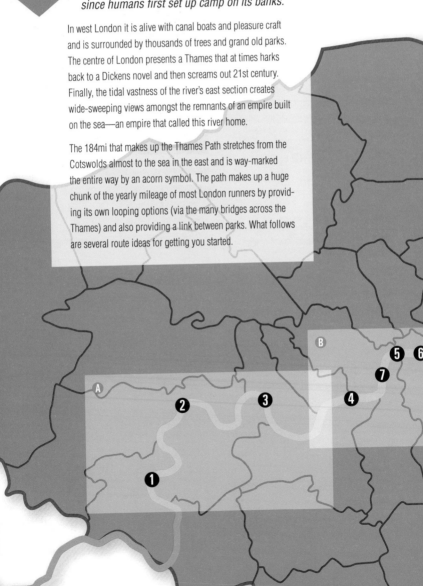

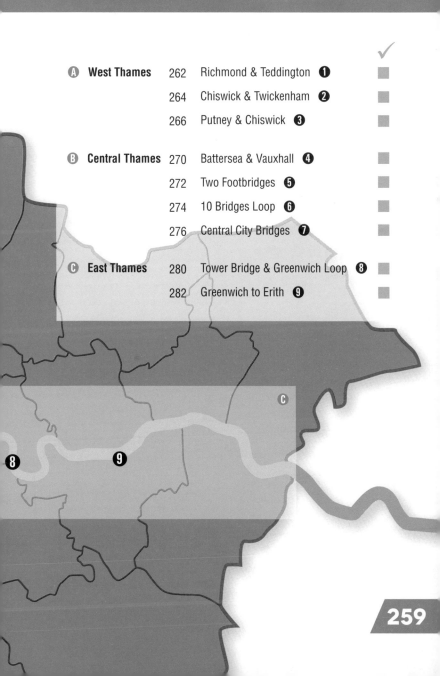

C

8 **9**

Richmond riverside.

THAMES PATH : WEST

Certainly the greenest stretch of the Thames Path in London, this western section also provides excellent links to the many mind-blowing parks that surround it.

MUST KNOW ▶ The Thames Path enters London from the west at Hampton Court on the north bank only. At Kingston-Upon-Thames it then swaps to the south bank (or east bank as it appears here). Then from Teddington Lock it follows both sides of the river right through to Battersea (which is where our central London Thames Path guide begins).

North Bank Detours (from W to E) | From Teddington the Thames Path follows streets a block or two back from the river until Orleans Gardens—about 2mi in total. Then again, north of Twickenham Bridge, the path follows a series of streets into the fine grounds of Syon Park.

Exiting the park into the centre of Brentford the path takes a zigzag route through a confusing industrial port section of the River Brent. For an easier option, cut this out by following Brentford High Street until you meet the Thames Path signs again.

In Chiswick, the path follows Hartington Road for about a kilometre (with a small break to explore the yacht basin) before returning to the river at Chiswick Bridge (and Duke's Meadows). It also cuts inland shortly east of here to navigate the rail lines.

In Fulham there are several short diversions inland, like going around Craven Cottage, the Fulham FC ground. Then just east of Putney Bridge is a 1mi diversion around The Hurlingham Club. Further east again are three more detours: 250m to skirt around a construction site (at the time of writing), 500m from Wandsworth Bridge to Sainsbury's, and 800m at Chelsea Harbour.

South Bank Detours | The riverside path along the south bank remains unbroken all the way from Kingston-Upon-Thames to Putney. Here it makes two short journeys inland between Putney Bridge and Wandsworth Park.

Shortly after Wandsworth Park there is a 900m diversion around a construction and industrial area (and to cross Bell Lane Creek). Finally there are three more short detour sections between Wandsworth and Battersea Bridges. On the whole, however, you'll find the running on this stretch quite pleasant with long periods on the water's edge.

1. Richmond & Teddington Loop
2. Chiswick & Twickenham Loop
3. Putney & Chiswick Loop

WEST THAMES FAST FACTS

- The Thames passes through seven counties in total. Can you name them all? Hint: The first is Gloucestershire.

- The Thames River Trust has created a twin relationship with the River Ganges (India) to develop new conservation strategies for both rivers.

- In 2006, Lewis Pugh became the first person to swim the river's length. It took 21 days.

- As well as the many shorter races you can run on the Thames Path, the Royal Parks Ultra and Thames Path 100 (miles) will give you your money's worth of riverside views.

THAMES PATH
Public Footpath

The River Thames from Strand on the Green.

Thames Path, Richmond.

Teddington Lock.

261

RICHMOND & TEDDINGTON LOOP

7.2mi / 11.6k

The homeward journey in particular (on the Richmond side of the river) is nothing short of spectacular: trees galore, plenty of soft gravel surfaces, palaces, and the ideal riverside spot for post-run refreshments at Richmond.

LOCATION ▶ Richmond Station, Richmond, TW9 (9.1mi W of central London)

MILE–BY–MILE ▶ Start: Richmond Station. Alternatively you can just as easily start from Twickenham, Strawberry Hill, or Teddington Stations (or at various car parks along the way), but as most runners will be coming from the city, we'll start at Richmond. Follow Kew Road south-west to make your way to Richmond Bridge.

0.5mi: Richmond Bridge. Cross the bridge and then drop down to the Thames Path to your left in order to follow the river south.

1.2mi: Marble Hill House Park. This inviting

Richmond Bridge.

park with several sports fields and some nice dirt and sealed trails could well entice you away from the riverbank for a short add on.

1.6mi: Orleans Park. This small park has toilets and a cafe if you need to make an early pit stop.

2.2mi: Diamond Jubilee Gardens. There are also toilets and a cafe here. From the Gardens the trail moves back from the river to follow Cross Deep (the street).

2.6mi: Radnor Gardens. Make a little detour through this small park before following Strawberry Vale south (which becomes Twickenham Rd and then Manor Rd).

3.7mi: Ferry Road. Turn left here and make your way across the Thames at Teddington Lock. Once across, turn left to follow the Thames Path north.

5.5mi: Ham House. Continue following this incredible riverside trail and take a moment amidst your puffing and panting to soak up your surrounds.

6.2mi: Buccleuch Gardens. The Thames Path passes through these riverside gardens that also host a set of toilets.

6.7mi: Richmond Bridge Again. Run under Richmond Bridge and on past the riverside bars and restaurants (unless you want refreshments). Then turn right at Water Lane (just before The White Cross). At the northern end of Water Lane, retrace your steps back to the rail station.

GETTING THERE ▶

Rail: Richmond Tube/National Rail Station (London Overground, District, & South West services).

Bus: 33, 65, 190, 337, 371, 391, 419, 490, 493, 969, H22, H37, R68, R70, & N22.

 ▶ A very special section of the Thames.

▶ The stretch of Thames Path near Teddington which is largely separated from the river is not particularly exciting (we're speaking relatively here of course).

Terrace Gardens, Richmond.

263

CHISWICK & TWICKENHAM LOOP

9.1mi / 14.6k

Cute cottages and riverside pubs, the impressive Syon Park, and then a long, uninterrupted, leafy trail on the south bank past Kew Gardens. Add to all this the 6.4mi turn-back option at Kew Bridge and there's very little not to like about this river loop.

You could equally use Kew Gardens, Gunnersbury, or Chiswick Stations as your start/finish point, or one of the many car parks on the course. There is also parking and showering facilities a few hundred metres up Chiswick High Road at the leisure centre.

LOCATION ▶ Kew Bridge Station, Hounslow, TW8 (7.7mi W of central London)

MILE-BY-MILE ▶ Start: Kew Bridge Station. Make your way south to the river. Turn right to follow the Thames Path west along the riverbank.

0.4mi: Watermans Park. After this riverside park the Thames Path takes a rather confusing zigzag route. Instead we'll just stick to Brentford High Street and run directly to the entrance of Syon Park (where we'll rejoin the Thames Path).

1.5mi: Syon Park Entrance. Turn left into the park entrance. There are toilets and a cafe near the garden centre. Once past Syon House, use the trail to your left as a softer under foot option.

2.2mi: Park Road. Turn left after exiting the park and be sure to carefully follow the Thames

Path signs over the next mile or so as you swap between streets and waterfront paths.

3mi: Isleworth Promenade. Back alongside the river, carry on past Richmond Lock to Twickenham Bridge. To reduce your run by 600m you could use Richmond Lock (closed at night) to cross the river. And to add on a mile, carry on to Richmond Bridge.

3.4mi: Twickenham Bridge. Cross the bridge and then turn left to follow the south bank towards Kew and Chiswick along this beautiful, tree-friendly trail.

6.1mi: Kew Bridge. Run under the bridge, following the riverside trail. Alternatively, cross Kew Bridge and head back to the station to complete a 6.4mi run.

7.3mi: Chiswick Bridge. Cross the Thames here to the north bank and then turn into Hartington Road (first on your left). Here the Thames Path ducks into the yacht basin for a quick diversion, but to keep it simple keep following Hartington—you'll meet the Thames Path signs shortly.

8.3mi: Riverside. You'll leave the road here and be reunited with the river, which will accompany you all the way back to Kew Bridge. Head back up to the station to complete your 9.1mi loop.

GETTING THERE ▶

Rail: Kew Bridge National Rail Station (South

West service).

Bus: 65, 237, 267, 391, 440, & N9.

👍▶ The soft gravel trail on the south bank from Twickenham Bridge to Chiswick Bridge.

👎▶ The Thames Path maze through Brentford means that following High Street is the best option.

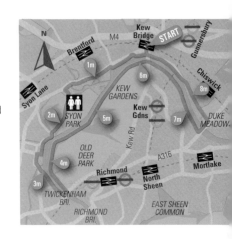

Strand-on-the-Green (north bank of the Thames), Chiswick.

PUTNEY & CHISWICK LOOP

8.4mi / 13.5k [!] [▦] [⊞] [🏃]

A section of river that holds much significance in rowing (Oxford vs Cambridge Boat Race) and football (you'll jog around the home of Fulham FC), but its sweeping views of the river, abundance of trees and bird life, and easy navigation make it great for running as well.

The leafy Thames Path near Barn Elms.

Sunset at Hammersmith.

LOCATION ▶ Putney Bridge Station, Hammersmith & Fulham, SW6 (5.0mi SW of central London)

MILE–BY–MILE ▶ Start: Putney Bridge Station.

Exit the station and follow the rail lines south to the river and to join the Thames Path. Start running west (to your right) to reach Putney Bridge. Run under the road to Bishop's Park.

0.3mi: Bishop's Park. You may want to fill in an extra mile or so in this exquisite riverside spot (which also has toilets). Otherwise continue on the river, making three short detours from its banks between here and the distinctively green Hammersmith suspension bridge.

2.9mi: Chiswick Mall. The Thames Path takes a step back from the river for a few hundred metres here and then follows an easy course alongside the Thames to Barnes Bridge.

4.3mi: Barnes Bridge. Cross this combined foot/rail bridge and begin your downstream journey on the south bank (heading east towards the city). Navigation from here couldn't be easier.

6.2mi: Hammersmith Bridge. The 10k point of your run. Continue following the river eastward.

7.9mi: Putney High Street. Back at Putney Bridge, cross the river and retrace your steps under the road and back to Putney Bridge Station to complete your 8.4mi run.

To add on, consider checking out Hurlingham

Park (700m further E from the station following the Thames Path), Wandsworth Park (700m further E from the S end of Putney Bridge—there are toilets here as well), Barnes Common (either as an add-on or a shortcut from Barnes Bridge to Putney) and of course Bishop's Park and neighbouring Fulham Palace Gardens.

GETTING THERE ▶

Rail: Putney Bridge Tube Station (District line).

Bus: 14, 22, 39, 74, 85, 93, 220, 265, 270, 414, 424, 430, 485, N22, & N74.

👍 ▶ Easy navigation and plenty of nearby diversions for longer runs.

👎 ▶ The adjacent Wetland Centre (south bank) is paid access only.

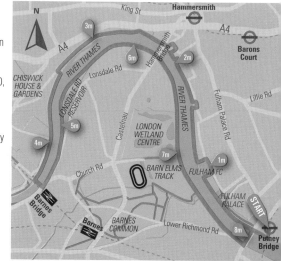

Hammersmith Bridge by night.

267

Millennium Bridge with St Paul's and the familiar sight of cranes adorning the skyline.

THAMES PATH : CENTRAL

Aside from the Royal Parks, the Thames Path is where central Londoners do most of their running. Being largely free from traffic and with wide sweeping vistas of the city, it's easy to understand why.

Bridge in the west through to Tower Bridge there are a total of 13 bridges spanning the river (that are navigable on foot). They combine to provide an abundance of looping options when running central London's Thames Path.

Surfaces are generally sealed, tiles or cobbles, so can become slippery when wet or icy. However, the main factor to be aware of is the foot traffic from tourists and commuters alike. Sometimes you'll be reduced to a walk (particularly near the London Eye and the Tower of London). Best way to avoid the crush is to run early mornings at the weekends.

There are plenty of toilets on this section of the Thames Path. However, many are paid so it can be wise to take a couple of 20p and 50p coins with you just in case.

North Bank Detours | The Thames follows the water's edge on the north bank all the way from Battersea Bridge until you reach the Houses of Parliament, which you skirt around before returning to the river.

Just after the Millennium Foot Bridge you'll a detour inland. Running from the west, you'll first encounter a restaurant hard up against the waterfront. It looks like you can carry on through here, but obey the Thames Path signs (it's just a dead end past the restaurant) and head inland on Broken Wharf. Then turn right and right again (on to Queenhithe) and you will be back on the riverbank.

South Bank Detours | The first diversion from the water on the south bank starts at the city end of Battersea Park where the Thames Path avoids the monolithic Bat-

tersea Power Station. This detour follows streets through an industrial area before returning to the river about 1km (0.6mi) later— easily the most unpleasant portion of the central London Thames Path.

The other detour is just after Southwark Bridge and is 600m long. The Thames Path heads south just before the Cannon Street rail lines, and then heads under those lines via Clink Street. At the Golden Hinde turn right, then turn left on to Montague Close, which will take you under London Bridge (the A3). 100m after exiting the tunnel follow the Thames Path sign left along the walkway back to the river.

4. Battersea & Vauxhall Loop
5. Two Footbridges Loop
6. 10 Bridges
7. Central City Bridges Matrix

CENTRAL THAMES FAST FACTS

- The distinctive bends in the river were used by WWII pilots to navigate during blackouts.

- In 1722, the old London Bridge became so congested that the mayor instigated the keep left rule to sort out the chaos on the roads. The rule has stuck ever since.

- There is a theory that the river got its name from the Sanskrit (ancient Indian) word "Tamasa", which means "dark water", and somehow that phrase spread amongst the Celts all the way from India to Britain.

- In 1858, Parliament was suspended because of the almighty stench wafting from untreated sewage in the river.

- It is far cleaner now with seals and dolphins regularly visiting the Thames estuary and occasionally venturing upstream (even as far as Waterloo Bridge).

BATTERSEA & VAUXHALL BRIDGES LOOP

5.4mi / 8.7k

An easy 5mi loop featuring beautiful bridges, the Battersea Power Station, and the riverside repose of Battersea Park.

LOCATION ▶ Vauxhall Station, Lambeth, SW8 (2.0mi S of central London)

MILE–BY–MILE ▶ **Start: Vauxhall Tube Station.** Cross the river at Vauxhall Bridge. Turn left to follow the Thames Path west on the north bank (firstly on a path next to the river and then on Grosvenor Rd).

0.8mi: Grosvenor meets the Thames. Once back to the river you'll enjoy a beautiful stretch of pathway with trees lining the road and great

views of the 1873 Albert and the 1937 Chelsea suspension bridges. At Chelsea Bridge you'll need to wait at the lights to cross the road, with there being no foot tunnel.

2.3mi: Battersea Bridge. Cross the river here, then turn left to follow the Thames Path east.

2.7mi: Albert Bridge. Cross the road and enter Battersea Park. At the city end of the park follow the Thames Path signs south to exit the park at its southeast corner.

3.9mi: Queen's Circus. Follow the signage around the back of the power station, through a couple of industrial streets and then back to the river.

Albert Bridge with Battersea Park and the disused power station.

5.1mi: Nine Elms Lane. Follow the river back to Vauxhall Bridge then turn right to find the station—completing the 5.3mi loop.

GETTING THERE ▶

Rail: Vauxhall Tube/National Rail Station (Victoria line & South West service).

Bus: 2, 36, 77, 87, 88, 156, 185, 196, 344, & 436.

👍▶ This is a stretch of river that oozes history, beauty and grandeur at every bend.

👎▶ The section behind the Battersea Power Station is this run's only blemish.

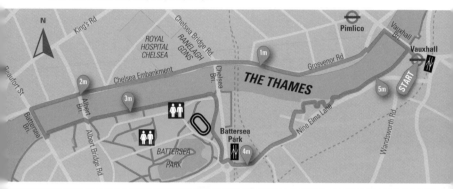

Chelsea from Battersea Bridge.

Millennium Bridge offers wonderful views and, if you get it at the right time, can be surprisingly absent of tourists and commuters.

TWO FOOTBRIDGES LOOP

2.7mi / 4.2k

Part of the attraction of the Thames Path is avoiding running near roads, and this loop captures that appeal perfectly by utilising two footbridges (Golden Jubilee and Millennium). It also passes some of London's most iconic buildings in just under 3mi.

LOCATION ▶ Temple Station, Westminster, WC2R (0.3mi E of central London)

MILE-BY-MILE ▶ Start: Temple Station. Exit the station and cross the road to be on the riverbank. Begin running west (clockwise) along the footpath. (You could also start this run from any number of other stations or locations on the banks of the Thames.)

0.5mi: Golden Jubilee Bridges. The second bridge you'll reach is the combo of Golden Jubilee foot bridges and the Hungerford rail bridge. Use the second (southern most) of the two Golden Jubilee bridges to reach the Southbank.

0.8mi: Southbank. Now begin heading east following the uninterrupted water's edge path.

1.8mi: Millennium Bridge. The dominating visage of the Tate Modern is the signal that it's time to cross back to the north bank, this time using the Millennium footbridge.

2mi: North Bank. Take the stairs at the end of the bridge back down to the Thames Path and start heading west again.

2.7mi: Temple Station. Cross Victoria Embankment to reach the station. Alternatively, why not do another lap?

GETTING THERE ▶

Rail: Temple Tube Station (Circle & District services).

👍▶ Visitors will definitely want to bring a camera—this is running selfie central.

👎▶ Tourists and commuting pedestrians often bring runners to a stand still, so run early in the morning..

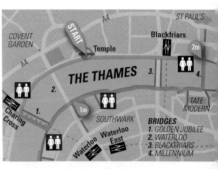

The iconic dome of St Paul's Cathedral.

273

10 BRIDGES: VAUXHALL TO TOWER & BACK

9.4mi / 15.0k

This run can be started from any of the several tube stations along the Thames. It crosses the river at every second bridge, crossing 10 bridges in total (as you may have already deciphered from the name) but each bridge only once.

LOCATION ▶ Vauxhall Station, Lambeth, SW8 (2.0mi S of central London)

MILE–BY–MILE ▶ Start: Vauxhall Station. Head to the Thames and turn right, running northwest along the south riverbank.

0.7mi: Lambeth Bridge. Head straight on,

remembering that you're crossing only every second bridge that you encounter.

1.1mi: Westminster Bridge. To avoid crossing the road later, go under the tunnel and use the stairs to get on to the bridge. Cross the river and continue in the same heading on the north bank.

2.0mi: Waterloo Bridge. Cross the road and use the stairs to get on to the bridge. Cross the river to carry on running on the south bank.

3.1mi: Millennium Bridge. Use this stunning footbridge to make your way back to the north bank and continue running east.

3.9mi: London Bridge. Run under the bridge and then take the stairs up to road level and cross to the south bank (use the stairs to get back down to the river).

4.7mi: Tower Bridge. The most eastern point of your run. Cross back to the north bank and then begin following the Thames Path westward, past the Tower of London.

5.8mi: Southwark

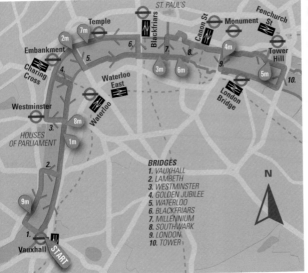

BRIDGES
1. VAUXHALL
2. LAMBETH
3. WESTMINSTER
4. GOLDEN JUBILEE
5. WATERLOO
6. BLACKFRIARS
7. MILLENNIUM
8. SOUTHWARK
9. LONDON
10. TOWER

London Eye, Westminster Bridge and the Houses of Parliament.

Bridge. Cross over again. This is your sixth bridge.

6.4mi: Blackfriars Bridge. Head under the bridge and then use the stairs on its west side to get up to street level and cross to the north bank.

7.5mi: Golden Jubilee Bridges. Use either of the two footbridges to cross back to the south bank.

8.4mi: Lambeth Bridge. Head under the bridge and come up on the left hand side of the road. Cross over to the north bank for the final time.

9.1mi: Vauxhall Bridge. Make one last crossing of the Thames to find your way back to Vauxhall Station, 9.3mi later.

GETTING THERE▸

Rail: Vauxhall Tube/National Rail Station (Victoria line & South West service).

Bus: 2, 36, 77, 87, 88, 156, 185, 196, 344, 360, & 436.

👍▸ Views galore and a lot of distance covered in a relatively small area.

👎▸ Busy foot traffic and not the best run for getting into your rhythm.

This run is another excuse to cross this funky bridge.

275

CENTRAL CITY BRIDGES

The beauty of the inner city Thames Path is its huge array of bridges and the limitless potential for creating your own favourite bridge-to-bridge loops.

In order for you to create these loops or figures-of-eight, use the table opposite to judge approximate distances for looping any two par-

ticular bridges together. (Note: Stairs, crossings and foot traffic will affect the actual distances that you travel.)

Alternatively, use the table to construct runs of a specific distance. For example, to do a 6mi run from London Bridge run a loop to Westminster Bridge and back (4.4mi) and then loop east out to Tower Bridge (1.6mi) and back.

London's central city bridges serve to connect the city's mosaic of the old, the new and the futuristic.

TOWER	LONDON	SOUTHWARK	MILLENNIUM	BLACKFRIARS	WATERLOO	GOLDEN JUBILEE (STH)	WESTMINSTER	LAMBETH	VAUXHALL	BRIDGE — Loop distance in miles / *Loop distance in kilometres*
7.6 *12.3*	**6.5** *10.5*	**5.8** *9.3*	**5.3** *8.5*	**4.7** *7.6*	**3.7** *6.0*	**3.2** *5.2*	**2.4** *3.9*	**1.4** *2.3*	/	VAUXHALL
6.5 *10.5*	**5.4** *8.7*	**4.7** *7.5*	**4.2** *6.7*	**3.6** *5.8*	**2.6** *4.2*	**2.1** *3.4*	**1.3** *2.1*	/	**1.4** *2.3*	LAMBETH
5.5 *8.9*	**4.4** *7.1*	**3.8** *5.9*	**3.3** *5.1*	**2.7** *4.3*	**1.6** *2.6*	**1.1** *1.8*	/	**1.3** *2.1*	**2.4** *3.9*	WESTMINSTER
5.0 *8.0*	**3.9** *6.2*	**3.2** *5.1*	**2.6** *4.2*	**2.1** *3.3*	**1.1** *1.7*	/	**1.1** *1.8*	**2.1** *3.4*	**3.2** *5.2*	GOLDEN JUBILEE (STH)
4.5 *7.3*	**3.5** *5.6*	**2.7** *4.4*	**2.1** *3.4*	**1.6** *2.6*	/	**1.1** *1.7*	**1.6** *2.6*	**2.6** *4.2*	**3.7** *6.0*	WATERLOO
3.2 *5.2*	**2.2** *3.5*	**1.4** *2.3*	**0.9** *1.5*	/	**1.6** *2.6*	**2.1** *3.3*	**2.7** *4.3*	**3.6** *5.8*	**4.7** *7.6*	BLACKFRIARS
2.7 *4.5*	**1.7** *2.7*	**0.9** *1.5*	/	**0.9** *1.5*	**2.1** *3.4*	**2.6** *4.2*	**3.3** *5.1*	**4.2** *6.7*	**5.3** *8.5*	MILLENNIUM
2.2 *3.5*	**1.1** *1.8*	/	**0.9** *1.5*	**1.4** *2.3*	**2.7** *4.4*	**3.2** *5.1*	**3.8** *5.9*	**4.7** *7.5*	**5.8** *9.3*	SOUTHWARK
1.6 *2.6*	/	**1.1** *1.8*	**1.7** *2.7*	**2.2** *3.5*	**3.5** *5.6*	**3.9** *6.2*	**4.4** *7.1*	**5.4** *8.7*	**6.5** *10.5*	LONDON
/	**1.6** *2.6*	**2.2** *3.5*	**2.7** *4.5*	**3.2** *5.2*	**4.5** *7.3*	**5.0** *8.0*	**5.5** *8.9*	**6.5** *10.5*	**7.6** *12.3*	TOWER

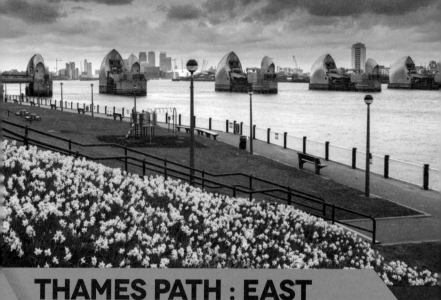

Thames Barrier Park (north bank).

THAMES PATH : EAST

With several notable exceptions, the Thames Path east of Tower Bridge is more industrial and exposed than its much greener counterparts further west. However, there is still plenty of good running to be had and its comparative solitude can make settling into your running rhythm much easier.

MUST KNOW ▶ The Thames Path carries on from Tower Bridge on both the north and south banks. However, the northern path comes to an end at the Greenwich Foot Tunnel (which connects to the south bank Thames Path) at the southern tip of the Isle of Dogs (Island Gardens).

From here the singular southern Thames Path carries on all the way around the O2 Arena, past the Thames Barrier and Woolwich Arsenal to Erith. East of the Thames Barrier the way-markers switch from the acorn symbol to a Thames barge symbol.

Back on the north bank, you can also follow the East Extension from the Island Gardens to East India Docks (follow the barge symbol here again). There are plans to extend the north bank Thames Path further east past the Royal Docks.

North Bank Detours (from W to E) | Between Tower Bridge and Canary Wharf there's plenty of cutting to and from the riverbank. It pays to keep your wits about you to make sure you spot the Thames Path signs.

Tower Bridge from the south bank.

From Canary Wharf you're mostly running with apartment blocks on one side and the tidal Thames on the other. There are however two sections, the first 800m long and the second for 300m, where you'll be running on streets a block back from the river. The second of these diversions takes you to Island Gardens where you'll find the 400m foot tunnel (open at all times) under the river to Greenwich.

South Bank Detours | The section from Tower Bridge to Greenwich, like the north bank, navigates many docks, waterways, and riverfront properties. So, again, you need to stay alert to spot signs and change directions often. Then, about 2mi before you reach Greenwich, there's a larger 1mi diversion from the river.

From Greenwich until you reach Erith the path is relatively straightforward, although there are a lot of industrial and construction zones, some of which may have temporary diversions and don't make for the most scenic running terrain.

8. Tower Bridge & Greenwich Loop
9. Greenwich to Erith (south bank)

EAST THAMES FAST FACTS

- 1.25 million Londoners live at risk from the Thames flooding. The Thames Barrier (opened in 1982) helps protect them.

- In 1545, Henry VIII established an ammunitions store at Woolwich. By WWI the Royal Arsenal reached its height, employing 80,000 ordnance workers.

- The O2 Arena has a walkway going over it, but it's not for running, you'll need a harness and a spare £33.

St Saviour's Dock, Bermondsey.

TOWER BRIDGE & GREENWICH LOOP

11.4mi / 18.3k

A longer run through the former industrial ports of east London that are now gradually becoming fashionable apartments and office blocks. For most of the way on this anti-clockwise loop the Thames Path takes a haphazard course, so keep a keen eye out for way-markers.

LOCATION ▸ Wapping Station, Tower Hamlets, E1W (3.2mi E of central London).

MILE-BY-MILE ▶ Start: Wapping

Station. Exit the station and turn left to follow the Thames Path west on Wapping High Street.

1.1mi: Tower Bridge. Cross this iconic bridge and then begin heading east along the Thames Path through the twisting ports and passageways of Bermondsey.

2.3mi: King's Stairs Gardens. This small waterfront park serves as an entrance towards Southwark Park (see p.48) which you can link through to nearby Greenland Dock as an alternative to the Thames Path. Otherwise keep following the zigzagging nature of the riverside way-markers.

4.3mi: Surrey Docks Farm. Here you are given two options. If it's between 10am and 5pm you'll be able to run through the farm. But if it's closed there's a short detour around it.

5.4mi: Pepys Park. This park marks the start of a large 1mi diversion inland that passes through several small parks and twisting streets.

7.1mi: Greenwich Tunnel. When you reach the Cutty Sark (the old ship in a glass house) look to your left and you'll find the entrance way to the Greenwich Foot Tunnel. Use it to cross under the Thames. When you pop up in the Isle of Dogs, follow the Thames Path signs to your left and begin your westward journey home.

9.3mi: Canary Wharf. At publication there was a large construction area that you need to run around where Canary Wharf meets the Thames.

10.3mi: Limehouse Basin. From this dock there are two canals (Regent's Canal, see p.58; and Limehouse Cut, see p.239) that head north and are ideal for adding on extra miles.

10.9mi: Shadwell Basin. You're almost home, just a little more twisting and turning through

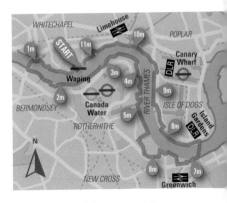

east London streets before you complete your 11.4mi.

GETTING THERE ▶

Rail: Wapping Station (London Overground).

Bus: 100 & D3.

👍▶ At times a scene from a Dickens novel and at other times a bustling financial district.

👎▶ A lot of twisting around narrow, cobbled streets (watch your footing when it is wet or icy).

GREENWICH TO ERITH

13.3mi / **21.4**k 🗂 🔲 🗂 🏃 ❓

Soak up the wide open skies of the tidal Thames of east London, from Royal Greenwich to industrial Erith, in one big point-to-point run. Catch the train home or, for the crazy, clock up a solid 27mi out-and-back.

LOCATION ▶ Greenwich Station, Greenwich, SE10 (5.8mi SE of central London).

MILE–BY–MILE ▶ Start: Greenwich Station. Exit the station onto Greenwich High Road, head to your left (north) and follow this street as it becomes Evelyn Street and then Greenwich Church Street. You'll soon reach the Cutty Sark and the Thames Path.

0.5mi: Cutty Sark. There are toilets here if needed, otherwise follow the Thames Path signage east, past the Naval College.

1.0mi: Lovell's Wharf. Major construction works are common between here and the O2. Lovell's Wharf is one spot that may have a diversion.

2.7mi: The O2. Enjoy the views over the water to Canary Wharf, east toward the Emirates Air Line, and of course south to the mega structure itself that is the O2.

4.7mi: Thames Barrier. This is the largest moveable flood protection system in the world. It also marks the official end of the Thames Path, however, the path continues along the extension to Erith swapping the acorn symbol for a barge on its signage. There is a 0.9mi diversion here that runs south to Woolwich Road and then left onto Ruston Road and back to the river.

6.1mi: Woolwich Foot Tunnel. This (along with the free ferry) provides an option to the north bank if you fancy following the roads back to the Greenwich Foot Tunnel.

6.5mi: Woolwich Arsenal. From here the navigation is nice and simple, just follow the river path all the way around to Erith. Keep in mind that this stretch can be quite lonely so company is always a good idea.

9.2mi: Thamesmead. This is one of the start points of the Green Chain that connects much of

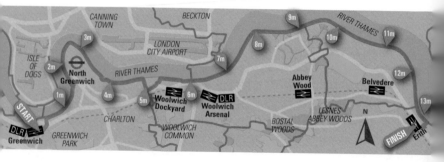

south east London's green spaces (see p.98). It makes a nice alternative inland route to Erith via the ruins and woods of Lesnes Abbey.

13.1mi: Riverside Gardens, Erith. When you reach the gardens look for the signage directing you inland to Erith Station (via Stonewood Rd, then under Bronze Age Way). You'll have run 13.3mi by the time you're at the station (which has toilets). From here you can catch the South-eastern back to Greenwich.

Options | You can retrace your steps back to Greenwich for an epic long run (perhaps opting for the alternative route back to Thamesmead via Lesnes Abbey on the Green Chain). Your other super long run option is to link this run with the Cray Riverway (see p.92 for details) at Erith.

GETTING THERE ▶

Rail: Greenwich National Rail Station (South-eastern & DLR services).

Bus: 177, 180, 199, & 386.

👍 ▶ A great stretch of river to clock up uninterrupted miles for marathon training.

👎 ▶ Some sections are exposed to the wind, are industrial or are lonely ... or all of the above.

The roomy vistas of the eastern reaches of the Thames Path.

283

LOCAL LEGENDS

RUNNING PROFILES

A BUSHY PARK TALE:
PAUL SINTON-HEWITT

It all started with a midlife crisis-inspired return to marathon running. Over-enthusiasm in the running led to an injury, which led to Saturdays spent wondering how to remain involved with running. Thus, began parkrun—probably the biggest organised running movement ever.

"This is the best job in the world. The best company I've ever worked for. The best people I've ever worked alongside. I'm really lucky. I never planned it," says Paul of the organisation he started on the back of a running injury.

It's funny how life can work like that; lemons turned into lemonade. parkrun is certainly one of those classic lemonade stories. Paul's own experience of birthing the organisation from the ashes of his marathon dreams is reflected in officialdom's initial resistance against parkrun, followed by an absolute embrace of the movement. parkrun has broken the mould of traditional running organisations and found an unlikely common ground between competitive and social running—a common ground that is booming.

We caught up with Paul to dig a little deeper into this worldwide running phenomenon that started right here in London's very own Bushy Park.

From one parkrun back in 2004, there are now over 600 around the world (and growing every week). What has this growth been like from your perspective?

Everything has been exponential. Even if you take the first year at Bushy parkrun, the growth was exponential. We began with 13 runners and one year later, 75. One year later again there were two parkruns. No matter what period you look at we've had an exponential curve on the number of events, on the number of people registering, on the number of PBs, you name it. It's quite phenomenal.

Jim [one of the original core group] approached me at some time in the second year saying this is something that people really want. We received feedback from people saying, "This is just brilliant. I'm not an athlete, I don't want to join a club but you make it possible for me to run. I'm getting fitter." Towards the end of 2006 Jim said, "Let's start another parkrun." So I worked on how to duplicate the parkrun experience.

Our second parkrun was in Wimbledon. We gave ourselves 12 weeks to find and establish a team. The good thing was it took six weeks to have a

285

LOCAL LEGENDS

completely self-sufficient team. So we had the basis for a model that we could cookie cut. In 2007 we went from one event to seven. Seven became 15 a year later. 15 became 35 a year later. And the rest is history.

With 46 parkruns within the M25 (so far), what is it about Londoners and parkrun?
London is a special case. Boris Johnson, the mayor, approached us and asked us to specifically create a parkrun in every borough. He invested to get them started. So London is the only place that we find the parks and then look for the volunteers before we get going. Whereas everywhere else in the country the model is organic where the volunteers approach us with requests to start a parkrun.

If I want to start a parkrun, what do I do?
There are usually three things required to start a parkrun. One is the land: a pleasant and safe public space. Another is the team: volunteers who understand the ethic of parkrun. And finally there needs to be some investment, a one-off charge of £3000 (covers start-up costs).

And who pays that one-off bill?
Most often, the council funds the development of a parkrun. This investment is an excellent way for local government to invest in their community and to improve health and wellbeing. It is rare but we occasionally receive these funds from a local benefactor and occasionally local enterprise comes together to make the investment.

When the council builds a fitness park they can make anecdotal references as to whether the park is useful or not. When they deliver a parkrun there is a record of everyone who took part, providing tangible evidence that their investment is worthwhile.

And is volunteering a way runners can contribute to the otherwise free event?
It all starts and finishes with the volunteers. I mean that's what I was for the first four years of parkrun [before becoming an employee in the organisation]. Everything I did I did for this community, there was no personal reward apart from the warm feeling in my heart knowing that I'm doing something right.

There are loads of people who volunteer hundreds of times. And then there are some people who volunteer once or twice. We ask folks to volunteer three times a year. We see this as their contribution to their local community.

Volunteering offers its own wonderful reward. Being a part of this local community is rather special. We don't try to force people to do this; it's a voluntary thing. We also don't treat them any differently where they have not volunteered. parkrun was created for people to run. While parkrun is not really about volunteering, we have found over the years that this is a fundamental aspect of our movement and without the volunteers there would be no running.

We are in the midst of a running renaissance. Has parkrun contributed to this revival?
The reality is that running is cheap and every-

PARKRUN FAST FACTS

- Started in October 2004 at Bushy Park, London.
- Seven parkrun locations by 2007.
- Female record is held by Hannah Walker (15:55) at St Albans.
- Male record is held by Andrew Baddeley (13:48) at Bushy Park.
- Over 474 events worldwide (as at December 2014) and growing weekly.

body's suffering financially. People are learning that running and walking are excellent ways to stay fit. And it's the cheapest and most accessible form of sport available.

So I wouldn't put it down to parkrun. We are a contributor because we make it possible for people to run with others instead of on their own and we record these activities. We're not revolutionary; we're just really simple, really easy, really fun-based community activity.

You encountered some resistance from others in the running world in the early days. What was that like?
When I started parkrun there was a natural aggression from the established running clubs and from the governing bodies. Now that's mostly changed.

In 2007 an official from a club up north went public in a newspaper saying that parkrun should be shut down, that it's not doing the right thing. He had so many letters back to the newspaper [from people supporting parkrun], it caused an absolute furore across the whole country, just slating him.

I talked to the chairman of the club and we resolved the differences. But the key thing is that the governing body stepped in and they've been going around the whole country talking about how parkrun fits. And to be honest now the clubs are coming to us saying, "We want parkrun." The evidence is that parkrun helps clubs to grow.

So where in the running landscape does parkrun sit? We fill the lower two thirds of the triangle. If you have the elite runners at the top, just below them you have your club runners, and below them you have the rest of us—joggers and walkers. parkrun is helping to fill the

Bushy Park parkrun on a rather brisk morning (not a day for a PB).
Photo: David Rowe Photography / parkrun

LOCAL LEGENDS

bottom of the triangle, which is filtering up into the clubs.

And how does parkrun affect other paid races (especially 5k events)?

The blatant answer to your question is that we make it very difficult for the regular 5k race. We don't intentionally do it, but if paid 5k races have to change because parkrun makes it possible for loads of people to run a 5k every week, then so be it. I don't think people should have to pay to run a 5k.

I've had conversations with race directors and I usually tell them to make it worthwhile for people to pay £15 to run a 5k. That's the first thing. The second thing is that many of the larger races associated with parkruns are selling out much faster than they ever did before. And it's a whole new audience participating.

The third effect is that where parkrun is established we have noticed that the local clubs have grown as a result of our association. And that is a fact. This is what we have recorded.

What excites you about working in parkrun?

parkrun is a real community. We are not a virtual community. We're a bunch of real people, staff, volunteers and participants. We make real bonds with each other in the process of getting healthier. It's not like Facebook or other virtual communities; this is about real people and I believe that is very valuable. It's incredible.

We get feedback from people every week that we are changing their lives.

Congratulations on being awarded the CBE, it's hugely deserved but did you see it coming? Can you describe the moment

Bushy Park has become the Mecca of parkrun. A must-run for any parkrun enthusiast.
Photo: David Rowe Photography / parkrun

Early autumn at Bush Park parkrun—perfect running conditions.
Photo: David Rowe Photography / parkrun

when that letter arrived in the mail?

I received a letter a month before the official birthday (14 May 2014). I wasn't expecting it and didn't pay any attention to it for a few days. It lay in the pile of invoices which I usually only open on a Wednesday. I was surprised and delighted to be recognised in this way. It's an honour to represent every parkrunner who contributed to our success. It's a kind of recognition that our movement is worthy and that we are being successful.

So where next for parkrun?

We're a not-for-profit organisation, so we're never going to be wealthy. And whatever we start we must be able to see through. So I've got to be careful about the growth. We're in it for the long-term.

However, my aspirations are that I would like every person in the world to know what parkrun is and be able to experience it. Nothing grander than that. There are no grand schemes, I'm not a Zuckerberg and never will be. I'm not looking for any public recognition or anything like that. What we're doing is real, and we're doing what any charity out there is doing. That's how I see it. ■ **www.parkrun.com**

PAUL'S TOP 3 LONDON RUNNING SPOTS ▸

3. Wanstead & Wimbledon | Equal third between Wanstead and Wimbledon Common.

2. Richmond Park | This is even more attractive. It has undulations and is a little more wild. It has everything you'd want in a running experience.

1. Bushy Park | Without any shadow of a doubt. You can break it into four or five different runs or you can do the whole thing. It's flat and the place I run in most frequently.

TAMING THE MARATHON: SCOTT OVERALL

In 2011 people were scratching their heads wondering who, if anyone, would step up as a serious marathon contender for the 2012 London Olympics. No Brit had run the A-standard of sub-2:12 since Tomas Abyu ran 2:10 way back in 2007. And few would've picked the then 5k specialist and proud Londoner, Scott Overall, to step up to the plate.

In Berlin, he sent worldwide message boards scrambling and search engines firing when he surprised everyone in his marathon debut. That day he ran 2:10:55 for an impressive fifth place (first non-Kenyan), stamping his ticket to run in a home Olympic Games.

We caught up with him to hear what it takes for a London kid to make it to an Olympic marathon.

How did this running gig start?

At secondary school I was in Twickenham, which is a big rugby area. I couldn't really play rugby so the other sports on offer were cross-country and in the summer, track. So I started running for the school. I was decent enough and that lead to joining a local athletics club and I progressed from there.

Kids often have dreams of making it big in sport, but when did your running dreams start coming in to the realms of possibility?

Probably not until I was 17 or 18. I was always ranked around the top ten as a junior and when I was 14 or 15 I started training with Mo Farah. Me and him were in the same club and trained together for years. Having a training partner like that can do wonders.

In 2004 you took a running scholarship at Butler University, Indiana. What effect did that have on your running career?

It was a new opportunity to study abroad and have a new experience. Going out there really changed my view of running and how hard you have to train to compete with the best guys.

The standard of [USA] college athletics is massive. It's a lot better than it is here. You have to run fast to compete. It definitely progressed me and helped me a lot more than it would have if I stayed in England.

And you stayed on in the States to train post–College?

Yeah, I finished Butler in 2007 and my coach Robert Chapman was setting up a post-collegiate training group in Bloomington, Indiana. So I stayed out there training trying to qualify for the Olympics the following year. That next year, in 2008, I ran 13:28 in the 5k, which was a B-standard. I didn't go to Beijing, but did go to the World Indoors in 2010 where I ran the 3k.

So when did this good 5k runner start thinking he could be an A–standard marathon runner?

In 2011 I was doing everything that I had previ-

SCOTT'S RUNNING STATS

Achievements

2009 5000m UK Champion; Multiple NCAA All-American (US College); 2014 Reading Half Marathon winner; 2014 Dublin Rock n Roll Half Marathon winner.

Personal Bests

Mile: 3:58.61 (indoors)
5000m: 13:28.33
10k: 28:49
Half Marathon: 1:01:25
Marathon: 2:10:55

Scott settling into his rhythm in the 2012 London Olympic Marathon.

ously done. Going up to Flagstaff every year training [at altitude] to run a 5k or 10k on the track. I ran 13:28 in 2008 and that's still my PB now so I didn't seem to get much quicker.

That year I went to Flagstaff in April with the aim of running a fast 5k in either Mt Sac or Stanford. But that didn't happen even though my training was going great. So then they had a half marathon in Indianapolis a week after Stanford and I decided to do it. I did and I ran 63:20.

That was off 5k training, so I thought if I actually trained for the half marathon and marathon I could actually run a bit quicker.

So I came back to the UK in June of 2011 and sat down with Dave Bedford about my ideas of running the marathon. Berlin was looking like the next opportunity for a very fast marathon and a decided to do that.

Going into Berlin were you thinking an Olympic qualifier was on the cards? Or were you just out to race for a place?
The way the training had gone I thought I was in shape to run 2:12. Berlin was simply to qualify for the Olympics and that's all I was thinking about. I didn't know I had finished fifth until someone told me. To me the position didn't matter so long as I ran the time.

And did you have to alter your training much from a 5k–focus to the marathon?
I've always been fairly high mileage, around 90 to 100 miles per week. So I didn't have to change a lot to be honest. Obviously the long runs got longer and tempos got a bit longer as well, doing that more marathon specific work.

Going into Berlin I thought I was in shape but having never done a marathon before you never know what's going to happen. I guess it was a good thing to go into it a bit naïve really. I didn't

know what to expect.

That naivety obviously worked and you are now an Olympian. What does the future hold for Scott Overall? The British marathon record?
I can definitely go quicker in the marathon. That 2:07 [GB record] is very good and obviously that shows because it was set quite a few years ago now. So that's definitely a target for me.

You've trained all over the world, how does London compare?
I grew up in the Teddington and Twickenham area in southwest London. It's probably one of the best places around the world that I've trained. You've got the variety of Bushy Park, Richmond Park, Home Park, and further afield you've got Wimbledon Common as well. You're kind of spoilt for places to run and of course you've got the track as well at St Mary's.

People ask "Do you live in London?" and they expect you to run in the city, but that's far from the case really. Bushy Park is great, especially on a summer's day, and it's also flat. In the summer months a lot of the Kenyans and the Australians come out here. And if you want to test yourself a bit more Richmond Park is very undulating.

As a marathon runner, what other places would you recommend fitting in those long sessions in?
Using the river is a way you can get more mileage. Now you can go out east along the river and up towards the Olympic Stadium or you can come west and enter Richmond Park via the river. The river is almost traffic free and you can just follow it in whichever way you want to go. Otherwise laps of Hyde Park and St James's Park.

OLYMPIC RECAP ▸

Unfortunately, the Olympics didn't pan out as planned for Scott. He ran the first half conservatively (which of course is a relative term when you're hitting 13.1mi in 65:30) and was sitting in a handy 29th place, just one-minute back from 10th—ready to strike as planned.

However, the heat and thirst got to him and he hit the proverbial wall at mile 18, going from running 15.xx-minute splits for 5k to between 18 and 20 minutes. He blogged later saying, "I had no energy left and I was just focusing on putting one foot in front of the other and getting to the finish line. … it's a tough pill to swallow knowing this has been my target for the past 8 months. … Still, I live to fight again, and I will be back from this."

Despite his obvious disappointment, he picked himself up to look on the bright side of it: "It truly is a once in a lifetime opportunity to compete in a home Olympics, and regardless of the result, one thing is for sure: no one can take away the fact that every athlete who competed is now an Olympian.

"… This time last year I had never even run a marathon and now I have run the Berlin and Olympic Marathons. I still have high aims for what I want to do. I can get this marathon business down. I can run faster and I will run faster."

Inspiring stuff. ■

www.scottoverall.com

SCOTT'S TOP 3 LONDON RUNNING SPOTS ▸

3. Bushy Park

2. Richmond Park

1. Home Park (Hampton Court Park)

293

Scott takes charge early in the Bupa 10k.

FROM MOUNTAINS TO MONDO TRACKS: JULIA BLEASDALE

A born-and-bred Londoner, Julia shares some of her thoughts and fondest memories of running in her hometown—everything from a double top-eight finish at the 2012 Olympics to traversing mountains and the joy of jogging through London's parks.

You really stamped your mark on world distance running at the 2012 Olympics, finishing eighth in both the 5000m and 10,000m [Julia and teammate Jo Pavey were the first non–Africans in both races], how did you enjoy your first Olympics?

It was a phenomenal experience being in front of a home crowd. It was my first major championship really so it was incredibly special. But it was also very intense. I was racing three times within eight days and covering 50 laps of the track in total.

I'd spent the last year building towards the Olympic Games, always with the aim of peaking at the right time in August. So I got to the Olympic Village knowing I was 100 per cent ready to go.

It was great having Jo Pavey as company because she had been there and done that before. I was also relatively unknown so there were no expectations; I didn't feel any weight on my shoulders.

In fact they didn't introduce me to the crowd. They introduced Jo because she's a well-known name and when everyone cheered for Jo I took on board some of that energy and sound. I was raring to go.

With such massive support, was it tricky keeping a clear head to focus on that first race?

The 10,000m is about 30 minutes of running so you've got to control your emotions and be sensible about it. It's a long race.

It was a matter of settling in. At times I thought, "Wow this is the Olympic Games and listen to that noise." And at other times I felt, "Well this is just another race." Fortunately it all went incredibly well. I had a great run and had a Mexican wave following me around the track.

After finishing the 10k it was lovely to do that lap with Jo thanking the crowd for their immense support.

Then just a few days later you had the 5k. How did your recovery go?

After the 10k, running 25 laps, you always come off it a little bit sore. So I spent a lot of time in the medical centre with the British team trying to sort out my calves.

It was great to have the opportunity to double up and experience the stadium as much as possible. The noise of that 5k heat when I was kind of in the lead at the last 100 was the loudest I'd heard in the stadium. It was a deafening, ear-ringing sound. You feel a surge of energy going through you when you hear it. I hope I'll experience it again one day.

Your Olympics results surprised many, did you surprise yourself?

Well, I was in Melbourne on New Year's Day [2012] and I watched the sunrise and knew that 2012 would be a very special year.

At that point I wasn't thinking top eight because you've got to do the systematic steps to get there. First, it's running the qualifying time, then it's qualifying, and then it's getting to the start line injury free. If you can get to there then things become possible.

Rather than jumping three steps you've got to do it step-by-step. That's exactly what I did with the help of my team. We just ticked the boxes and moved onto the next step.

Before going into the Games I said to my close team "sub-31 [10,000m] and top eight that's the aim" [Julia ran 30:55.63]. I've learnt over the years to understand and know my body. And, from the training he's set me, my coach is very

good at assessing how fit I am. So although it's been a surprise for many people, it wasn't unexpected amongst my close circle. It's what we've been planning and it was just nice to execute it according to the plan.

As a London girl, how did you discover this whole running thing?

I've been running since the age of six. My father could run a sub-30-minute 10k as a young man and he used to go jogging to keep fit, so I asked him if I could come with him. It was probably only a one or two-mile jog.

[When I was younger] I didn't train very much as some athletes do now. I was a county standard athlete and if I could finish in the top 100 at the national cross country I was pleased.

I always enjoyed running but I was doing a lot of different things. It wasn't until my 20s that I started making inroads and training more.

What do you like about running?

For me it's about being out there in nature in the fresh air. I don't run with music. I just enjoy the sounds and sights around me. It's a great time to think and relax.

In London I spend a lot of time running in the parks, in Bushy Park, Richmond Park and Home Park. You've got the view, you've got the fantastic undergrowth and wild grasses, and you can kind of get lost in the park.

It's time to yourself, away from it all. When you're fit you're flowing through the undergrowth, and up and down the hills. It's quite special.

I've spent time running in the Alps and running across the mountains. So that's where my joy in running comes from. Track and field is fantastic but my initial love and feeling for the sport was being out in nature.

JULIA'S RUNNING STATS

Achievements
8th 2012 Olympic Games 5000m
8th 2012 Olympic Games 10,000m
4th 2012 European Championships 5000m
1st 2014 Carlsbad 5000 (California)
2011 UK 5000m Champion
Third fastest Briton all-time over 10,000m

Personal Bests
3000m: 8:46.38
5000m: 15:02.00
10,000m: 30:55.63

So do you have a soft spot for hills?

Hills are my kind of running. I'd love to do mountain running. But you can't do everything at once. There's no Olympic mountain running. So for the next four years I'll be track and field. But after that I'd love to have a mountain running season.

When you're running through the Alps you don't feel the need for any competition, you just compete against yourself. It's running free.

Outside of fun runs, competitive running can be quite male–dominated, what advice would you give to aspiring girls wanting to race and train more?

I've been part of Thames Hare and Hounds, which is now my second claim club, but in that club there was a fantastic group of women who run together regularly. We have women of absolutely every standard and men of absolutely every standard. And you don't have to be of a particular standard to enjoy taking part in a club.

Also the parkruns are fantastic for getting people out there on a regular basis. It's semi-competitive because everyone has their personal best on the different courses.

It'll be interesting to see what happens off the back of the Olympics if people are inspired to go running.

Since the 2012 London Olympics Julia has battled injury in 2013 and 2014, however, early in 2014 she had a great return to form in winning the prestigious Carlsbad 5000 (5k road race) in California and also winning the off road Greensand Marathon in an outright race record (for both women and men). Her main goal is the 2016 Rio Olympics.

www.juliableasdale.com

JULIA'S TOP 3 LONDON RUNNING SPOTS ▸

3. Ruislip Woods | I grew up in West London, so did a lot of my running in Ruislip Woods. And whenever I return home, one of the first things I do is run there.

2. Hampstead Heath | I also have really fond memories of running on Hampstead Heath, competing there and winning the South of England Championship for the first time. There's this great hill and you've got this massive South of England Championships where everyone starts at the bottom of the hill and charges up.

1. The Parks | My number one general area is Richmond Park, Wimbledon Common, Bushy Park, Home Park [Hampton Court Park]. I try to combine all the parks in one run. Every time I do it I feel really blessed that I have such a fantastic place to run. And the surface is really good underfoot so you can do it at quite a pace. [See p.151 for details of this run.]

Introducing

THE AUDIO RUNNING COACH

Turn your MP3 player into your own personal technique coach. *Runner's Guide to London* author and coach Hayden Shearman presents a series of 50-minute audio workouts to help you build a smoother, more efficient running style.

USE THE CODE "RUNLONDON" TO SAVE 30%.

EPISODES INCLUDE:
TECHNIQUE 101
INTRO TO SPEED
HILLS, HILLS, HILLS
RACE PACE PRACTICE